DOING
OUR OWN
THING

ALSO BY JOHN MCWHORTER

Towards a New Model of Creole Genesis

The Missing Spanish Creoles:
Recovering the Birth of Plantation Creole Languages

Word on the Street:
Debunking the Myth of a "Pure" Standard English

Spreading the Word:
Language and Dialect in America

Losing the Race:
Self-Sabotage in Black America

The Power of Babel:
A Natural History of Language

Authentically Black:
Essays for the Black Silent Majority

DOING
OUR OWN
THING

The Degradation of Language and Music
and Why We Should, Like, Care

JOHN McWHORTER

GOTHAM BOOKS

GOTHAM BOOKS
Published by Penguin Group (USA) Inc.
375 Hudson Street, New York, New York 10014, U.S.A.
Penguin Books Ltd, Registered Offices: 80 Strand, London WC2R 0RL, England
Penguin Books Australia Ltd, 250 Camberwell Road, Camberwell, Victoria 3124, Australia
Penguin Books Canada Ltd, 10 Alcorn Avenue, Toronto, Ontario, Canada M4V 3B2
Penguin Books (NZ) Ltd, Cnr Rosedale and Airborne Roads,
Albany, Auckland 1310, New Zealand

Published by Gotham Books, a division of Penguin Group (USA) Inc.

First printing, October 2003
1   3   5   7   9   10   8   6   4   2

Permissions are on page 279 and constitute an extension of the copyright page.

Copyright © John McWhorter, 2003
All rights reserved

Gotham Books and the skyscraper logo are trademarks of Penguin Group (USA) Inc.

LIBRARY OF CONGRESS CATALOGING-IN-PUBLICATION DATA
McWhorter, John H.
Doing our own thing : the degradation of language and music and why
we should, like, care / by John McWhorter.
        p.   cm.
Includes bibliographical references.
ISBN 1-59240-016-7 (hardcover : alk. paper)
1.   English language—Variation—United States. 2.   Popular music—United States—
History and criticism. 3.   English language—Written English—United States. 4.   English
language—Spoken English—United States. 5.   English language—Social aspects—United
States. 6.   English language—United States—Usage. 7.   Language and culture—United
States. 8.   English language—United States. I.   Title.
PE2808.8.M38 2003
427'.973—dc21   2003011487

Printed in the United States of America
Set in Giovanni Book with Crane Light and Copperplate
Designed by Sabrina Bowers

This book is printed on acid-free paper. ∞

I dedicate this book to that cheery, weary town,
New York City

Contents

Introduction

I am first putting pen to paper—or, really, finger to keyboard—for this book on September 10, 2002, in New York City. Tomorrow, the city will witness a commemoration of the terrorist attacks on New York and Washington, DC, a year ago. A certain feature of the ceremony has occasioned an amount of discussion: There will be no original speeches given. Instead, various dignitaries will read stirring speeches from the past.

And in today's American culture, the fact is that this feels "right" somehow. Commentators have opined that the horror of the events of September 11, 2001, was too profound for mere words to express. And many Americans would share a sense that on such an occasion, "speechifying" would seem a tad purple, something better suited to a wedding or the grand-opening celebration of some mall.

But this sentiment is more local to our time and place than it might appear. Nobody felt this way, for example, on the Gettysburg battlefield in 1863. Over seventeen times the number of people who died in the World Trade Center—51,000 men—had died in three swelteringly hot days of gunfighting, along with 5,000 horses left rotting along with them on the battlefield. Yet, Abraham Lincoln, of course, presented some thoughts composed for the occasion. And no one is recorded as questioning the appropriateness of his doing so, or suggesting that he should have instead just read off the names of the dead as former New York City mayor Rudolph Giuliani will initiate tomorrow. On the contrary, Lincoln's Gettysburg Address is now considered one of the masterpieces of human expression. For him to have instead read off a speech George Washington had made decades before and then pulled out a list of the dead to start reciting would have been inconceivable to the spectators that day.

More to the point, though, the main course of the Gettysburg ceremony was the man who spoke before Lincoln. Edward Everett has been enshrined as a prototypical historical footnote for giving an address that lasted two hours—the length of a movie!—to a rapt audience. The content itself was no great shakes. Everett recounted the events of the battle and some political issues surrounding it. But he was not especially cherished for his political insights, and it's no accident that no one quotes his speech today. Nor had Everett contributed to the life of the nation in any really significant way. By this time near seventy, earlier in life he had been governor of Massachusetts, president of Harvard, and secretary of state for about five minutes apiece, not having particularly distinguished himself in any of those or assorted other capacities. If he hadn't happened to speak before Lincoln delivered his Gettysburg Address, Everett would not even have wangled his historical footnote.

Yet at the time, Everett was by no means just Lincoln's opening act; he was a national celebrity in his own right. Not for having an affair with a president, not for marrying curiously often and having a large behind, not for relatives blockading him in a house in Miami to keep him from going back to Cuba to live with his father; Everett was famous for being a good talker.

Certainly he had his political stances, and often used his speaking talents to broadcast them. But he was not famous as, say, a Unionist, and a good thing too, since he's so good with the words! Everett was a nineteenth-century rock star simply because he was a man who could really *talk*, whatever the topic, period. For us, Tiger Woods is famous for his way with the golf clubs, Mariah Carey for her singing gift, Michael Jackson for being staggeringly peculiar. In the same way, for audiences in the antebellum era, Edward Everett was famous as an orator. He could go on tour orating and rake in big bucks just like Carey can now and Jackson wishes he still could. Everett was a master of eloquent phraseology, and complimented it with a beautiful voice and a flair for the dramatic. Here is the opening of his Gettysburg oration:

> Standing beneath this serene sky, overlooking these broad fields now reposing from the labors of the waning year, the mighty Alleghanies

dimly towering before us, the graves of our brethren beneath our feet, it is with hesitation that I raise my poor voice to break the eloquent silence of God and Nature. But the duty to which you have called me must be performed;—grant me, I pray you, your indulgence and your sympathy.

Yet, let's face it—to the modern American eye or ear, the first impression this excerpt lends is logorrheic: too windy, too puffed up. It doesn't even look sincere—language like this smells of snake oil to us. But that's just us: Audiences at the time were quite stirred by this speech. Phraseology like this had been typical of public addresses in America since the founding of the Republic and would continue to be for a long time afterward. And to the extent that we can stand back a bit and assess the excerpt simply as language, there is considerable beauty in it. The rhythm, the imagery, the precise choices of words—this is poetry. The Gettysburg audience stood there listening to a man declaiming in prose that bordered on free verse. For *hours.*

But however we feel about poetry, most of us will have a sense that words like *reposing* and *brethren* are overdoing it, a bit much. But really, why? What is it about those sequences of sounds—*ree-POE-zing, BREHTH-rin*—as opposed to *REH-sting* and *BRUH-therz*—that is somehow inherently "fake?" Nothing, obviously. And to the extent that Everett was using such words to lend a sense of grandeur and ceremony, why, exactly, do we feel that to do so is somehow a pose, a kind of verbal monocle?

After all, meat-and-potatoes folks standing there on November 19, 1863, did not. And it's not as if they inhabited a society so different from ours that we can only hope to understand their lives through an anthropological lens, like an England in which Queen Elizabeth only bathed once in her life. The people who gratefully listened to Everett run his mouth for as long as it would take us to watch *Pulp Fiction* had magazines, trains, surgery, classical music, theater, Congress, a stock exchange, zoos. They bathed at least once a week. They spoke essentially the English we speak—we could converse with them with no trouble, though they would draw a blank on the likes of "Let's do the dinner thing." Although, actually I once caught that last expression used as early as a silent film from 1917, when most of the Gettysburg spectators would have still been alive. And while we're on that, many who heard Everett's oration as teens lived to see movies, radio, and Franklin D. Roosevelt's election, and some few who fidgeted through it as tots lived to see John F. Kennedy's election on television.

All of which is to say that in the grand scheme of things, November 19, 1863, was not really *that* long ago. It was just over 140 years ago as you read this, not even 150. Seven little generations. Which leads to a question: Where are our orators like Everett in America today? Can you name any public figure who is best known for being a fine talker?

Yes, Jesse Jackson can certainly stir a crowd. Only a corpse could fail to respond to such music on some level. But Jackson's medium is the African-American (or more broadly, fundamentalist) preaching style. A talent this is—not just anyone can do it. But as I will revisit in Chapter Two, this style is more about arousal than exposition, the punchy over the considered, the riff over the paragraph, the gut over the head. The "Ah, but is it art?" question is tricky, but we can acknowledge that as brilliant as John Lennon and Paul McCartney were, it would be hard to say that there is no difference in the intricacy of construction between the Beatles' recording of "Eleanor Rigby"—achingly perfect though it is (that cello writing!)—and a Beethoven string quartet (*that* cello writing!). In the same way, there is an obvious difference in level of craft between a speech by Jackson ("I am somebody!") and one by Everett.

And in any case, the black preaching tradition is embedded in one subculture of the American fabric. What about oratory on a national, mainstream level? Sure, we have the occasional stirring speech. After Jackson, many people mention Mario Cuomo's "City on a Hill" speech to the Democratic National Convention in 1984. And that was certainly a fine one, but note how it stands out. We have the *occasional* stirring speech—while oratory was a core component of American public discourse in the past. Cuomo's speech would have seemed downright ordinary in 1863. Everett was but one of legions of professional "talkers" of his era, when a gift for gab was a prime qualification for a life in politics. It's significant that, meanwhile, most readers still will be seeking in vain just one Everett equivalent around today.

Can we really say that the speeches Peggy Noonan wrote for Ronald Reagan, deft though they could be, would strike anyone as poetry? Yes, "Mister Gorbachev, tear down that wall," perhaps—but that was just one nugget; what about the other 98 percent of the speech? Will anything Mark Gerson writes for George W. Bush stand as the equal of the Gettysburg Address in the history books of tomorrow? Lincoln concluded with

"We here highly resolve that these dead shall not have died in vain, that this nation under God shall have a new birth of freedom, and that government of the people, by the people, for the people shall not perish from the earth"—enough said. Now back to the future: Bush concludes a *nationally celebrated* speech with "We have our marching orders, my fellow Americans. Let's roll." Cute—but different. Very different. If Lincoln had ended his speech with "Let's roll"—really; imagine it: ". . . that government of the people, by the people, for the people shall not perish from the earth. Let's roll"—he would have been assassinated two years earlier.

He might not have even made it off of the lectern. And the fact is this: If we went back in time to Gettysburg on November 18, 1863, spent the night with an ordinary middle-class family, and tagged along with them the next morning to attend the Battle of Gettysburg do, most of us would be squirming a half hour into Everett's speech, desperate after an hour, sobbing quietly after an hour and a half, and needing therapy by the time he finished. But our hosts, while perhaps flagging a tad as the second hour wore on, would be engaged with Everett's words for much longer than us, perplexed at our antsiness, and would applaud with a sincere lustiness at the end, as happy they came as we would be attending a taping of *Letterman*.

What is it about us? And it's not just that the media have shortened our attention spans—because *most of us would feel funny hearing anyone talk like Everett for even ten minutes.*

Why?

The reason is that in America today, the proper use of English has gone the way of the dodo, with our most prominent pundits butchering . . . no, actually—sorry. This will not be one more book claiming that "English is going to the dogs." I will most certainly not be doing John Simon and his ilk here. The actual issue is quite distinct from the fact that people so often say "Billy and me went to the store" instead of "Billy and I went to the store" and so on. The notion of sentences like this as mistakes is a complete myth, as any professional linguist will readily tell you. Many readers are likely thinking at this point "But *me* isn't a subject!"—and in the following chapter, while laying out some other fundamentals for understanding what has happened to English in America today, I will explain why this is a garden-path analysis despite its seductiveness.

But no matter how carefully linguists present this kind of argument, the people Steven Pinker calls "language mavens" insist that there remains a legitimate concern for clarity in word usage and graceful composition. No linguist would disagree. But modern linguistics focuses on speech rather than writing, specifically, the internal structures of language as spoken spontaneously. Linguistics is a geeky affair, as much science as humanities, that has little to do with etymologies and nothing to do with rhetorical eloquence in speaking or writing. As such, the truth is that most linguists have little interest in such things—the person who does will not usually become a linguist. When the language maven goes on about maintaining the artful aspects of language, deep down the linguist's eyes glaze over—most of us have no more interest in Strunk & White than a molecular biologist has in dog training. Thus it is that linguists' common consensus—to the extent that the subject is considered of any import among us—is that all claims that there is a qualitative decline in the use of English are benighted non-starters.

But I write this book out of a sense that the issue actually does bear some more examination. As far as casual speech is concerned, no, Americans never have and never will "let the language go," any more than any of the 6,000 languages in the world have been discovered to have suffered such destructive uncorseting over the years. But casual speech, despite being what academic linguists find most interesting, is just one of many layers of what English or any language consists of. And beyond the realm of six-pack, cell-phone "talk," there is indeed something that we are losing in America in terms of the English language. Namely, a particular kind of artful use of English, formerly taken for granted as crucial to legitimate expression on the civic stage, has virtually disappeared.

The rarity of the elaborately composed speech is just one example. The contrast between then and now permeates American society. When I am at a conference and have to get up early, I often watch CNN *Headline News*. One of the anchors is Robin Meade. So spellbindingly pretty she looks like a computer composite, she first struck me visually, I must admit, and so I started tuning in to CNN in hotel rooms to watch her when I am getting ready for the day. But it's harder to look at the screen while you're shaving, and she soon began to strike me just as much aurally. Overall, she is the typically white-bread poised, coiffed American anchor. But here and there she casually contracts –*ing* to –*in'* ("We'll be seein' you after the break"), and in one interview with an official, she referred to his organization as "You guys." She ends up sounding like a woman you lived down the hall from in college.

Now, from a linguist's perspective, it's not that Meade is lapsing into "bad grammar" in saying *seein'*. If loaded up with some Xanax after Everett's oration we then jumped into the time machine and made a stop further back in the past to 1700, we might encounter a Jonathan Swift who felt it as crude to pronounce a word like *rebuked* as *rih-BYOOKD* as opposed to what he saw as the proper rendition, *rih-BYOO-kid*. As Swift soberly expressed it: "By leaving out a vowel to save a syllable, we form so jarring a sound, and so difficult to utter, that I have often wondred how it could ever obtain." But nevertheless the pronunciation of the *-ed* ending changed anyway. We do not find it at all "jarring" or "difficult" to say *rih-BYOOKD*, or what Swift disparagingly wrote as *drudg'd, disturb'd,* and *fledg'd*. The globe kept spinning with no detriment to English perceived, and *seeing* and *seein'* exist today in the same relationship as *rih-BYOO-kid* and *rih-BYOOKD* did three hundred years ago. Just as we cannot accept that today we are all wrong in saying *rih-BYOOKD*, there are no logical grounds for designating *seein'* as decayed. Language changes, and with each change, Stage B—no more illegitimate than the one-hooved horses that evolved from ones with a hoof flanked by two toes—coexists with Stage A.

Nevertheless, for a good while a society usually feels the newer, "other" version of a word as more casual, more dress down. That's just a take-it-or-leave-it fact that no linguist denies. And here is where Meade's use of language is interesting when we compare then and now. She likely sees her colloquial tilt as lending a note of warmth. "Why can't we loosen up a little?" one imagines her objecting if someone called her on it. Okay—I get it; folksy it is. But it's interesting that this folksiness would have been unthinkable of a news personality in the 1950s. If Chet Huntley had ventured a "you guys" on the air, while he wouldn't have been shot on sight, he would have been reprimanded. Certainly Betty Furness (remember her? If you are a person of a certain maturity you will recall her "You can be sure if it's Westinghouse" ads; with a tad less maturity you may recall her subbing for Barbara Walters on the *Today* show; otherwise just imagine a deathlessly poised, profoundly unethnic lady with an immovable head of hair) could not possibly have maintained a social life always talking the way she did on television. The crucial distinction is that as a person of her era, Thoroughly Modern Meade intuitively senses less of a distinction between her private and public linguistic faces. When the teleprompter went off, as long as she was still in front of a camera, Furness spoke; Meade talks.

Or take a letter Washington Roebling, who supervised the building of the Brooklyn Bridge, wrote to his fiancée in 1864:

> My candle is certainly bewitched. Every five minutes it goes out, there must be something in the wick, unless it be the spirit of some man just made perfect, come to torment me while I am writing to my love. Are any of your old beaus dead? If I wasn't out of practice with spiritual writing I would soon find out.

Just imagine writing an e-mail—or even letter—like that to someone you were interested in today. But here is the crucial thing: Neither the rococo tone of Roebling's letters, the stiffness of the lithograph drawings of public figures in his era, nor his first name being "Washington" must mislead us into supposing that he used such language on a casual level while quaffing ale with his chums. In the same letter he mentions that he had been "building bridges and swearing all day." We can be quite sure that Roebling was cussing along about what he was *seein'* and how *you guys*—or in his day, *you fellas*—could have been doing better. The interesting thing is, rather, that for him, switching from everyday speech to so formal and composed a tone in letters to his beloved was such a natural choice. Even, a required choice—for a man of his day, this kind of language was as essential to a respectable man's wooing kit as a condom is today. On the other hand, for the modern American man desirous of channeling the bewitched state of his candle, writing to women in language like this would all but ensure his dying alone.

The issue, then, is that in earlier America it was assumed that a certain space in society required that English be dressed in its Sunday best, complete with carnations and big hats. It's no accident that in another letter to his fiancée, Roebling mentioned that he had just heard an oration by—three guesses—Edward Everett, commemorating the taking of Fort Duquesne. Linguistically, this was practically a different planet. The tone of Everett's speeches as well as Roebling's letters makes it unsurprising that in the nineteenth century, poetry was a bestselling genre rather than the cultish phenomenon it now is. Talking was for conversation; in public or on paper, one used a different kind of language, just as we use forks and knives instead of eating with our hands.

Surely on the everyday level English was used much as it is now, in all of its fluid, vulgar splendor. And just as surely, the educated and more fortunate were more comfortable in the "higher" mode than others (although its usage permeated further down the social scale than we might expect, as we will see later). But modern America has all but eliminated this kind of English, with any remaining sense of its Sunday best now being at most a button-down shirt. Most of us sense carefully wrought phraseology as corny. Where for earlier Americans ornate language corresponded to gravity, today we sense it as insincere—a change similar to that undergone by the tuxedo.

And this is indeed an American issue: To be a modern American is to lack a native love of one's language that is typical of most humans worldwide. In general, I suspect many Americans reading this do not consider themselves as feeling much of anything about English pro or con—and that is exactly the point. It's one of those "fish don't know they're wet" issues—we have to step way back to realize that anything is afoot.

One often hears foreigners praising the beauty, the majesty, the richness of expression, of their native languages—both in and away from their homelands. And this is not limited to the "developed" world. The linguist is familiar with finding that speakers of the obscure indigenous language they are documenting have whole fables or poems about how wonderful their tongue is—and composed not as modern statements of cultural assertion, but as in-group libations created long before English and other imperial languages began edging smaller languages aside.

Americans are an exception. We do not love English. We do not celebrate it overtly, nor do we even have anything to say about it if pressed on the point. Sucking slowly on a cigarette and misting up a bit, the foreigner muses "There's nothing like hearing my native language." But it almost strains the imagination to hear this said in an American English accent. The utterance would be almost as bizarre and unprocessible as someone responding to your "Good morning" with "I've been told they were mostly *bald* cooks." Certainly some of this is because we are not obliged to learn foreign languages since we can get along in English almost anywhere in the world, and thus are not faced with the contrast between our own language and others' as urgently as most of the world's peoples are. But as I will show later, a hundred years ago Americans could be heard expressing a specific pride in English that would ring oddly now. And it's also indicative that today, to the extent that we might suck on a cigarette and mist up about anything having to do with language, it would most likely be to praise a *foreign* one.

And that, more than anything else, consigns an Edward Everett to the antique. In today's America, it would be quizzical if there did remain any place for grandiloquence. But this relationship to our language—or lack of one—is a new development. What gave us Americans a tacit sense that to wield the full resources of our native language is tacky?

Various factors tempt us as explanations that in fact cannot help us because the timing is off. The grand old American tradition of anti-intellectualism, for example, is fundamental to the very warp and woof of the Republic, hardly a new development. It was an antiintellectual America that thrilled to the strains of Edward Everett's orations. We might suppose that American individualism discourages allegiance to a standard imposed from on high. True, but again, that individualism traces back to our beginnings, while for centuries afterward, "high" language was one standard that Americans readily accepted. Mass culture and its focus on the lowest common denominator? Timing again: for example, when sound films began, mass culture had already turned American life upside down. Yet there were elocution coaches all over Hollywood training actors to sound like characters in Noel Coward plays, and this artificial diction and blackboard syntax—Bette Davis, despite her plummy tones in performance, was born and raised in Massachusetts—was coin of the realm in American films well into the 1960s.

I think we get closer to the McGuffin in another September 11 commemoration that will take place tomorrow, at the University of California, Berkeley, where I teach. It has been decided that there will be no patriotic songs sung and no American flags waved at the ceremony, out of a sense that this would be "too political." For the conveners this is an utterly natural position, and they have been surprised at the minor barrage of criticism the right fired at them recently. Nor would the position exactly shock most educated Americans today given that we live in an America where many consider it an essential part of education to learn that our country has been responsible for a great deal of misery and injustice both here and worldwide. For today's thinking American, if their sense of patriotism is not a quiet one held with significant reservations, then they likely sense themselves as part of an embattled minority, or are perhaps recent immigrants whose perspective on America is couched in a contrast with the starker misery and injustice elsewhere that drove them to pick up stakes.

Of course, few people actually walk around saying "America is too morally corrupt to merit anything but the most coded of celebrations by anyone with half a brain." Every political sentiment will always have its fringe of strident firebrands, but generally, this filtered patriotism is deeply entrenched enough that most educated folk barely consider it a position at all. It is considered by many as a part of basic human enlightenment, which one votes on the basis of, incorporates into the upbringing of one's children, and assumes as common knowledge at parties.

My goal here is not to attack this position. As with all political standpoints, what initially broadens horizons can end up contracting them just as much. But an educated class of modern Americans as chauvinistically patriotic as Theodore Roosevelt would be a troglodytic one. I do not believe that humans have yet devised a political system that yields as much good for as many as democracy and capitalism. But these systems hardly tamp down greed and cruelty, and the damage that America has inflicted in many parts of the world as well as at home is well-documented.

Rather, the current state of American patriotism is useful here because it offers an explanation for why we no longer have orators, and for many other things we now take for granted in America that would perplex the Gettysburg citizen who jumped into our time machine to look at our modern society.

Here, the timing is just right. Obviously, events in the sixties deeply transformed Americans' conventional wisdom regarding the legitimacy of their ruling class and the very concept of authority. Basic cynicism about Washington and politicians has always been old news—the Constitution and the *Federalist Papers* design our political foundations upon just such an assumption, after all. But before the 1960s, the conviction that the American experiment itself was fundamentally illegitimate was largely limited to certain political sects and intellectuals. After Vietnam and then Watergate, a less focused form of this sentiment became a conventional wisdom among the educated, and proceeded to become a general cultural zeitgeist. The Civil Rights movement and growing awareness of the systemic nature of poverty painted mainstream America as irredeemably immoral. And these sea changes came along after earlier in the sixties, best-selling books like Thomas Szasz's *The Myth of Mental Illness* popularized a trope that mental illness was a societal construct, and that society shackled the human spirit from rising to the higher plane of self-expression. Plays like Herbert Gardner's *A Thousand Clowns* were the product of this new idea blowing in the wind, and R. D. Laing's *The Politics of Experience* (1967) helped set it in stone.

Importantly, it is in the 1960s that the space for high language starts wasting away—and even more specifically, the late 1960s. Earlier in the decade the old linguistic culture was still in place. John F. Kennedy's State of the Union address in 1961 was a speech in the old-fashioned sense, standing on its own on the page as prose:

> We cannot escape our dangers—neither must we let them drive us into panic or narrow isolation. In many areas of the world where the balance of power already rests with our adversaries, the forces of freedom are sharply divided. It is one of the ironies of our time that the techniques of a harsh and repressive system should be able to instill discipline and ardor in its servants—while the blessings of liberty have too often stood for privilege, materialism, and a life of ease.

Thirty-two years later, a State of the Union address by our second president to be raised under the new linguistic regime has a distinctly different flavor. The Kennedy passage is a minor piece of art. The words appear set just where they should be. One senses the hard work it took to craft it—coffee and cigarettes long into the night, yellow pads. The Bush *fils* passage is competent but perfunctory; there is no love of language in it. Bush's speechwriters work hard, but their sense of goal is different from their predecessors like Ted Sorenson. Remember also that this passage is not one more "Bushism" revelation because these addresses are carefully written out beforehand and then read aloud:

> Now, in this century, the ideology of power and domination has appeared again, and seeks to gain the ultimate weapons of terror. Once again, this nation and all our friends are all that stand between a world at peace, and a world of chaos and constant alarm. Once again, we are called to defend the safety of our people, and the hopes of all mankind. And we accept this responsibility.

At no point did the Kennedy speech ever feel like this, nor at any point did the Bush speech venture into artful language. As late as the early sixties, language like Bush's would have been as off-key as going to work without a jacket and tie. Meanwhile, for a presidential candidate to communicate to the public in language like Kennedy's today would ensure his defeat. Al Gore's almost studied articulateness is certainly one of the major factors that has blocked him from winning the presidency.

The late sixties is also when casual speech penetrates American cinema in a real way—when movie actors start letting their hair down and sounding like normal people instead of stage players. Peter Fonda and Dennis Hopper mumbling their way through *Easy Rider* in 1969 can be thought of as the totemic inauguration of this new linguistic order, the film being the first major release to celebrate the countercultural ethos in all of its grimy vitality. Yes, by then we had heard voices like this on the big screen now and then. But this was in characters like those played by Marlon Brando and James Dean, presented as forces of nature shouting into the wind at odds with an America where everybody else still talked like Ozzie and Harriet. In *Easy Rider*, for the first time a truly natural, shambling, almost telegraphic way of talking is not a character marker but common coin, with those using it presented as heralds of a brave new world. It is also at this time that in popular music, crisp diction and carefully wrought lyrics become the exception rather than the norm—as witnessed by the funky songs featured on *Easy Rider*'s soundtrack, on which Cole Porter would have sounded as incongruous as Puccini.

This mainstreaming of the counterculture actually *predicts* that linguistically, every day would become Casual Day in America. Formality in all realms, be it sartorial, terpsichorean, culinary, artistic, or linguistic, entails the dutiful acknowledgment of "higher" public standards considered beyond question, requiring tutelage and effort to master, with embarrassing slippage an eternal threat. The girdle might slip, you might step on your waltzing partner's toes, the soufflé might not rise, the water in the landscape painting may not shimmer just right, the *mot juste* might elude one. Formality means caring about such things, and being driven to avoid them in favor of making a pretty picture.

Certainly, then, formality was a sitting duck under a new Conventional Wisdom that saw being American less as a privilege than as something to gingerly forge a relationship with, and mainstream American behavior as something to hold at half an arm's length, on the pain of one's inner spirit being suffocated under a burden of Velveeta and Pat Boone. At such a cultural moment, formality becomes repressed, boring, unreflective, and even suspect, while Doing Your Own Thing is genuine,

healthy, engaged, and even urgent. As such, the only accepted commu-
nality is being united against The Machine. Hence, the ironic sameness
of dress, opinion, and attitude among the folks stretching across the
country from the East Village through Ann Arbor and Austin, Texas, to
Haight Street, who pride themselves on marching to the beat of their
own drummers, or an antigovernment sentiment among modern academics consistent enough to qualify them as "a herd of independent
minds."

Journalist and speechwriter Hendrik Hertzberg's comment about the
muteness of New York City's 9/11 commemoration nicely captures the
countercultural consensus and how it discourages public celebration of
our nation: "To say something worthwhile, you'd probably have to say
something that not everyone would agree with." Indeed, as Nathan
Glazer tells us, *We Are All Multiculturalists Now* in part because with all
that has happened and all that has been said, it can be so challenging for
many of us to embrace our own culture. And on the linguistic front, in a
way We're All Dennis Hopper Now. The transformation in Americans'
conception of themselves and their country is reflected not only in how
we listen to music, dance, have sex, raise children, and vote, but in
how we feel about English.

Our national shift from a written to an oral culture has had broad and
profound effects, but the point is a highly specific one. It hinges on a distinction that most of us have little reason to be consciously aware of on a
day-to-day level unless we are linguists. To the extent that we are aware
of the fact that there is the way we talk and the way we write, we have an
understandable tendency to underestimate the depth of the difference
between the two poles.

Yet the argument will not be simply that we have lost "rhetorical eloquence" in America. This is because eloquence is possible both in the
formal, carefully revised language of writing, and in the more spontaneous, flexible realm of speech. For example, Martin Luther King, Jr.'s "I
Have a Dream" speech was surely eloquent—but it was couched in brief,
repetitive phrases that, in terms of written English, are quite elementary. I will show that our marginalization of the written can indeed com-
promise eloquence of certain kinds. But eloquence alone is a highly
subjective concept, such that an argument focusing on this in itself
would be an unavoidably preachy, tendentious screed.

For example, nineteenth-century listeners found Edward Everett thoroughly eloquent while even literate modern Americans, admiring Lincoln's masterfully concise Gettysburg Address, find Everett's language inflated and affected. But who are we to indict all of those people who listened to Everett as somehow aesthetically challenged? This is an issue of style and gut preference. Then today, B. R. Myers's famous essay "A Reader's Manifesto" in *The Atlantic Monthly* has accused fiction writers like Annie Proulx and David Guterson of "bad writing" because he finds their metaphors "mixed" and misses the flinty clarity of earlier writers like Henry James and Virginia Woolf. But this judgment on eloquence is again a matter of taste, submitting to no unequivocal metric. Millions of intelligent and artistically sensitive readers and thinkers deeply value the prose of the writers Myers dismisses. The fact that their aesthetic sensibility had yet to hold sway in 1910 does not qualify as a conclusive dismissal of their acumen.

Our issue will be what *kind* of eloquence Americans currently value most, and why—to wit, the new American tendency to increasingly distrust forms of English to the extent that they stray from the way we use the language while Doing Our Own Thing as we gab. As linguistic scientist and cultural historian, I am fascinated by single phenomena that explain several developments that otherwise appear disconnected. The written-to-spoken shift, while hardly something that the non-linguist has much reason to notice beyond its most strident manifestations (e.g., profanity on television and in the movies), makes various current American developments predictable. We are neither heedless of "grammar" nor deaf to the power of words in themselves. Yet there has nevertheless occurred a strange reverse progression in our linguistic time line, whose origins and nature reveal much about who we are as Americans.

The counterculture's permeation of the national consciousness, then, has created a new linguistic landscape in this country, demanding exploration as much as the many other effects that the late sixties has had upon our culture. In some ways, the change has allowed space for more voices than was possible in the past and has blown away some cobwebs we are well rid of. But in just as many ways, the new linguistic order compromises our facility with the word and dilutes our collective intellect. Our new sense of what American English is has upended our relationship to articulateness, our approach to writing, and how (and whether) we impart it to the young, our interest in poetry, and our conception of what it is, and even our response to music and how we judge it.

A society that cherishes the spoken over the written, whatever it gains from the warm viscerality of unadorned talk, is one that marginalizes extended, reflective argument. Spoken language, as I will show in the first chapter, is best suited to harboring easily processible chunks of information, broad lines, and emotion. To the extent that our public discourse leans ever more toward this pole, the implications for the prospect of an informed citizenry are dire. The person who only processes information beyond their immediate purview in nuggets is not educated in any meaningful sense. On the contrary, this person is indistinguishable in mental sophistication from the semiliterate Third World villager who derives all of their information about the world beyond via conversation and gossip. And a culture that marginalizes the didactic potential of written-style language in favor of the personal electricity of spoken language is one whose media becomes ever more a circus of personalities rather than a purveyor of information and guide to analysis.

We often hear about how wealthy, how adaptable, how individualistic, how open to enterprise this noble mess of an experiment called America is. Less often do we realize that Americans after the 1960s have lived in a country with less pride in its language than any society in recorded history. A modern man who wrote love letters sounding like Washington Roebling's to a woman would never hear from her again, and Roebling would need smelling salts on finding out that we consider Bob Dylan an artist. In the grand scheme of things, Roebling's America was the normal one, while our America is the anomaly.

CHAPTER ONE

People Just Talk: Speech Versus Writing

Have You Seen Any Swamp People?

Some years ago, an undergraduate student in a course I was teaching gave me a tape she had made of an elderly black woman reciting a folktale. The woman belonged to a group the student had described called "Swamp People," living on the outskirts of Greenwood, Mississippi, where she had grown up, who dress in unusually colorful clothes, and have a way of speaking unique to themselves. The woman on the tape's speech sounds like a bizarre casserole of Jamaican patois and Haitian Creole, a dash of Black English, and a sprinkling of something somewhere between Cesaria Evora and God.

Missing links always exert their fascination, and as paleontologists hope to unearth a skeleton of the first dinosaur, some Black English specialists have long hoped that in some remote district of the South, a proto–Black English might turn up. There is a theory that Black English has its roots in the Euro-African hybrid creole language Gullah. Gullah is a variety of West Indian patois spoken right here in America, on the Sea Islands off the coast of the Carolinas and Georgia, and in some places a bit inland. But many theorize that black Americans once spoke Gullah more widely, across the South or possibly as far north as Pennsylvania.

Gullah speakers have indeed been found in one little town in Texas—but there is a well-documented after-the-fact historical migration from Georgia that explains it. A pocket of people still speaking a deeply Gullah-fied Black English somewhere, with no evidence that they had roots in today's Gullah-speaking region, would be a kind of missing link for someone like David Sutcliffe of Pompeu Fabra University in Spain, who has long sought evidence that Black English began as Gullah. David was electrified when I sent him a copy of the tape. For years, he has been mining recordings of ex-slaves made in the 1930s for evidence of Gullah in their speech, but this modern recording of an aged, rural, black woman speaking something that sounded rather Caribbean was something else again. What lent even more of a sense of drama was that the student graduated soon thereafter and all attempts to locate her were in vain. All we had was a post-office-box address for the woman that she had included with the cassette.

To make a long story short, a few springs ago David, I, and some other interested parties wound up shuttling around Greenwood, Mississippi, in a van trying to find the Swamp People. Really, the tape has never sounded like Gullah to me. The student certainly had no reason to make the Swamp People up or fake the tape, and I would love to know who this old woman was and what she was speaking. But to get to the bottom of it we would have needed more than a post-office-box address that ended up not corresponding to any actual residence. Yet I came along, because we had all been at a conference nearby and I wouldn't have wanted to miss just *maybe* taking part in a really neat discovery.

But it was a long shot—Greenwood is no swamp, but a modern town. I can only be thankful that there is no filmed record of me and the others bumbling all over it asking ordinary black people buying groceries, sitting in their cars listening to CDs, or tending stores "Have you ever heard of the Swamp People?" I could only laugh along with them, and our search for the woman or any other Swamp Person was fruitless.

It was a long day. But one interview we did with an elderly black woman yielded an observation that has never left me. Trying to nudge her into giving us some clue that could lead us to people speaking some unusual dialect, we asked her whether she knew of any people in the area who "talked kind of funny." Our hope that she would say "Oh, yeah—those weird folks out there in the swamps with funny cloths on their heads" was not rewarded. But she did say "Well, seems like most folks, they speak pretty good English, but some people, it seems like they just talk." She proceeded to give a couple of examples of good-old ordinary Black English dialect.

But the way she put it captured, as it happened, a basic truth about human speech. On the one hand, there is "speaking," a kind of effort or nicety that lends itself to ratings such as "pretty good." On the other hand, there is "talking"—people just letting language fall out of their mouths, with no conscious effort, no striving toward any ideal, just doing what comes naturally.

In the Beginning Was the Mouth

This woman was referring to her immediate context, where African-Americans negotiate a continuum between the standard English of the printed page and the Black English dialect of the familiar realm. In the Mississippi Delta, as in all black communities, Black English is the default, while standard English is something one switches in and out of according to topic, attitude, who one is speaking to, and personal background. But this switch-hitting is a local rendition of how language is used in all literate societies. The written variety penetrates the speech of ordinary people to varying degrees. No black Mississippi Delta resident can help dipping daily into *isn't* versus *ain't* or *he goes* versus *he go*. The spoken/written boundary is more penetrable in some places than others—the local dialect of Arabic an Arab learns on his mother's knee is as different from the standard Arabic used in writing and most public language as Latin is from Italian. But worldwide, the use of a language that has both written and spoken varieties entails constant choices between the two toolkits.

But the oral toolkit is ontologically primary. Writing is just a method for engraving on paper what comes out of our mouths.

A modern literate person can barely help but see it the other way around. Taught to write from an early age, when we haven't even fully mastered speech, we naturally tend to process speech as an oral rendition of the "real" language on the page. "The language" is imprinted, nice and tidy, on paper—indelible, authoritative. Talking seems a mere approximation of that, gone as soon as it comes out, and only fitfully as well-turned as the "real" language sitting on paper as a model. When we utter a word, we cannot help but mentally see an image of its written version. In our heads, what we have "said," or, to get the point across, "sayed," is that sequence of written symbols. When we say "dog," a little picture of that word flashes through our minds, *Sesame Street*–style.

But for all but a sliver of human history, this experience would have been as alien as being "beamed up" to the starship *Enterprise* would be to us. An estimate for how long human language has existed that few would have their tenure revoked for is 150,000 years. But writing did not exist until about 5,500 years ago in what is now the Middle East. This means that if humans had existed for twenty-four hours, writing would only have come along around 11:08 P.M. For the twenty-three plus hours—or to come back to reality, 144,500 years—before this, language worldwide was spoken only. That is, *all* humans had the relationship to language that only illiterates have today. Imagine saying "dog" and only thinking of a canine, but not thinking of the written word. If you're reading this book, it follows that you couldn't pull this off even at gunpoint. But for most of human history, no one on earth could even imagine any such failed effort because, from womb to tomb, they just talked.

For us, one way to peel away the layers of the onion and get into a real sense of what language really "is" is through music. Even in a literate population, the proportion of people who do not read music is larger than that which is illiterate, and even those who read music can fairly easily imagine what it would be like to not be able to. Take singing "Happy Birthday." If you do not read music, then you know that although it corresponds to a sequence of written musical symbols, for you this is a mere abstraction given that you just render it out of your head and larynx on the requisite occasion. You might even do this quite well—fine musicianship does not require musical literacy (Barbra Streisand does not read music). If you do read music, while you know that "Happy Birthday" can be written as a sequence of written notes, you can pretty easily put yourself into the mind of someone who just sings the damned thing—especially since you probably remember not being able to read music as a child. And although the women who wrote "Happy Birthday" were musically literate, theoretically the song could have been produced orally—just as, for example, the little "Ring Around the Rosy" tune that goes with the children's taunt "Nyah nyah-nyah nyah nyah" most likely was.

Dancing is another example. Dancing can be notated on paper, but such notation plays a relatively marginal role in the dance world. Dancing is, after all, something you just do, isn't it? If it's a planned-out affair, like a ballet, as often as not the creator or a disciple just teaches it to the dancers by demonstration bit by bit. And certainly when dancing socially at some party or club, we do not see ourselves as executing a version of an activity whose "real" representation is on the page. Of course, someone *could* videotape us wiggling around for fifteen minutes and encode it in a language designed to register each step, each swing of the arms, and each toss of the head. And on being presented with the transcription, we would be a tad perplexed, perhaps even a little uncomfortable, and not give it a moment's thought the next time we went out dancing. Dancing is something we *do*, not write down.

Language is exactly like singing and dancing. Printing and the spread of literacy happen to have created a First World in which the written version of language infuses our very souls, in a way that musical transcription only does for a few, and dance transcription for even fewer. But properly speaking, that is a historical accident. The capacity for language that we are, most likely, genetically specified for is an *oral* one. Just as we have no genetic endowment for driving, although many of us do it daily, we have no genetic endowment for reading (which in fact damages our eyes) or writing (which is hard on the hands and, on keyboards, now gives millions carpal-tunnel problems).

In fact, most of the 6,000 languages in the world remain, for all intents and purposes, exclusively oral in their usage. Of course by now most of them have been transcribed onto paper in some way—brief word lists in some cases, longer word lists and short grammatical descriptions in many others. For hundreds of languages there are these plus, say, Bible translations and some transcriptions of folktales. But even in these cases, the very sight of the language on the printed page is something of a novelty for its speakers, commonly evoking a certain marvel and gratitude. For them, the language remains fundamentally oral, used casually at home or with friends. They rarely read it, especially since there is so little to be read—no newspapers, magazines, or novels. How deeply can a word list permeate daily life? Few of even us speakers of written languages are given to curling up with a dictionary and a cup of hot cocoa on a blustery night. Speakers of oral languages commonly use one of the world's "big" languages for reading and writing.

But these "Berlitz" languages are very much the exception among the 6,000. Only about two hundred languages are regularly taught in writing to children, and only about half of them are represented by piles of works on a wide range of subjects to the extent that we could say that they have a literature. For most of the languages in the world, if you learn it, it'd better be in order to talk to its speakers, *a lot*—because there's barely anything in it to read. Language is talked. If it's written, that's just an accident.

Literates Don't Know They're Wet:
"Real" Language and "Trick" Language

We tend to see the oral languages as undeveloped, not measuring up to the state achieved by the written ones. Think of the frequent designation of such languages, quietly condescending, as "dialects" or "tongues." But since speech rather than writing is what all humans share, we can also see the oral languages as representing the bedrock of what human language consists of. And that bedrock is something quite different from what we are conditioned to see as what language is. Casual language and formal language are different animals, much more so than we are usually aware of on a conscious level, especially those of us in highly literate, First World societies.

How Many Words Can You Know?

For example, the multivolume, shelf-straining *Oxford English Dictionary* contains about 500,000 words. If we added all slang words and acronyms, the count would hit about a million. Written languages with substantial literatures tend to have vocabularies of comparable size. But this is a mere historical contingency, printing having allowed so many words that enter a language to be recorded indelibly and thus passed down as eternal "parts of the language." It is significant that no one person knows all of those million words in English. Estimates of how many words individuals control are tricky and controversial, but even those for highly educated people average somewhere between 50,000 and 100,000. And even they learned these from a lifetime's engagement with the printed page—as humanity goes, a recent appearance of a highly artificial nature, and available to an elite few.

But in "real" (that is, oral) languages, as new words and meanings enter a language, they often ease old ones aside. And these old words, without the artifice of writing to preserve them, gradually vanish from communal memory instead of living on as useless synonyms (*lift* versus *raise*) or obscure alternates (*dipsomaniac,* which now has an air of Fitzgerald about it, versus *alcoholic*).

We can see words hovering between the life support of big dictionaries and utter disappearance in the language used by talking drum players among the Lokele in the Democratic Republic of the Congo (Zaire). The drum language is not ordinary conversation, but a poetic, formulaic level of speech, and no living person recalls the meaning of many of its words. The words were current when the formulas were composed, but have since faded away except when caught, like flies in a window screen, in the special, archaic, drum talk. For English speakers, nursery rhymes provide some rough equivalents—what exactly is a *tuffet*? And if there were no dictionary to remind us, would we have any way of knowing? Ethan Allen doesn't sell *tuffets*.

But only so many such words happen to get snared in drum talk, traditional songs, or folktales. As such, an oral language typically has some thousands of words or, at most, some few tens of thousands. Even in these, there are still synonyms, words with similar but subtly different meanings and connotations, and layers of vocabulary used only in stories or ceremonies. But there is less of a difference from one person to another in command of "fancy" words. Only dictionaries give people beyond a small, learned elite ready access to a rarified layer of obscure words whose very use is more of a party trick than a neutral utterance. Take *ruth,* "mercy," that is, the noun that *ruthless* is based on—it's in the dictionary, but can we really say this is now a word in our language in anything but an ostentatious sense? There is, quite simply, no oral language with hundreds of thousands of words. "Who could remember them all?" we think—and indeed, none of us remember all of English's. But English is written. Most languages are not, and without writing, the memory is all there is.

Strung Out Short and Sweet: Sentences in Real Languages

In oral languages, sentence construction is also looser and less carefully planned out than in written varieties of language. Writing is a slow, conscious process that allows forethought and editing, and reading also allows careful savoring and, if necessary, backtracking. This is what allows elaborate passages like Everett's send-off:

Wheresoever throughout the civilized world the accounts of this great warfare are read, and down to the latest period of recorded time, in the glorious annals of our common country there will be no brighter page than that which relates *The Battle of Gettysburg*!

Everett wrote that out beforehand. Of course, a lifetime's acquaintance with written language may give one a knack for spinning out sentences like this spontaneously. But then this requires the previous existence of the written model. People speaking purely oral languages do not structure their sentences in this way.

It's not that they don't have grammar—au contraire. Purely oral languages tend to be spoken by smaller groups, and the fewer and more isolated a language's speakers are, the more frighteningly complex their grammar is likely to be in terms of conjugations, genders, and other bric-a-brac (I explored this in *The Power of Babel*). My linguist's sense is that if a language is unwritten, it will most likely have so many bells and whistles that it will leave me wondering how in the world any human being could actually speak it.

Yet, speakers of such languages do not typically wield their grammars within tapeworm sentences full of clauses layered all over one another. I see this all the time in my pet language, Saramaccan. It is a creole hybrid of English, Portuguese, and African languages, spoken by about 20,000 people in the Suriname rain forest, and written only by missionaries and linguists. Overall, Saramaccan is just talked; literate Saramaccan speakers usually read and write in Dutch, the language of the country that colonized Suriname from 1667 to 1975. And as a "talked" language, Saramaccan sentences are generally on the streamlined side compared to language like Everett's. Here is part of one folktale told to me by a native speaker. Notice that the information is nicely parcelled out among short sentences:

Anasi dε a wã kↄndε. Nↄↄ hε̃ wε wã mujεε bi dε a di kↄndε nããndε. Nↄↄ di mujεε, a pali di miii wã daka. Nↄↄ di a pali, nↄↄ dee oto sεmbε u di kↄndε, de a ta si ε̃ u soni. Hε̃ wε a begi Gadu te a wei. Hε̃ wε a go a lio. Nↄↄ di a go a lio, dee Gadu ko dε̃ε̃ wã mujεε mii.

Anancy (the spider) was in a village. And a woman was in the village there. And the woman bore a child one day. And when she gave birth, the other people in the village didn't want to have anything to do with her. Then she prayed to the gods fervently. Then she went to the river. And when she went to the river, the gods gave her a girl child.

The conventions of punctuation must not give the impression that Saramaccans putter through their folktales at the halting pace of synthesized speech. The sentences are threaded into fluent paragraphs complete with vivid intonations, etc. Yet all of this is accomplished within these bite-size sentences.

A different feel indeed from just one sentence from the beginning of the fourth Harry Potter installment: "They were rewarded for leaving their firesides when the Riddles' cook arrived dramatically in their midst and announced to the suddenly silent pub that a man called Frank Bryce had just been arrested." When asked to translate sentences like that into Saramaccan, invariably the speakers I work with spontaneously split it into smaller pieces. The Rowling passage would come out something like "They got a reward for leaving their firesides. The Riddles' cook came in to them dramatically. Then everything got quiet. Then the cook told them 'They just arrested a man called Frank Bryce!' "

If I present the speakers with a cooked-up Saramaccan passage structured as in written English, I and the graduate students working with me are now familiar with a certain bemused smile and shake of the head, followed by the response we now almost chant along with: "Well, if you said that people would *understand* you, but . . ." It's always clear that they are quietly thinking "What in God's name is this screwed-up (you know the word I really want to use) Saramaccan they come up with?!" And note that the speaker will say "If you *said* that"—because the language for all intents and purposes does not exist on paper, beyond some religious and teaching materials and collected folktales. To us, Rowling's phraseology seems ordinary, but it is actually only so in a written language.

Indeed, it is only *possible* in a written language. Imagine hearing the Rowling passage spoken to you casually, assuming—as will require a stretch for all but about seven people by now—that you had never read a Harry Potter book. And remember that language is spoken quickly. One's response would likely be "Hold on!"—so much packed into one sentence, with that "the suddenly silent pub" feeling especially "jammed in." This is why oral languages are not spoken in this way—in them, uttering a sentence like this would qualify at best as a stunt. The language's grammar overall will most likely be a nightmare—*fireside, cook, pub,* and *man* might all have different gender markers; the way the language expresses "had just been arrested" might be one of eight different types of past tense. But the event would *not* be described in one tapeworm sentence.

It's Always All About You

These kinds of contrasts between an oral language like Saramaccan and the written mode of English also hold between the oral and written varieties of one and the same language. A "Berlitz" language is in a way two: the natural oral one and the constructed written one.

A Vocabulary-Type Thing

Vocabulary in the spoken variety of a language, for instance, is smaller than in its written variety. One way to harness this to numerical demonstration is with a ratio between the number of different words in a passage and the total number of words in it. For example, the total number of words in that last sentence was twenty-nine, while the number of *different* words is twenty-two, yielding a ratio, rounded down, of .76. Of course, with whole paragraphs the ratio is much lower than this, as the *of*'s and *a*'s and *the*'s multiply, for example.

But Wallace Chafe and Jane Danielewicz found that the ratio in academic prose is, on average, still larger by a third than in speech—including even professors' speech as they lecture. The *Oxford English Dictionary* sits on library shelves, but when speaking live and in the moment, we cannot command its 500,000 words, or even the fraction of this that we wield when writing. Instead, when we talk, we select our words from a much smaller set, comparable to that used by the speaker of an oral language.

We reveal this limited choice in our tendency to bedeck our speech with hedges like, well, *like,* and *sort of,* and others when choosing words. Chafe and Danielewicz give conversational examples like:

She was still young enough so I . . . I just . . . was able to put her in an . . . uh—*sort of* . . . sling . . . I mean one of those tummy packs . . . you know.

Aaand the graduate students are *kind of* scattered around.

That last one might be rendered in writing as something like "The graduate students are thinly dispersed," but *dispersed* did not occur immediately to the speaker, as it very well might not to us if we were talking in the moment. And I must admit a certain curiosity as to just what kind of "tummy pack" the previous speaker was referring to, but the upshot is that the speaker's immediate access to vocabulary did not, at least in that segment of their utterance, even succeed in conveying just what they meant at all. And that's despite that Chafe and Danielewicz are academics, such that the people most readily available for them to record were naturally all educated, articulate people.

A modern example typical in the speech of people about thirty-five and under is "type thing": "So we had a debate-type thing where we hashed it all out," someone says, when what transpired was nothing so formal as a debate, but a concentrated dwelling upon an issue by people with disparate opinions. A more considered rendition might be "So we explored the issue in an extended fashion." It's no accident that we do not write "type thing"—it's something oral language needs, but written English, which gives us time to think, does not.

And all languages, written or not, have similar hedge markers—learning them is part of really speaking any language (along with being able to readily render *I sank in the mud up to my ankles* and *Get that out of my hair!*). Russian speech is sprinkled, for example, with their *like* equivalent *značit*, "it means . . ." To hedge is human—in *oral* language.

I Talk Like *That*?

Spoken English also spreads thoughts out into more clauses and sentences, Saramaccan-style, than written English. Here is a thoroughly ordinary bit of something someone said somewhere sometime. If you can bend yourself into imagining how you really talk on an everyday level, what really comes out of your mouth, you can imagine yourself saying something like this, say, on the phone:

> I had to wait, I had to wait till it was born and till it got to about eight or ten weeks of age, then I bought my first dachshund, a black-and-tan bitch puppy, as they told me I should have bought a bitch puppy to start off with, because if she wasn't a hundred percent good I could choose a top champion dog to mate her to, and then

produce something that was good, which would be in my own ken-
nel prefix.[1]

That, ladies and gentlemen, is how English speakers talk, all over the
world. Any sense we have of how the person "should" have said it reflects our immersion in a print culture, where we see a gussied-up version of language on paper day in and day out. But composing that takes
a kind of effort only possible when we have time to reflect. For example,
here is how linguist M.A.K. Halliday rephrases this, quite plausibly, in
formal written English:

> Some eight or ten weeks after the birth saw my first acquisition of a
> dachsund, a black-and-tan bitch puppy. It seems that a bitch puppy
> would have been the appropriate initial purchase, because of the
> possibility of mating an imperfect specimen with a top champion
> dog, the improved offspring then carrying my own kennel prefix.

Two sentences and out. But no one talks like this all day, or at least we
hope they don't. These sentences took some doing—they are a different
kind of English, the written variety.

Some readers may be skeptical that they, or most people, actually
talk along the lines of these choppy passages. But if I may be so bold,
you do, unless you are singularly given to linguistic self-monitoring. It
can be shocking to see how we actually talk when our casual speech is
transcribed word for word. This is no holier-than-thou book, and I can
use myself as an example. I once participated in a free-form discussion of
a then-hot topic scheduled after a conference, and the session was later
transcribed word for word and included in a volume gathering the papers that had been delivered during the days before the final session. In
the live situation, I held my own well enough. But I can hardly bear
reading myself in the transcription where, on the page, at times I almost
look like I have a speech disorder.

But actually I was just talking the way all of us do day-to-day, and
many of the participants look about the same on the page. Live speech is
not only sparse-ish with its vocabulary and airy in its sequencing of

---

[1.] "Bitch puppy" does not sound quite everyday to most of us, but is natural to dog
breeders and is in general used more conventionally as a term for female dogs in
England, where this person lived.

packets of information, but full of fillers, expressions like *you know* that check that the listener understands, and half-cocked utterances that would qualify as "sentence fragments" or "run-on sentences" in written language.

Only rarely is spoken language written down word for word, but when it is, the result is always a tad unsettling. Written English is tidy, and meanwhile literacy leads us to harbor in our minds an image of what we say as cast in writing (the d-o-g phenomenon I mentioned). It's a short step from there to assuming that we talk like we write. But here are two students in a junior college in California in the early 1970s, taped in running conversation:

A.   On a tree. Carbon isn't going to do much for a tree really. Really. The only thing it can do is collect moisture. Which may be good for it. In other words in the desert you have the carbon granules which would absorb, collect moisture on top of them. Yeah. It doesn't help the tree but it protects, keeps the moisture in. Uh. Because then it just soaks up moisture. It works by the water molecules adhere to the carbon moleh, molecules that are in the ashes. It holds it on. And the plant takes it away from there.

B.   Oh, I have an argument with you.

A.   Yeah.

B.   You know, you said how silly it was about my, uh, well, it's not a theory at all. That the more pregnant you are and you see spots before your eyes it's proven that it's the retention of the water.

A.   Yeah, the water's just gurgling all your eyes.

That is how the people in the Norman Rockwell painting were talking over that Thanksgiving dinner, how two bank tellers talk on a smoking break outside by the ATM machines, how you and your friends in a dorm room talked (don't I know—I made such a tape of my college friends and me in the early eighties and was flabbergasted by how messy our speech was). And yet, just imagine how bloody with red ink a composition teacher would leave this if it were presented as written English:

A.   On a tree. (*frag.*) Carbon isn't going to do much for a tree really. Really. (*repetitious*) The only thing it can do is collect moisture. Which may be good for it. (*frag.*) In other words in the desert you have the carbon granules which would absorb, collect (*choose one word*) moisture on top of them. Yeah. (*No.*) It doesn't help the tree but it protects, keeps (*choose one word*) the moisture in. Uh huh. (*Uh uh*) Because then it just soaks up moisture. (*frag.*) It works by the water molecules adhere to (*awk.*) the carbon moleh, molecules (*stutter*) that are in the ashes. It holds it on. (*repetitious*) And the plant takes it away from there. (*awk.*)

B. Oh, I have an argument with you.

A. Yeah.

B. You know (*if he knows, why tell him he does?*), you said how silly it was about my, uh, well, (*what is your "uh well"?*) it's not a theory at all. (*overall, awk.*) That the more pregnant you are and you see spots before your eyes (*very awk.*) it's proven that it's the retention of the water.

A. Yeah, the water's just gurgling all your eyes. (*eyes are not gurgled*) *Come see me.*

And this oral/written split is human, not particular to English. We see it with Russian in Tolstoy's *Anna Karenina*, in a chapter where, for example, gentlemen farmers talk casually among themselves. Here is one statement by one of the farmers. Note the short clauses, a kind of series of verbal explosions:

Ja požalujus'?	I lodge a complaint?
Da ni za što v svete!	Nothing in the world!
Razgovory takie pojdut, što i ne rad žalobe!	The way conversations like that go you aren't even glad of the complaint!
Vot na zavode—vzjali zadatki, ušli.	Take at the mill—took the advance, took off.
Što ž mirovoj sud'ja?	The justice of the peace, what?
Opravdal, tol'ko i deržitsja vse volostnym sudom da staršinoj.	He acquitted—the only thing keeping any kind of order is the communal tribunal plus the village elder.

Etot otporet jevo po-starinomu.	That'll beat some sense into them the old-fashioned way.
A ne bud' etovo—brosaj vse!	And without that—toss it all!
Begi na kraj sveta!	Run to the other end of the earth!

On the other hand, Anna's husband always talks in ornate sentences such as "Though indeed I fail to comprehend how, with the independence you show, informing your husband outright of your infidelity and seeing nothing reprehensible in it, apparently, you can find anything reprehensible in performing a wife's duties in relation to your husband." This is one of many ways Tolstoy highlights the man's coldness. Even to intimates, he doesn't talk like a normal human being, instead, maintaining the self-monitored pose of written language.

But Karenin is an outlier, as well as a fictional creation. Overall, human beings just talk all of the time, the world over.

Caveat Lector: "Bad" Grammar Versus Spoken Grammar

Before we move on, I should make clear that our issue is not, as it may reasonably appear, the difference between "bad" grammar and "proper" grammar.

Indeed, sentences like "Billy and me went to the store" instead of "Billy and I went to the store" and constructions like "less books" instead of "fewer books" are much more likely in spoken English than written. But the sense that utterances like these are errors is, while understandable, mistaken, as I and a busful of other linguists have argued in various books over the decades. The blackboard grammar rules that we are chided about by people with a bee in their bonnet about grammatical correctness are myths, mostly cooked up by a few self-appointed grammarians in the 1600s and 1700s. The very idea that grammatical "mistakes" eternally tempt the unwary is the spawn of three illusions that seduced these bewigged martinets.

One was that all languages should pattern like Latin even if, well, they weren't Latin. This meant that double negatives like "I never go nowhere" were wrong because Latin did not have them, though most of the world's languages do—and most varieties of English always have.

The second was that when a grammar changes, it must be decaying rather than just, say, changing. So we were taught to lasso and hold on to *whom,* though at the time it was fading from English just like all the other words and constructions that differentiated Modern English from Old English—a foreign tongue to us that none of us feel deprived in not speaking.

The third was that grammar must always be strictly logical. Naturally, then, we must say "Billy and I went to the store" because "*I* is a subject," although this leaves behind other illogicalities no one complains about, such as that "I and Billy went to the store" sounds like a Martian's rendition of English even though *I* is used as the subject, or that if someone asks "Who did this?" and you answer "Ahem—*I!*," you'd better look over your shoulder for men in white coats, though your "I" would be very much a subject.

When linguists make such observations, outside observers often read it as an expression of the leftist tilt in academia. Innumerable commentators suspect that behind the calls to "Leave Your Language Alone" lurks a reflexive animus toward The Powers That Be. But while the leftist bias in academia is real, the kinds of arguments I just galloped through are based on logic, pure and simple. Some readers will be aware that my politics tilt rightward as often as leftward, and as such, I am not exactly primed to embrace arguments just because they "feel good." Yet I have spent portions of some of my books outlining the hollowness of blackboard grammar (*The Word on the Street* gives special attention to the point).

The unequivocal fallacy in the proper English/bad English dichotomy is especially clear when we look at some of the things language purists were complaining about in the past that are universally accepted today. At this point, linguists, including me, tend to go back several centuries. (Note how awkward "... linguists, including I, tend to go back ..." would have looked, and yet *I* is a subject after all! ...) But, actually, the case was well made as recently as the era when Everett and Lincoln spoke.

One of my favorites is that as late as the 1800s, many stewards of "good English" considered a sentence like "A house is being built over there" wrong, with "A house is building over there" being correct. "The book is being printed" was "vulgar," "The book is printing" was "right." The year after Gettysburg, one grammarian was groaning about this particular "inaccuracy" that had "crept into the language, and is now found everywhere." In 1883, *Harper's Weekly* presented a "joke" in which this "inaccuracy" impeded communication across the generations:

Old Gentl.—Are there any houses *building* in your village?

Young Lady—No Sir, there is a new house *being built* for Mr. Smith, but it is the carpenters who are *building*.

Well, har *har!*—there's wit for the ages. Or not—the joke is opaque to us and anyone now alive (imagine it as a quick blackout exchange between Artie Johnson and Goldie Hawn on *Laugh-In* followed by them breaking into "The Swim" to that bouncy, saxy music!). This is because now "The house is being built" is ordinary and "The house is building" sounds like something from the same Martian who would regale us with "I and Billy went to the store." Language changes whether we like it or not. What look like rules from on high within our lifespans are always, in grand view, rationalizations that we superimpose upon language for impressionistic reasons, just as we think of a tomato as a vegetable instead of a fruit. Edward Everett and Abraham Lincoln probably sensed "The house is being built" as newfangled, but now we don't—life went on and, really, we have bigger things on our plates.

Certainly there are *real* mistakes, like saying "boy the," lvng out vwls, or talking backward. Or less hyperbolically, saying things like "Me wants candy" or one of my favorites, in response to my saying to someone new to English that I liked dinosaurs, her smiling and exclaiming, "I like dinosaurs either!" But no one makes true mistakes like this in any language unless they are children ("Me wants candy"), foreigners ("I like dinosaurs either"), or brain-damaged (the language of many people who have recently suffered strokes, for example). Beyond these subsets of a population, there is, quite simply, no such thing as a human being walking around using bad grammar.

Important: my argument is not that people need not be taught standard English in school; they do and likely always will. My point is more specific: The casual speech constructions that we use alongside standard English, that we are taught, are illogical; wrong, and mistakes, are in reality just alternates that happen not to have been granted social cachet.

Language from 11 P.M. to 11:30 P.M.

And with that we return to my observation that just talking (albeit not in "bad grammar") casually is all anyone does all over the world. Or has ever done, for that matter. It can look as if in the past, everybody talked like a book and that the way people talk today is a decline. But that's just an artifact of technology.

How Did George Washington Talk?

It's sobering to realize that short of that time machine, we will never hear an actual human voice from before 1877, when Thomas Edison recited "Mary Had a Little Lamb" on a cylinder wrapped in tinfoil. (This is a truly haunting few seconds—a man talking 125 years ago as I write, a man talking *when Rutherford B. Hayes was President*—and Edison sounds almost frantic, as if he knew that he was about to turn the world upside down.) For all of the time before that, we can only engage people verbally on the page—and that automatically means that their thoughts have been translated into the written variety. Vital, oral language only peeks out here and there when someone decides to quote someone directly now and then, but this is rare. Of course, fiction writers often put language into the mouths of their characters that is intended as natural. But as often as not, the result is as much caricature as depiction. And since conscious awareness of the systematic differences between oral and written language is largely confined to linguists and social scientists, these linguistic portraits usually only approximate the patterns of actual human speech. Mark Twain's Huck and Jim, for instance, for all of their dialectal pronunciations and grammar, express themselves in longer, tidier, better planned-out passages than any humans, educated or not, do on an everyday basis.

And our access to casual speech is even narrower than the 1877 date suggests, because until just a few decades ago, all but a sliver of recordings of the human voice are speeches and performances. Thomas Edison didn't record himself kibbitzing with his family. In ancient silent-film clips from the turn of the twentieth century, we can see ordinary folks walking around chatting, but no one dragged out a phonograph recorder to record what they were saying. Sound films start in the twenties, but again, they were all of people performing. "Photoplays," as they were called in the press for a while, were a commercial product, and nobody was going to pay to watch people off of the street gabbing about where their shoes pinched and wondering when somebody was going to invent the computer. If you wanted to listen to a *spontaneous* conversation in America as late as 1950, where would you hope to find it? If you have been around long enough to remember people talking casually that far back, think about it—who ever *recorded* your Uncle Max teasing Aunt Bella about how she cooked?

Most of the language of the distant past comes down to us spruced up in its Sunday best—either written up nice and clean, or, if oral, then from people declaiming from scripts or reading off of written notes. Naturally, then, from our vantage point the raggedness of oral language looks like a new development.

Early Writing: Talking on Paper

But viewed more closely, the historical record reveals the truth. In the few languages that developed written varieties, the process took time. As one might predict, the people who first wrote languages down could hardly have yanked Ciceronian syntax out of the air. Instead, they wrote largely the way they spoke. A good example is, of all things, the Bible. Modern translations of the first lines of Genesis read as we expect prose to:

> In the beginning, when God created the heavens and the earth, the earth was a formless wasteland, and darkness covered the abyss, while a mighty wind swept over the waters. Then God said "Let there be light," and there was light.

But this is not how the original Hebrew version scanned at all. The Bible was written down in a culture just past "real" language, the spoken variety in all of its choppy, meat-and-potatoes majesty:

> *Bereshit bara Elohim et hashamayim ve'et ha'arets.*
> *Veha'arets hayetah tohu vavohu*
> *vechoshech al-peney tehom veruach.*
> *Elohim merafechet al-peney hamayim.*
> *Vayomer Elohim yehi-or va-yehi-or.*

> In the beginning God created the heavens and the earth.
> And the earth was formless and empty
> with darkness on the face of the depths.
> God's spirit moved on the water's surface.
> God said "There shall be light" and light came into existence.

No *when, while,* and *then* to knit things together like cheese in a casserole. Four sentences instead of two, presented with a spareness that to us constitutes its own kind of drama. But as Walter Ong observes in his splendid *Orality and Literacy* (a truly consciousness-altering book I highly recommend), there was nothing special about this scansion to ordinary people alive when it was written. Written-style prose was in its infancy; they were just talking. In other words, the Hebrew Bible is a useful source not only of moral and literary wisdom, but of the heart of human linguistic expression—the orally based style. To us, the original phrasing almost feels like a folk song, and with good reason—it reflects how language is produced by folks.

Even later writing often retains an air of oralness about it, reflecting a world when writing actually still was what we tend to mistakenly think it is now—speech transcribed onto the page. As late as the early Middle Ages, in his *Summa Theologica,* Saint Thomas Aquinas presented his arguments not as endless successions of paragraphs of bald exposition, but as if he were engaging in an oral debate. "Whether love is a passion," one section is titled. Following are three objections to that thesis: "Objection 1: It would seem that love is not a passion. For no power is a passion. But every love is a power, as Dionysius says (Div. Nom. iv). Therefore love is not a passion." And then two other objections presented similarly. "On the contrary," Aquinas declaims, "The Philosopher (by which he meant Aristotle) says (Ethic. viii, 5) that 'love is a passion'." Then, as if he were taking the floor from Aristotle speaking, he writes "I answer that: Passion is the effect of the agent on the patient . . ." and follows with an elegant argument concurring with Aristotle. He then presents discrete replies to each of the three objections in sequence: "Reply to Objection 1. Since power denotes a principle of movement or action, Dionysius calls love a power, in so far as it is a principle of movement in the appetite," and so on.

Philosophers don't write like this today. They typically write in lengthy, abstract paragraphs of ratiocination, with no such explicit flagging of the guideposts of their argument. Thomas Aquinas wrote this way because in his time, written conventions had yet to jell to the extent that they have today. The fact that we see his presentation as bracingly clear reflects its roots in spoken exchange, which indeed evolved for clarity and processibility since live communication leaves no space for rereading and musing.

Mumbling Monks: Between Orality and Literacy

"Peev'd" by Jonathan Swift's disparagement of our speech and strapping ourselves into that time machine to travel back further, we could have gotten another glimpse of the oral-to-written transition: noisy libraries. Silent reading was a gradual development throughout Europe: at first, writing was thought of as something to recite from, not to sit alone reading in one's head, initially seen a rather odd-duck thing to do. In other words, writing was still processed as speech transcribed onto paper rather than as the way language "really is." Inevitably, at this intermediate stage between orality and modern literacy, it felt natural to translate writing back into actual speech when reading.

We recapitulate the development from pure orality to today's hyperliteracy when we mouth the words as we first learn to read, and we can spot an inexperienced reader by their doing so. But in a world where reading was rarer, medievals quite literate by the standards of their day went through their whole lives gaily mumbling away when buried in a book. The originals of classical Latin and Greek texts were written with no spaces between the words—just as, if you think about it, there are no   actual   pauses   between   words   when   we   speak. It was assumed that the text would be read aloud, such that where the words stopped and started would be toocleartorequireindicationonthe-page (see—it made sense). And even by the early Middle Ages, at a cloister library monks read out loud to themselves, with carrels separated by stone walls to muffle what was considered a thoroughly ordinary noise, like a car alarm in Manhattan set off by someone sneezing in Connecticut.

Chaos Down Below: Fossils of an Oral Past

Even individual words shed light on the path from oral to written. Written language bears ample footprints of a chaotic oral past, abruptly frozen in place by print and tradition as if by some freeze ray out of Marvel Comics. Peering through a microscope at seemingly faceless words reveals written language as a kind of frozen smile, a public face for something harder to pin down if we are allowed a greater intimacy and look more closely. Take a rather formal English phrase, "often ahead, seldom behind." It is full of fossilized remnants of the nature of spoken as opposed to written language.

We'll proceed backward. *Behind* is one of a set of words expressing position with the prefix *be-* and a root word. In the case of *below* and *beside*, the roots *low* and *side* are still used. *Fore*—well, dictionaries have it, but outside of the expression "to the fore," most of us would be hard pressed to recall when we ever heard it used alone beyond a golf course. But where is *hind*? Yes, we have it in "hind leg"—but as it happens, this arose as a shortening of good old *behind*. The original word *hind* was lost to the ages before widespread literacy and comprehensive dictionaries came along to encase words like it in amber. Or *between*—what's *tween*? An old word for *two*, whose only remnant now is *twain*, which like *ruth* is "in the dictionary," but is utterly unusable outside of a highly arch poem. *Beneath's neath* is also restricted to poetry, in which case we sense it less as a word of its own, but as a mannered elision of *beneath*—we do not say "I stuck the gum to the table's *neath*." And where is "betop?" Who knows? In earlier English, an oral language, some words lived, some died. *Behind, between,* and *beneath* retain echoes of words lost back when English speakers, like most people, just talked.

Seldom started out as *seldan*. No one knows just why it became *seldom*. This kind of morphing is ordinary in languages in which printing and literacy have not enshrined certain forms of words as official, lending a sense that to depart from them is to err. In our world, when George in Edward Albee's play *Who's Afraid of Virginia Woolf?* pronounced *bourbon* as "bour-gon" as a boy, he was jeered into falling in line. But smallish transgressions like that still manage to seep into the language here and there. How many people really say "COME-fer-ta-bull" as opposed to "CUNF-ter-bull" for *comfortable*? A Martian who came down and composed a word list of English without access to a dictionary would certainly, upon listening to hundreds of American English speakers, record the word as something like "cunferble"—even if all he heard were university faculty meetings. *Seldan* underwent a similar process, crunched around in early medieval mouths less concerned with the printed page than we can easily imagine.

Ahead—again, pull back the camera and logic fades away. *Ahead*, yes, and also *aside*. *Aback*, however, is either *Li'l Abner* (*aback of the house*) or ghettoized into the one expression *taken aback*. *Atop*? Poetry only. And there is no *aneath, alow,* or *atween*. They either didn't happen or faded away—and no one cared, because the language was in the mouth, not on the page. We have *above*—but what are *boves*?

And finally *often*—we are familiar with the poetic *oft*, and in fact this is the original word. Where did the *-en* come from? As far as we know, people started tacking it on because it seemed right since the same ending hung on the end of *often*'s opposite—*seldan*! *Often ahead, seldan behind*—but then *seldan* morphed into *seldom* and left *often* with a little appendix, as meaningless as the organ that sits in us courting infection.

Write Makes Might

Just as no human community can keep track of a million words, none can police even 30,000 words for changes, nor police its grammar to keep it faultlessly logical. Oral language lives not to please language mavens or our sense of linguistic feng shui, but to communicate, to maintain social ties, to live life from mundane moment to moment. Those functions require geometrical tidiness no more than singing or dancing do. It is common today to hear someone talking on a cell phone announce "I'm in a store." That's what oral language is for—to announce that even though you're in a store, you are still on tap to play your role in the social fabric—that you *are*. Without spoken language, you *are* not. It is how—or since all humans use language, it is *what*—we *be*.

But we would sense it as rather trivial to *write* "I'm in a store," or even "I *was* in a store" earlier today, even in the hastiest e-mail message. In McLuhanesque terms, written language is cooler than oral. It is less something that we *be* than something that we *do* after having "been," that we execute in order to record the worthier portion of what we have "been." Written language, then, selecting from reality and then ordering and airbrushing it, is an art. In the fifteenth century, when English was still primarily an oral language, pioneering printer William Caxton bemoaned that English had no "*art* of rhetoric"—italics mine.

But then passages like the written version of the one about the bitch puppy—"Some eight or ten weeks after the birth saw my first acquisition of a dachshund"—might suggest that *artifice* rather than *art* would be a better term. There are those who sense an air of the Marx Brothers' ritzy foil Margaret Dumont in this kind of English, and question its status as progress. Swift was one, skeptical of the written variety jelling as he lived. He thrilled to the majestic tread of the English-language Douay Bible translation of 1610, which stuck closer to the original Hebrew phraseology (although rendered secondhand through the earlier Latin translation):

I doubt whether the alterations since introduced, have added much to the beauty or strength of the English tongue, though they have taken off a great deal from that simplicity, which is one of the greatest perfections in any language . . . No translation our country ever yet produced, hath come up to that of the Old and New Testament . . . I am persuaded that the translators of the Bible were masters of an English style much fitter for that work, than any we see in our present writings, which I take to be owing to the simplicity that runs through the whole.

More recently in the late 1960s, William Labov, who was instrumental in bringing the structredness of casual speech to the attention of linguists and beyond, ventured that the written style is "turgid, bombastic and empty" compared to the vividness of spontaneous utterances.

Doubtless, written language deserves that condemnation at times—the opacity of so much modern academic prose is an example, and would be virtually impossible in a strictly oral language. But there is always the fly in the ointment. Overall, written language is a distinctly *useful* art.

Written Language Is Leaner and Meaner

For example, casual speech is full of repetitions. In high-speed scenes in early Hollywood cartoons, a character often does something funny not once, but three times—stretching their legs like rubber hoses over a rock as they ski out of control down a mountain, etc. Early animators did this to save time and money by reusing footage, but many of us know people who seem unable to resist making a rather mundane point at least three times, although money is not an issue and they have little apparent interest in time-saving. And all of us do this to some extent when talking—speech reflects our emotions, which do not evaporate just because we have vented them one time. Here is a real-life utterance from a British teenager, with the repetitions in italics:

Well it should do but it don't seem to nowadays, like there's still murders going on now, any minute now or something like that they get people don't care they might get away with it then they all try it and it might leak out one might tell his mates that he's killed someone *it might leak out* like *it might get around* he gets hung for it like that.

That passage hardly sounds unusual as casual speech goes, nor does this guy even sound like the type with a particular broken-record tic. It's just how people talk. As sociologist Basil Bernstein put it about casual speech, "The thoughts are often strung together like beads on a frame rather than following a planned sequence. A restriction in planning often creates a high degree of redundancy. This means that there may well be a great deal of repetition of information, through sequences which add little to what has already been given."

But idle repetition is much less common in written English. However moved or excited one might be about the subject, writing a statement out once discourages writing it again. With the statement sitting engraved forever on the page instead of floating out of our mouths into instant oblivion, it's strikingly obvious that, well, we already said it. Plus, writing takes effort, and in all human endeavors, the principle of least effort has a way of looming ever large. As a result, written English is generally cleaner, more economical, than spoken English.

Written Language Spells It All Out for You

Bernstein became famous for his exploration of a larger distinction between the oral and the written. He noted that speech is "event-oriented," designed for the here-and-now, while written language is "extended argument–oriented," encompassing the past and the future as well as the present, designed to express a broader canvas of experience. More properly, Bernstein was concerned with the oral reflection of written language, the kind of speech that results from constant immersion in print. He distinguished what he termed the "restricted code"—"in an, uh, sort of sling—I mean one of those tummy packs, you know"—from the "elaborated code" that children steeped in print acquire naturally.

It would be more exact to say that Bernstein became as much infamous as famous, as he couched his argument in the tripwire issue of class. He saw working-class children as hampered scholastically by their greater comfort with the restricted rather than elaborated code. He had the misfortune of presenting his work in the early 1960s, soon after which a Political Correctness took hold of academia and cast his "deficit model" of the lower classes as morally suspect. It was his "elaborated code," for example, that sparked William Labov's dismissal as "turgid, bombastic and empty."

Bred in Great Britain, where class is so immediately felt that a scholar is especially likely to address it, and couching his ideas in the donnish terms typical of British scholars of his vintage, Bernstein unwittingly made his own bed to an extent. Only with our historical-perspective glasses on can we moderns read proclamations about working-class people like "Relative to the middle classes, the postponement of present pleasure for future gratifications will be found difficult" without flinching. Because of passages like this, and others where he casually refers to the "backwardness" of working-class children, even today Bernstein's thesis is taught in many classes on sociolinguistics with a certain aggressive skepticism.

But much of the problem is mere change in fashion as terms go. In his sociological treatises of the turn of the twentieth century, W.E.B. Du Bois dwelled casually in terms quite similar to Bernstein's, and often more nakedly judgmental. In this, he was simply typical of his Victorian era, and yet is revered as one of humankind's visionaries. If Bernstein were writing today, he would likely substitute something like "natural code" for restricted code, and thus raise fewer antennas.

In any case, Bernstein was no conscript in the culture wars. At the end of the day, his observations represented the sincere concern of a specialist in the sociology of education about disparities in performance between lower- and middle-class students. After the initial onslaught against his ideas from the New Left, he doggedly clarified in later work that he never meant to imply that the elaborated code was utterly foreign to working-class children, but that middle-class children were more accustomed to using it actively.

And whatever one's views on the class aspect of the issue, linguistically, Bernstein was on to something real. His ultimate point was that casual speech is more telegraphic than written language because shared experience between speakers obviates the need for explicitness:

> A restricted code will arise where the form of the social relation is based upon closely shared identifications, upon an extensive range of shared expectations, upon a range of common assumptions . . . Such codes will emerge as both controls and transmitters of the culture in such diverse groups as prisons, the age group of adolescents, army, friends of long standing, between husband and wife . . . meaning does not have to be fully explicit, a slight shift of pitch or stress, a small gesture, can carry a complex meaning.

Bernstein also captured the issues of vocabulary size and tight structural planning that distinguish the written from the oral:

> Meanings which are discreet and local to the speaker must be cut so that they are intelligible to the listener, and this pressure forces upon the speaker to select both among syntactic alternatives and encourages differentiation of vocabulary.

Anna Karenina, of all things, neatly captures what Bernstein meant. In the passage before in which the farmer complains, I provided my own translation, designed to correspond as closely as possible to each chunk of this highly oral kind of Russian, and convey the true nature of the utterance. I did this because official translations tend to convert passages like this into more elaborated language, filling in background information intuitive to the Czarist Russian reader, but unrecoverable to readers outside of Tolstoy's time and place. For example, the farmer precisely says, "The justice of the peace, what?" and this is what I gave. But this could theoretically mean "Why do they have this justice of the peace there?" or "What about the justice of the peace—wasn't he available to do something?" or any number of things. Rosemary Edmonds's classic translation has "And what did the justice of the peace do?," filling in just how this utterance connects with what precedes and comes after.

A useful comparison is a hypothetical statement by a modern American:

> "Internet? Forget it! I start out—hundred thousand a week, easy. Two years later, thirty thousand dollars' debt, a secretary, us and two temps. 'Cyberspace will bring us all together'—yeah, right. Early retirement—*that* was some dream."

Familiar with the recent boom and bust in the Web start-up world, that telegraphic barstool gripe will make sense to American readers today even on the page. But if someone picks up this book in a library in twenty years, the passage will already convey fewer immediate impressions, especially if the reader is too young to have lived through the turn of the millennium as a mature person. Back to the time machine— imagine eavesdropping on a drunken businessman complaining under gaslight about what happened to them on the commodities market in the Panic of 1893. In a similar way, the young reader of 2024 will not re-member the NPR pieces about "dot-com millionaires," the classic image of the once-bustling dot-com office space now full of empty cubicles, *Wired* magazine's gee-whiz gushing about the impending "cybercommu-nity," the sexy archetype of the thirty-something Internet millionaire cash-ing it all in and spending the rest of his life investing in other people's ventures, or meeting people at parties in 2001 and 2002 out of work af-ter the dot-com they worked for went bust.

Thus, if a character in a novel written now uttered that passage, then a Russian translation by Rosemarija Edmondskaya in 125 years would have to render it along the filled-out lines of "People say the way to riches is the Internet? A ridiculous notion! When I started out, my com-pany was making a hundred thousand dollars a week with no trouble. But then just two years later, we were thirty thousand dollars in debt, and our staff was reduced to one secretary . . ." and so on.

Written Language Rises Above It

It follows that written language is also a better vehicle for objective argument than speech. Casual speech is shot through not only with the bread-and-butter "parts of speech", à la *Schoolhouse Rock* ("a noun is a person, place, or thing") but with flags of how we feel about what we are saying. You can wrap your head around this by imagining how unlikely it would be to read in a newspaper a sentence like "The senator just never attended the meeting." There is a lot in that little word *just*: it lends a sense that the senator should have attended, and that opting not to was a rather unusual, and even socially maladroit, choice. That sense of judgment is a personal one, which is why the *just* injects the writer's soul into the statement and makes the sentence feel more alive than "The senator did not attend the meeting." But we expect newspaper writers to be as objective as possible, and hence how rare it is to see them use these flags of personal orientation in their sentences.

Nothing bars these flags from written language in the strict mechani-cal sense. To write "The senator just never attended the meeting" takes no special effort. But if a literate society values that there be a space for objective argument, as Western societies tend to, then it grants writing pride of place within that space, rather than speech. This is because writ-ing is better suited than speech for this focus on the logical over the felt—a focus that is properly a distortion of "real" language, but is as useful as it is artificial. One simply could not be a human being and *speak* without using words like *just*; we feel while we talk, or if we don't, we are distinctly unwell. But writing, deliberate and piecemeal, allows the editing of the heart from one's prose, leaving just the head.

For all that, such language lends itself to charges of coldness, the maximum objectivity that scientific discourse strives toward would be impossible without it. It also allows at least the pretense of journalistic impartiality. Certainly this goal is consistently undershot and probably unattainable, but few would argue that inserting *more* personal sentiment would lead us any closer to the ideal. And as for Orwell's exploration of the exploitative potential of "doubletalk," the wariness of "big words" and tricky phrasing that his warning creates is healthy to an extent. But then lying and dissimulation hardly require elevated language—for 150,000 years people have been doing it using the humblest of speech as well ("It depends on what *is* is"). Its pitfalls acknowledged, written language has enabled literate societies to immeasurably enrich the human experience with the artful manipulation of a genetic endowment.

Talk Marches On

Yet, we must remember that languages keep on being talked even after the written variety becomes established. The repetition, the here-and-now focus, and the messy subjectivity hang in there on the day-to-day level. And there is always that mushy changeability: recall things like "The house is building" that randomly fell by the wayside in the 1800s.

But then that construction sounds rather formal to our ear, encouraging that sense that in the old days people talked like books. One way of getting at the relentless coexistence of scruffy speech and starchy writing is through sounds. They're fragile creatures, and the correspondence between how words are written century after century and how many people actually pronounce them is always approximate.

An example are the explorers Lewis and Clark. We see them in noble paintings, read that they were close confidants of Thomas Jefferson, and spontaneously imagine that they must have spoken in the language style of the Declaration of Independence—"Hark, Merriwether: a mallard flyeth above that may provide us ample provision for supper!" But they were actually men of modest education, and in conversation sounded more *Dukes of Hazzard* than *1776*. We see this in their diaries, where they tended to write words as they actually pronounced them, lending us a rare glimpse of how ordinary people actually talked in the early 1800s. To Lewis, a cliff was a "clift" and *when* was "whin"; Clark wrote of "furin" things for foreign ones, sounding like a Kentucky Chrysler salesman talking about Nissans, and in his writings we see a man who "gits" tired of the infernal "musquiters" always biting him.

Though even this was a time when higher education was limited to a small elite, such that we might see Lewis and Clark as remnants of a time when written language simply had yet to penetrate society conclusively. But even after this had happened, we can see talked language living on. Sinclair Lewis in *Main Street* gives a nice portrait of banter between teenaged boys of the sort who smoked, played pool, and whistled at passing women. Lewis was renowned for his Balzacian talent for painting anthropological pictures of the American scene he knew, and was also a talented mimic in real life. Thus, we can be confident that this linguistic sketch pretty well reproduces what humble young men in small Midwestern towns sounded like just before World War I:

> "Hey, lemme 'lone," "Quit, dog-gone you, looka what you went and done, you almost spilled my glass swater," "Like hell I did," "Hey, gol darn your hide, don't you go sticking your coffin nail in my i-scream," "Oh you batty, how juh like dancing with Tillie McGuire last night? Some squeezing, heh, kid?"[2]

You can almost smell these guys, and the passage shows that everybody in the book's Gopher Prairie, Minnesota, did not talk like prim protagonist Carol Kennicott.

Old-TV buffs are familiar with the factoid that *Candid Camera* began

---

[2.] Lewis actually slipped here, I think—I suspect it would have been *squeezin'*, but no matter. While we're on the subject, elsewhere in the book Lewis casually notes that the stereotypical sense of small-town Midwesterners' speech—presumably in the teens when he wrote the book—included people saying the likes of "Wal, I swan." Eighty years later "Wal, I swan" is by no means one of the phrases I associate with the *Fargo* dialect that the descendants of Lewis's *Main Street* characters speak, nor with "hicks" in general. What in the world did "Wal, I swan" mean? (This just in: an unusually engaged copy editor dug up that "Wal I Swan" was a pop song of 1907. The phrase was apparently an interjection of some kind: the lyric goes "Wal, I swan, I must be getting on . . ." But still—what in God's world did it mean?)

as a radio show, *Candid Microphone*. The ten surviving episodes of the radio show are a precious document of ordinary people talking spontaneously before tiny portable tape recorders made recording live speech more common. Here is a New York City cab driver annoyed that host Allen Funt has given him a twenty-dollar bill to make change from for a quick, twenty-five-cent ride. It's 8:30 in the morning, and there are no stores open to get a smaller bill. The driver talks in rat-a-tat choppy phrases that could not pass muster in writing anymore than those of the junior college students. Incidentally, this is from the days when New York cab drivers were mostly working-class whites (the sitcom *Taxi* caught the tail end of this era). The man is not, as he would likely be today, a South Asian, Haitian, or African speaking English as a foreign language—he actually sounds a lot like Buddy Hackett:

Funt: Well, what can I do?

Driver: Well there's not a store in the neighborhood, you wanna wait, mister, I'll take ya for a ride, we'll go for change.

Funt: Why do you give me a big argument about it?

Driver: I'm not givin' ya a big arg- . . . , I'm just tryin' to explain to ya', youse fellas, ya always got da same habit—twenty dollas, twenty doll . . . where're we supposed to get change for twenty dollar bills?

The year was 1947, when among the nation's bestsellers were elegantly written novels like Sinclair Lewis's *Kingsblood Royal* and Laura Hobson's *Gentlemen's Agreement*, and non-fiction editorials like John Gunther's *Inside U.S.A.*, where run-on sentences and truncations like "big arg- . . . , I'm just . . ." were unheard of. Oral language roils apace, then, even as written language reigns serenely on the page.

Talking is fuzzy around the edges and tends to stray from the tenets of formal logic. It gets its job done nevertheless, and grandly so—without it our species would still be galumphing around savannas, dying young. Besides, to condemn talking as missing some mark is to condemn most of humanity, who speak oral languages natively, as slovenly of speech, as well as to judge a product of natural selection as faulty. Writing, however, has different and fussier traffic rules than talking, and coexists with it on its own track. Naturally, conventions of writing bleed into oral language, as educated people learn to wangle oral renditions of written style—elephantine vocabularies, clause-sandwich sentences—that could never have come to exist without the printed page. But in a schematic sense, a language with a literature comprises two equally legitimate brands, the oral and the written.

The theme of this book will be one of decline, but not of "the way people talk nowadays," because there has been no decline in that arena. Although it would have surprised him to learn this, in many ways the *Candid Microphone* cab driver talks the way the Bible was originally written. Wal, I swan, people have just talked since the dawn of humanity and continue to do so worldwide, from rain forests to boardrooms.

The change has been in the written variety: Modern America is a society that takes precious little joy in what Caxton called the "art of rhetoric." There are certainly legions of Americans who see themselves as lovers of language, and many would at this point dispute my claim. But we live in the present, and the current linguistic order has now reigned for as long as a great many Americans now in the prime of their lives have lived. History reveals a type and degree of language love in an earlier America—even one recent enough that today's grandparents grew up in it—that would be inconceivable today.

To take a cue from the word Caxton used, for example, whatever happened to "rhetoric" in America as an Edward Everett—or even a young Maya Angelou—would have understood it? For most of us today, the word *rhetoric* has specialized into signifying contentious declamations or political cant. In other words, the word has marginalized into an especially local, loaded meaning—because the larger, more neutral concept it used to refer to is a thing of the past. Back in the day, *rhetoric* was how we sang our language to the skies. In today's America, who'd want to do that?

CHAPTER TWO

Mere Rhetoric: The Decline of Oratory

B ack in the day, a joke used to circulate at UC Berkeley (and presumably, Dartmouth and other college campuses):

> **Freshman to Senior, on first day of school:** Excuse me, but can you tell me where the freshmen dorms are at?
>
> **Senior:** At Dartmouth, we never end a sentence with a preposition.
>
> **Freshman:** Excuse me. Can you tell me where the freshmen dorms are at, asshole?

Now, the preposition rule that people were taught in that era is, in itself, nonsense. One of the men who inflicted it upon us in 1762, Robert Lowth, labored under the assumption that English would be best off patterning itself after Latin, which happened not to allow prepositions to "dangle" at the ends of sentences. Lowth went so far as to emblazon the cover of his *A Short Introduction to English Grammar* with a quotation in Latin from Cicero. But even at gunpoint, none of us Americans could get through a half hour without ending a sentence with a preposition, no matter how passionate we were about using English "correctly." English has its own rules, and is no more beholden to Latin's rules than a dog is obliged to purr. Lowth neatly undercut his case by committing the very "error" while warning against it: "This is an idiom, which our language is strongly inclined to."!

But the fact remains that most educated people beyond the little world of linguists assume that rules like this are valid, and this reveals that old joke as a vital nugget of history. The joke hinges on the tension between the spoken and the written poles in a literate society. The freshman's retort confirms that casual speech is eternal, and that at no point have people in any society walked around sounding like books 24/7. Written language is an art(ifice). Yet it is significant that the joke even presents the mastery of written language—and its oral offshoot—as a distinguishing feature of an upperclassman. Surely, upperclassmen of the era reveled in casual speech in their off hours as much as freshmen, and the depiction of the senior thus qualifies as caricature. But humor is a refraction of truth. The very trajectory of the joke presupposes that linguistic formality looms as a force to be reckoned with, if only to be rejected. In the world the joke reflects, that rejection qualifies as a stance taken, against a custom perceived as having some sort of juice in society.

But among modern undergraduates at Berkeley and elsewhere, this joke would be all but opaque. It is almost as much a token of a bygone era as the "the house is building" joke. The college student concerned with using English "properly" in this sense is virtually inconceivable even as a marginal type. To the extent that some exist, they would not dare inflict their views on other students as the joke has the senior doing. And especially meaningless is the notion of upperclassmen having "mastered" formal English to a degree that underclassmen have yet to. Among the expectations that modern American undergraduates have of what their college education will yield, greater facility in speaking English is not one of them. We do not perceive the college graduate as being appreciably "better spoken" than they were as high school seniors—even in the sense of caricature.

The last thing I mean to imply is that an America where seniors walked around correcting freshmen's grammar would be preferable. For one, the rule the senior espouses is ridiculous. But even if he admonished the freshman to express himself in a thoroughly logical and valid sentence like "Excuse me, but could you be so kind as to inform me of the location of the dormitories allocated to freshmen?" the senior would be neglecting that casual speech, with its own complexities, has pride of place in human social interaction. The senior is indeed, well, an asshole.

But the very fact that a campus joke *ever* played upon the casual/formal opposition indicates the change I want to explore in this book. If our Martian came to earth and fashioned himself physically into a dead ringer for a modern undergraduate, somehow learned to speak perfect English, and moved into a freshman dorm, then one way he would start to give himself away as an alien would be the night he attempted to make a "joke" and told the one above. No matter how lustily he rendered it, after the dutiful chuckles he elicited, a person or two would think to themselves "Justin is kind of, like, weird." It'd be as if he was going to frat parties in sweater vests.

And this is a microcosm of a general fact about English in modern American life. America no longer values carefully wrought oral expression in the way that it did even in the recent past.

Homer on the Range

Many will think of the decline in educational standards in America at this point. But that is a symptom of a larger development, as I will revisit later. This book will not be one more brief against America's failing schools, and I will have failed to make my point if this is what the reader gains from the chapters that follow.

Here is the first of many indications we will see that the schools are a red herring: Even societies without writing very often cherish elaborated language. That is, even without formal schooling, humans can thrill to their language used with an artistic concentration beyond what is necessary to casual speech.

For example, for the linguist studying an unwritten language, one task in doing a really complete job is documenting the ceremonial—i.e., formal—level of the language. In a language without writing, formal language is not a matter of mile-long sentences with subordinate clauses piled all over one another. That kind of thing is only possible when there is writing, when the page allows the reader to parse layered sequences of phrases in a way that the rapid, here-and-now nature of speech does not allow. But there are other ways of making a language formal.

One of many examples is the Zuni Indians of New Mexico. Zuni is an unwritten language, beyond the grammatical descriptions and transcriptions of folktales written by scholars. But the Zuni switch to their equivalent of written language in their kivas, underground chambers used for councils and ceremonies. The casual word for "to live" is *ho''i* (where the apostrophes stand for glottal stops—the catch in the throat that we actually produce in place of the *t*'s in *button*; if you think about it, you do not actually say "buh-tuhn"). But in the kiva, for *life* Zunis do not use a form of *ho''i*, but the word *pinnanne*, which means roughly "a breathing into," out of a sense along the lines of English's "breath of life."

Then there are metaphorical epithets, rather like the classic Homeric "rosy-fingered dawn" in place of *morning*. The everyday word for "frog" is *takka*, but in the kiva one uses the phrase *woliye tinan k'ayapa* "several (of them) are in a shallow container."[3] Now, alone this looks colorful or creative, but deep down we might suppose that it also seems a tad child-like, as if Zunis' formal language entails fancy little storybook, nick-namey expansions of this thing or that. As such, it bears mentioning that in fact, epithets like this are also common in *casual* Zuni—the ordinary designation for the poisonous gila monster lizard is *čittol 'asipa*, roughly "rattlesnake with hands." Which means: The essence of formal Zuni is not just coming up with fancy epithets, because even the casual language is full of those. Rather, using formal Zuni requires knowing *the particular epithets required in the kiva*.

And this is closer to what we are used to in English than it might seem: The Zuni simply have casual/formal word pairs just like our *rest* versus *repose*. There is no inherent sense in which the sequence of sounds that make up *repose* are more formal than the sequence of sounds that make up *rest*. Someone who spoke no English, presented with both words, would have no way of deciding which one was more likely to be used at a black-tie affair. It's an arbitrary division of labor, which an En-glish speaker just picks up as part of how one uses the language formally. Thus, the Zuni who uses *takka* for *frog* when eating one, but *woliye tinan k'ayapa* when talking about one in the kiva is equivalent to Edward Everett using *repose* and *brethren* in his orations, though certainly not shuffling around his living room saying things like "When my older brethren get here from the train, tell them they can repose on the porch for a while."

In contrast to the freshman/senior context in the Dartmouth joke, ceremonial language is not a fraught issue among the Zuni, ripe for re-cruitment as joke material. As I will argue, our American discomfort with high language stems from a revolution in how we have come to conceive of class and authority since the 1960s. But ticklish class issues are largely

---

[3.] I have no idea.

alien to a small society like the Zuni (8000 people in 1990). The language has its slang just like any other, right down to much of it coming and going with generations of youngsters. But no Zuni gets called an asshole for using the kiva level of language. It is spoken best by elders and is a badge of prestige. Among many Native American languages of the Pacific Northwest, the formal varieties were explicitly taught—orally—to the young. (I use the past tense because all but a few Native American languages are no longer being learned by children and are, thus, moribund.)

"High" language, then, is by no means restricted to literate societies. It requires no schoolrooms or textbooks. It is a general feature of being human. Peoples do differ in how elaborated and strictly ruled their formal varieties are, and not all of the world's oral languages have formal varieties of any note. But a great many do. And in that light, American English has become one of the world's 6,000 languages whose speakers do *not* especially value elaborately stylized speech.

Rhetoric 101

In this, a vast weight of Western tradition in language use becomes foreign to us, and much more so than it would have been to many of Edward Everett's spectators. The movers and shakers of Ancient Greece took carefully structured use of oral language as essential to a man of influence, and not as a fashion statement, but for the simple reason that artful language use is the vehicle of effective argumentation. To the Greek, *rhetoric* was not the suspect term it is to us, but artful speaking. Their word *rhētorikē* came from *rhētōr* "speaker"—the same root, with an *o* added at the beginning, created the word *orator* in the Latin spoken on the peninsula next door.

Aristotle's *The Art of Rhetoric*, then, is a manual, categorizing stratagems of argumentation, such as the "from greater and less" technique, allowing the speaker to point out a person's inadequacy without seeming petty, by observing the same flaw in figures universally considered to cut a wider swath. "If not even gods know everything, hardly will men do so" is one of his examples. Then he points out logical pitfalls to avoid, as well as to catch one's opponents falling into, such as "giving the non-cause as cause, such as something's occurring at the same time or after the action; for men take its occurring *after* as its occurring *because."* Aristotle also gives advice on the use of maxims, and other techniques for swaying listeners to one's convictions.

Like Thomas Aquinas's, Aristotle's organizational style is odd to our eyes. There is a latent orality in his prose that suggests lecture notes rather than written exposition. This was natural in a society in which literacy was not yet widespread and written norms had yet to jell as completely as they would later. But the assumption that one must master an artful layer of speaking in order to wield influence effectively was central to medieval education in Europe, and continued in Western societies well into the twentieth century.

And for that reason, over the centuries there were thousands of books on rhetorical technique written in styles more accessible to us than Aristotle's. Paging through dusty tomes like this, we must adjust ourselves to the odd notion of education comprising taxonomies of argumentational technique with Greek names like *antinomasia* versus *pronominatio*. Walter Ong nicely captures that upon seeing "the universal and obsessive interest in the subject through the ages and the amount of time studying it, of its vast and intricate terminology for classifying hundreds of figures of speech in Greek and Latin," our first response might well be "What a waste of time!"

And it's true that to some extent, the oral tilt in Ancient Greek and medieval European intellectual life was a hangover from a world without writing that was still recent. Tradition dies hard. The first ball I had for my cat to play with happened to be a hollow one with little beans inside that made a rattling sound. As such, to signal to Lara that it was time to play with the ball, I would shake it before tossing it down the hallway for her to chase. Eventually, that ball got broken somehow, and her new ball happens not to have any beans in it. But before tossing this ball down the hall, I still reflexively jiggle the ball in my hand. This looks senseless unless you happen to know that Lara's first ball rattled.

In the same way, it took centuries for literate peoples to fully adapt themselves to the possibilities of print. And then the ancients and medievals were still bound by technology. Before printing and cheap paper, books were expensive, hand-scriven items that students could not afford. The university reader in Britain acquired this name at a time when his job was to read from a book while students took down as much as they could; for that matter, *lecture* comes from Latin's root for "to read." Meanwhile, education naturally concentrated on oral exposition and debate. Only an elite few owned books and there were only so many to be had. Writing was handy, but precious; even among scholars, talking was still the order of the day.

But even in our world of paperbacks, laptops, and beanless balls, if we can look past the old-fashioned language in old, rhetoric primers written by people with three names, we glean that such techniques could still be useful in sales meetings, political debates, or even discussions with friends about issues of the day. We could see *rhetoric* in its original sense, as a refinement of linguistic exchange granted us by writing. Ong notes that for the Greeks, rhetorical technique "provided a rationale for . . . something which had been a distinctively human part of human existence for ages but which, before writing, could never have been so reflectively prepared for or accounted for."

There is nothing inherently dusty or outmoded about such a thing, then. Like the Zuni, many preliterate societies value speech tailored to a level of structured eloquence beyond what is possible on the casual level. Of one of the Pomo languages spoken by Native Americans in northern California, in an interview in the 1920s a man recalled of his grandfather: "My grandfather made a long speech in the sweathouse; he spoke for about twenty minutes; oh, how he could speak! The words just flowed and flowed, so easy, so smooth; he was a great speaker." Note how difficult it is to imagine an American English speaker saying the equivalent. Even if one did hear someone giving such a speech, it is unlikely that the modern American would be moved to make this particular comment. We might if the speaker had lit up the crowd in a revivalistic, Jesse Jackson sense, but this is not what the Pomo man meant by "so easy, so smooth." He referred to word choice and graceful sentence construction. In those terms, we are not especially attuned to how deftly someone uses English.

The Gaslight Gift of Gab

Many would be tempted to attribute that to something American, but wait: There was a time when speeches artfully fashioned to convince the listener were ordinary—even in a nation every bit as antiintellectual and art-shy as it is now. One of the charms of Jack Finney's classic time-travel novel *Time and Again* is the little things his protagonist notices about 1882 that would not occur readily to us. Horse-drawn carriages, men with ample facial hair—those are easy. But Finney's Si is also thrown by seeing clothing stores full of fabrics, but not clothes—people still *made* most of their own clothes in 1882.

Something that would require the same kind of adjustment if we traveled with Si would be public speeches sounding much like orations of Ancient Greece and Rome. Part of why we are unlikely to say "Boy, could that guy talk!" is because it is so rare today that we hear English stretched to its limits.

A typical example was William Jennings Bryan's famous "Cross of Gold" speech against the gold standard that he made at the Democratic Convention in 1896. He opened with:

> I would be presumptuous, indeed, to present myself against the dis-
> tinguished gentlemen to whom you have listened if this were a mere
> measuring of abilities; but this is not a contest between persons. The
> humblest citizen in all the land, when clad in the armor of a righ-
> teous cause, is stronger than all the hosts of error. I come to speak to
> you in defence of a cause as holy as the cause of liberty—the cause of
> humanity.

He famously closed with "You shall not press down upon the brow of la-bor this crown of thorns, you shall not crucify mankind upon a cross of gold!" Aristotle would have praised Bryan's use of nimble juxtapositions (the humble good trump the powerful evil) and effective metaphors (us-ing a potent image suffused with Christian symbolism to move an audi-ence about an abstract financial issue). Also good is how Bryan sets off that final "the cause of humanity" with a dramatic pause, drawing atten-tion to this largest of concepts and setting a tone of gravity.

This kind of thing takes work. As corny as it looks to us, just imag-ine deciding to write a speech against the gold standard, of all things, and starting with a blank piece of paper. What would even your first sen-tence be? Bryan came up with several pages of language in the style of the paragraph above—and not written for laughs. This kind of oratory was art.

Bryan is especially revealing for two reasons. First, Bryan "The Great Commoner" was no genius by any account. "Almost unable to think in the sense in which you and I use that word," a sympathetic but honest acquaintance once said of him; "Vague ideas floated through his mind but did not unite to form any system or crystallize into a definite practical position." Bryan shows that old-style rhetorical ability was not merely an outgrowth of general intelligence. Intelligence certainly might help, but innumerable brilliant people would come up short trying to compose orations like Bryan's. Rhetoric was essentially a subject like math or history, a self-standing technique available to people of various ranges of mental agility, and one we have largely lost today.

Second, our modern sense of orator so suggests a paunchy windbag well into middle age that it is useful to observe that Bryan was only thirty-six when he gave the "Cross of Gold" speech. He was too young to have any but the dimmest memories of the Civil War. Yet, even in the baroque style of language that was normal for him, he did not address his audience as an elder speaking from on high. Certainly, thirty-six was a more mature age in his time, at which marriage, multiple children, and a permanent career choice were norms for men rather than the options they are today. But Bryan was still a youngish man by any standard, and had already mastered his craft at a young age, when he was known as "The Boy Orator of the Platte." In his time, rigorously yoking words to argumentational technique was not something associated with reaching an august state of life—it was the way people in the prime of their lives were expected to use language in public.

Or how about a man who didn't remember the Civil War at all? This level of oratory was even expected of the callow student. W.E.B. Du Bois was chosen as commencement speaker when he got his bachelor's degree (his second, actually) from Harvard in 1890. He spoke for ten minutes. It was actually a rather odd speech that fails to convince in hindsight—the title alone hints as to why ("Jefferson Davis As a Representative of Civilization"). But oh, the language! And following the era's conventional expectation of students delivering orations, he recited it from memory—reading it would have been as gauche as a concert pianist playing from the score in performance. Here is a representative passage:

So boldly and surely did that cadaverous figure with the thin nervous lips and flashing eye, write the first line of the new page of American history, that the historian of the future must ever see back of the war of Secession, the strong arm of one imperious man, who defied disease, trampled on precedent, would not be defeated, and never surrendered.

Du Bois was only twenty-two years old. But he was doing what was expected in his day. Anyone whose life or career lends them a familiarity with speeches of this era knows that this crafted style of oratory was typical of the period.

Significantly, in this America where linguistic ornament was valued so highly, one heard people referring explicitly to the quality of people's formal speaking skills more than today. One of many examples was, actually, Du Bois's eventual rival for black leadership, Booker T. Washington. The same year Bryan made his "Cross of Gold" speech, Harvard awarded Washington an honorary master's degree. In his autobiography, he describes how "President Eliot, in beautiful and strong English, conferred upon me the degree of Master of Arts." "Beautiful and strong English"? To imagine an undergraduate today even mentioning the quality of a college president's "English"—or, for that matter, their parents or anyone else at the ceremony doing so—brings our Martian to mind again.[4]

I Hear America Just Talking:
Speeches Shift to the Oral

Washington, as a man of accomplishment in his era, was attuned to language used artfully. But Americans' relationship to their language has changed vastly since then. We are much less likely to have an ear cocked in the direction Washington's was, regardless of our level of education or achievement.

As it happens, the President Eliot that Washington referred to was the butterfly whose wingflaps set in motion a series of events that led to a later hurricane. Charles W. Eliot had been entranced by the German educational system he had seen in his chemistry studies abroad, and when he became Harvard's president in 1869, he was determined to make the

---

4. As to the possible objection that Washington, having been born a slave, may have been especially impressed by standard English because of having worked to master it, this is certainly possible, but in fact feeds back into my general argument. We strain to picture an African-American today of disadvantaged background who grew up immersed in Black English marveling at a white official's "beautiful English." Rather, our times encourage such a person to see standard English as an uptight code imposed from on high, and to encourage our own Charles Eliots to loosen up and see the value in the vernacular.

curriculum over on the German model. He was particularly impressed by the German system's giving students advanced writing skills by the time they entered the university, obviating the need for remedial classes for freshmen (whose existence at this early date ought temper our convictions about contemporary educational decline, founded in fact though they are).

Harvard had traditionally put students through a four-year program in rhetoric that trained students in oral expression as much as written. That was typical of schooling in general in these days; even children's education was oral to an extent that would perplex us if we could be a fly on the wall of a schoolhouse at the time. Schools drilling the brute mechanics of clear diction? The McGuffey's readers, known to legions of American schoolchildren in the 1800s and well into the twentieth century did just this. McGuffey drilled the obvious to an extent, as in such useful instructions as:

> Inflections are slides of the voice upward or downward. Of these there are two: the *rising* inflection and *falling* inflection. Both inflections are exhibited in the following question: Did you walk ' or ride `?

This was like making darned sure schoolchildren knew that walking required putting one foot in front of the other. Yet McGuffey drilled away, as in pronunciation exercises with sentences like "O *breeze, t*hat waf*tst* me on my way!" and "*That m*orning, thou *t*hat slumber'd'st not before." McGuffey's concern with clear articulation was partly the product of an age before electric amplification, where public speaking required more attention to diction. But no one ever assumed that all schoolchildren had orating in their future. McGuffey's basic concern with elocution reflected that oral articulateness had a social capital, which it no longer does to us.

It was this pedagogical culture of stylized orality that Eliot's new writing program began eating away at. His model became the prototype for the "English Comp" classes familiar to us. The focus on writing marginalized the recitational one once ordinary. Eliot later went on to espouse Progressive Education, with its focus on teaching writing by encouraging expression of one's individuality rather than abstract addresses of larger issues. This paved the way for the writing of spoken language, in place of the speaking of written language.

But Eliot only planted a seed; schools were very slow to adopt these methods in any significant numbers. Du Bois's speech captures an America that was still a culture of traditional rhetoric three decades after Eliot's instatement, including at Harvard itself. This remained the case well into the twentieth century. In the 1940s, for instance, Maya Angelou was participating in oratory contests sponsored by the Black Elks club in the small Arkansas town she grew up in. Only in the 1960s would Progressive Education—albeit in a form that would have given John Dewey considerable pause—break through and become the dominant School of Education gospel. Here, education was not a prime mover, but just a symptom of a larger cultural development, the new vogue for Doing Your Own Thing and Keeping It Real. Inevitably, it was at this time that Progessive Education finally broke through, such that among the countless ways in which the culture changed, talking was elevated over speaking.

A nice way of seeing the results of this transformation is to compare the speeches of congressmen on December 8, 1941, arguing for the United States' entry into World War II, with those assessing whether or not our country should invade Iraq in October 2002.

Most of the graying people sitting in Congress in 1941 had grown up in the 1870s and 1880s, likely using the McGuffey's Readers, reciting in front of classrooms, and preparing mini-orations in college. And the records of their speeches in the *Congressional Record* show what they considered a speech in Congress to be, even having had but one night to prepare one. Congressman Joseph Martin, from Massachusetts, intoned:

> Mr. Speaker, our nation today is in the gravest crisis since its establishment as a Republic. All we hold precious and sacred is being challenged by a ruthless, unscrupulous, arrogant foe.

Charles Eaton, of New Jersey, almost rivaled Bryan with his:

> Mr. Speaker, yesterday against the roar of Japanese cannon in Hawaii our American people heard a trumpet call; a call to unity; a call to courage; a call to determination once and for all to wipe off of the earth this accursed monster of tyranny and slavery which is casting its black shadow over the hearts and homes of every land.

Those passages were chosen more or less randomly; the majority of the speeches made that day sounded like this.

We might suspect that there may have been a big difference between what the congressmen submitted to the *Congressional Record* volumes and what they actually said live. But in fact, radio recordings exist of the House session that day, and confirm that the printed versions usually reflect almost exactly what these people got up and said. They composed carefully written texts and read them aloud, only departing from them slightly—Eaton said "we American people heard a trumpet call" in place of "in Hawaii our American people heard a trumpet call," for example. And pointedly, most of them spoke in an aroused, theatrical tone as if they were on stage—Joseph Martin actually trilled his r's, and in his speech Eaton pronounced the *a* in "a world civilization" as "ay," rather than the casual "uh."

Fast forward to October 2002 on the Iraq Resolution. Some of the congressmen rose to the occasion with crafted prose of a sort, although never as ornately as their predecessors of 1941. But just as many congressmen came close to "just talking." In 2002, crafted oratory is Godiva rather than Hershey. Here was Senator Sam Brownback, of Kansas, in an excerpt typical of the whole speech:

> And if we don't go at Iraq, that our effort in the war on terrorism dwindles down into an intelligence operation. We go at Iraq and it says to countries that support terrorists, there remain six in the world that are as our definition state sponsors of terrorists, you say to those countries: We are serious about terrorism, we're serious about you not supporting terrorism on your own soil.

On paper we see a mess of fragments and run-ons, and a colloquialism like *go at* that congressmen in 1941 wouldn't have dreamed of using in a public statement. Actually, to give all due credit to Brownback, inflection, gesture, and context made it a thoroughly comprehensible speech—not polished, but hardly of the sort that would leave you shaking your head. After all, remember the transcriptions of casual speech in the previous chapter! We can be sure that congressmen Martin and Eaton sounded at least something like them when smoking cigars after sessions. But the point is that they did *not* talk this way when making speeches.

I hardly mean to single Brownback out, because he was typical. But that typicalness is just what indicates the shift in America's relationship to the language it speaks. We find the same shift in how our presidents speak to us on grand occasions. In 1942, Franklin D. Roosevelt made his

State of the Union address a month after the Pearl Harbor attack. Here is the passage that was remembered most:

> We have not been stunned. We have not been terrified or confused. This reassembling of the Seventy-seventh Congress is proof of that; for the mood of quiet, grim resolution which here prevails bodes ill for those who conspired and collaborated to murder world peace. That mood is stronger than any mere desire for revenge. It expresses the will of the American people to make very certain that the world will never so suffer again.

This is a carefully crafted piece of expression. Any speech that includes a sequence of words like "quiet, grim resolution which here prevails bodes ill" took some doing. It made a great impression on those who heard it.

But then fifty years after this in 1992, George Bush the Elder's State of the Union address was a different thing entirely. No, the man was not known as terribly articulate off the cuff. But this was a prepared address— he had time to plan this out:

> And you know, it's kind of an American tradition to show a certain skepticism toward our democratic institutions. I myself have sometimes thought the aging process could be delayed if it had to make its way through Congress. But you will deliberate, and you will discuss, and that is fine. But my friends, the people cannot wait. They need help now. And there's a mood among us. People are worried. There has been talk of decline.

Or more to the point, decline of talks. The throughline meanders: the people can't wait, they need help, *plus* they're worried. But don't impatience and need presuppose worry? Repetition substitutes for careful word choice: will people really be *both* deliberating and then taking a deep breath and switching to the distinct activity of discussing? One simple phrase follows another like toy train cars. No resonant words like Roosevelt's "resolution," "prevail," or "bode." Or, why is skepticism "kind of" an American tradition? That's the kind of polite hedge we use when talking, but time was that in speeches, one declared in a firm voice. And then there is even the smoking-room familiarity of the joke about how slow Congress is.

Sure, in 1942 there were as many people who lacked the gift of gab as in 1992. But custom required disguising the fact in public speeches much more than today. A presidential address like Bush's simply would not have been socially appropriate in 1942—oratorical craft was a kind of linguistic deodorant. Roosevelt would have been perplexed to read Bush's son's speechwriter Mark Gerson saying, "The President's style is a mix of very straightforward language with elements of elevation, and so at our best, when we have the time and the moment to do that, that's the mix we strive for."

A "mix?" Just "elements" of elevation? What happened between then and now?

Tune In, Drop Out, Talk Down

There is a hint of the answer in what we expect today even of humbler speeches. The modern American speechmaker tends strongly to operate under a guiding imperative *not* to sound too high a note. For the author invited to "share their thoughts," the speaker at a business convention, etc., the tacit running message is "I'm just like you." No one expects the speaker to bring potato chips or take off their shoes, but the speaker seeks, and is praised for, maintaining as much warmth and familiarity as possible despite the formal nature of the occasion. This inherently discourages speaking in elegantly crafted sentences and ten-dollar words, and thus the modern American speaker is less likely than a nineteenth-century one to craft a treatise that could stand alone as good reading.

The key concept here is formality: It is part of the modern American soul to distrust it, and since the 1960s has been much more so than ever before. But the formality issue connects to something larger, in a way that comes through especially clearly on the student-protest scene. Vocal student protest has been a staple at Berkeley since the Free Speech Movement of 1964. While I have taught there, the 1995 ban on racial preferences in California has occasioned ongoing controversy, the events of September 11, 2001, have sparked serial antiwar rallies, heightened tensions between Israel and the Palestinians have roused partisan groups to a fever pitch, and graduate teaching assistants have been engaged in a continued fight for unionization. As such, many Berkeley professors become accustomed to rallies reducing attendance in their classes by half roughly once a semester, and anyone affiliated with the school hears impassioned public speeches out on Sproul Plaza by students and affiliated activists on an almost weekly basis.

I can honestly say that in my years at Berkeley, while I have seen considerable charisma, street theater, and sincere indignation at injustice on Sproul, not once have I heard an *oration* delivered in any sense that a pre-1960s America would recognize. I assume it may well have happened while I wasn't around. But the fact that I have never caught a *"speech speech"* when I *was* around is suggestive that a standard has changed—crafted oratory is definitely not common coin on Sproul.

Given that the people I have heard have spoken so recently, it would be inappropriate, I believe, to give any transcriptions here. The speakers are still alive and usually not even far past the stage of life they were in when they spoke. Especially given how messy *anyone's* spoken language looks on the page, I am not comfortable with the thought of one of these people by chance reading this book and seeing themselves in print looking like Rain Man. Word-for-word transcriptions are hardly vital to making the case here; I will just describe instead.

Typically, the student or even professor standing at the microphone has a three-by-five index card in their hand with a few general points to hit. Just as often they have empty hands. The usual address begins by listing assorted factoids pertinent to the topic, and then proceeds into a succession of phrases of indignant complaint, often culminating in calling someone a name or hitting a potent buzzword, which whips spectators up into applause. The phraseology is generally ripe with repetitions and *like*-style hedges. Especially among the younger speakers, any sense of the diction that McGuffey taught is long gone. The microphones ensure that we can understand what the speaker is saying anyway, but a microphone cannot create the melody of intonation wielded to highlight and sway and compel. Undergraduates usually speak in a flat tone not far removed from the one they would use in a dorm room, and even graduate students and professors usually display little of the sense, now archaic, that making a speech is something vastly different from talking.

In other words, the spoken/written dichotomy that earlier American public speakers assumed—albeit largely unconsciously—has vastly narrowed. And in college students, the leitmotif of the convictions they are expressing makes this narrowing predictable. The speaker on Sproul Plaza is almost always one with a major brief against the American Establishment. And because the Establishment has traditionally been the steward of formal conventions in its language, to hold the Establishment in contempt all but entails rejecting those conventions. Elaborate language in America has always been associated with the national machine, and identification with accomplishment within it. When rejecting the Establishment as not worth taking one's place in becomes a sign of the times, then naturally the would-be orator sounds like Dennis Hopper. "Articulate"? Fuck that schoolteacher bullshit, man. Even in a speech. Just as naturally, the meaning of the word *rhetoric* shrinks and sours into signifying an oral snow job. Old-style formal rhetorical facility was a dress-up affair, taught and cherished by the higher-ups. It's a short step from "Don't trust anybody over 30" to uttering the word *rhetoric* with a sneer—speaking is dishonest and oppressive; just talking is where it's at.

And now we all process the oratory of Bryan, Du Bois, and the 1941 congressmen as almost laughably quaint. Of course, most Americans aren't walking around fuming at The Powers That Be, any more than they ever were. We are simply creatures of what has become a general context. Throughout history, what begins as a response to a clear-and-present stimulus drifts into unconscious fashion. Why did old cars, slung a few inches above the ground, have running boards when all a passenger had to do to get into them was slide in and sit down? Because horse-drawn carriages, slung a yard above the ground and requiring the passenger to clamber up into them, had had them, and so it seemed natural to include them in any vehicle, even if they were decorative instead of functional. I shake Lara's ball because her old one had beans in it, but a child who grew up watching me jiggle the new ball before throwing it might well do the same thing for years, simply because I was the only person they ever saw throwing a ball for a cat.

In the same way, in the 1960s the Civil Rights movement and the Vietnam debacle pushed thinking Americans' politics further to the left than had ever been the case before. College protesters were only a strident manifestation of a larger trend, and Watergate went on to cast it in stone. People already of age in the sixties, then, were responding to a stimulus. But people growing up in the era instead of living through it never knew the former America. They simply imbibed the assumptions and customs of the new America from childhood, and this included a basic sentiment that the formal is to be avoided, that real life is a dress-down affair. One generation put their fedoras and jackets in the closet as a sign of the times, embracing a new informality. But the next generation never knew anything else: I do not wear fedoras and avoid jackets except on formal occasions because I never knew a world in which they were required attire, and thus process them as a queer something else—like most professors of my generation.

It was the same with language. In the 1960s, inevitably fancy talk came to seem corny and backward compared to loosening up and telling it like it is, and people suckled on the old-style rhetoric let it go. But people who were children in the sixties or later never knew an era when the gap between casual and formal language was the one the 1941 congressmen took as a given. You speak the language you grow up with, including how it is used—and ours today is one in which formal language is restricted to a very narrow space. Thus, all we know is that the formal language that a Booker T. Washington admired is stiff, irrelevant, even laughable—just because, well, to us that's just how formality *is*. We've never known anything else. The very core of our beings now leans toward the spoken, in a way that would perplex William Jennings Bryan or even FDR.

So the die is cast. I am not exactly a countercultural sort of person. A family legend recalls a family reunion when I was nine and my sister was five. We were given slices of watermelon, and while my sister immediately began eating her slice with her face, I casually reached for a plastic fork.[5] Thus I am not one who senses the American government or the Western educational canon as an oppressive straitjacketing of my true self. But I did grow up in the 1970s. And as such I openly admit an impatience with stuffy language that would set me off from, say, W.E.B. Du Bois, if I could live out my fantasy of going back to the aughts and meeting him. I strive for a casual tone in my undergraduate lectures, and would never dream of reciting my lectures from notes, or even speaking to classes in language anything less than breezy and accessible. I don't know how Senator Brownback eats his watermelon, but while the 1941 congressmen had grown up in the Gilded Age, Brownback, born in 1956, grew up in the Age of Aquarius. Whether or not he participated in it, it deeply stamped his sense of linguistic decorum. After all, he has never known anything but his own time. It is unlikely that a senator despises the very Establishment he is sitting smack in the middle of, but Brownback lives in an age where even a senator can "just talk" without attracting notice. Linguistically, America eats with its face now.

---

5. My sister is today an elegant young woman who is not given to eating with her face. (And no, she didn't tell me to write that.)

The Times A-Changin'—
A Closer Look at the Shift

My argument is that the 1960s' rejection of formality and its elevation of Doing Your Own Thing was a major turning point in the style of American speechmaking. Yet already, by the middle decades of the century, almost nobody was making speeches that Aristotle would have recognized as oratory. As with most historical changes, the seeds had already been set long before.

William Jennings Bryan's way of speechifying already sounded a little old-fashioned by the twenties, for example. Here fits, for instance, Eugene O'Neill, scorning the broadstroke grandiloquence of the stage dialogue fashionable when his father made a career of playing the Count of Monte Cristo from the 1880s through the aughts. O'Neill was writing plays in a language closer to the ordinary as early as the teens. At this time, Edna St. Vincent Millay did some acting at the Provincetown Playhouse where O'Neill was presenting his early work, and when her sister came to live with her, Edna warned her that in Greenwich Village profanity was more *au courant* than a proper girl from Maine might expect. Sister eased sister into gutter talk while darning socks: "Needle in, shit. Needle out, piss. Needle in, fuck. Needle out, cunt. Until we were easy with the words."

But this first bump after the Great War actually feeds into my point. The Roaring Twenties were the prequel to the 1960s countercultural revolution, complete with new sexual freedoms (necking and petting!), an expanded role for women in politics (the suffrage), open celebration of intoxicants as a respectable indulgence (hooch), and reflexive skepticism toward society spreading from artistic bohemia to thinking people in general ("It's the bunk" was the current equivalent for our "It's bogus"). Certainly these were just beginnings: overall, the 1920s was just two decades after the turn of the century. But young moderns of that time felt themselves as throwing off the shackles of the past as urgently as those of the sixties would four decades later, such that the mood foreshadowed the era of the Flower Children culturally and linguistically. Some even argue that without the interruptions of the Depression, World War II, and the Cold War, The Sixties would have happened two or three decades earlier.

Electric amplification also played a role. Before the twenties, the public speaker had to reach a mass of hearers with the naked voice. This required high volume, which in turn favored a theatrical tone, majestic pacing, and planned phraseology. When speaking as loudly and clearly as possible—say, shouting down an elevator shaft—one is less likely to insert hedges like "you know" and string phrases together in quick succession without considering their strict logical coherence. To wit, yelling discourages one from just talking. Plausibly, speakers who encountered the microphone in midlife retained the elevated phraseology out of blind tradition, but later generations settled into a style better suited to the technology and cut the drama. Franklin D. Roosevelt straddled the eras nicely, sounding the proper theatrical note in public speeches, but adopting a more intimate, down-to-earth style in his radio Fireside Chats.

But while the baroqueness of speeches decreases from the turn of the century to the sixties in general, the space for crafted oratory in society still remained much larger than we today are used to. For one, generations overlapped. At any given time, plenty of older people were still alive making speeches the way they had been taught as students. Even many men of O'Neill's generation (O'Neill was born in 1888) or the one before made lofty speeches in Congress in 1941 that James O'Neill would have thrilled to. Even the two generations after Eugene O'Neill often carried a muted, but recognizable version of the old style well past the sixties, although the new climate made them stand out as anachronisms. West Virginia Senator Robert Byrd, born in 1917, today retains a semblance of the grand old oratory, complete with classical references—but not only does it come off as pretentious, but it seems to trace in part to his windy, imperious persona. In, say, 1910, his speech style would seem ordinary, and he would have to come up with other ways of expressing narcissism.

But most important, there was a particularly sharp change in the 1960s. Let's take a look, for example, at a famous speech from just the decade before, Senator Joseph McCarthy's notorious "I have in my hand" speech of 1950 warning of the infiltration of Communists into the American government. McCarthy was just an average speaker, and his speech that day represents the state of the art for public addresses of the time:

The reason why we find ourselves in a position of impotency is not because our only powerful potential enemy has sent men to invade our shores, but rather because of the traitorous actions of those who have been treated so well by this Nation. (. . .) It is the result of an emotional hangover and a temporary moral lapse which follows every war. It is the apathy to evil which people who have been subjected to the tremendous evils of war feel. As the people of the world see mass murder, the destruction of defenseless and innocent people, and all of the crime and lack of morals which go with war, they become numb and apathetic. It has always been thus after war.

Hardly ringing oratory, but still quite different from casual speech: "impotency," "traitorous," "always been thus," lengthy sentences that require a certain command of intonation to render effectively. McCarthy, born in 1908 and thus a product of the teens and twenties, was definitely "making a speech".

Now let's move ahead to the very early sixties, when the general standard in public speeches was still similar. One of the most famous speeches of the time was FCC chairman Newton Minow's "vast wasteland" speech to the National Association of Broadcasters in 1961:

I invite you to sit down in front of your television set when your station goes on the air and stay there without a book, magazine, newspaper, profit-and-loss sheet or rating book to distract you—and keep your eyes glued to that set until the station signs off. I can assure you that you will observe a vast wasteland. (. . .) We all know that people would more often prefer to be entertained than stimulated or informed. But your obligations are not satisfied if you look only to popularity as a test of what to broadcast. You are not only in show business; you are free to communicate ideas as well as relaxation. You must provide a wider range of choices, more diversity, more alternatives. It is not enough to cater to the nation's whims—you must also serve the nation's needs.

Minow's speech had a certain intimacy lent by his direct address of the audience as *you*. Yet his word choices and graceful sentences reveal a man who was still, despite having come of age in the forties (he was born in 1926), essentially reading written English. "I can assure you," "would more often prefer to be entertained than stimulated or informed," "your obligations are not satisfied," are all "written" language. The final sentence I quote is Rhetoric 101—two phrases carefully balanced in weight for euphony and the persuasion it can lend. Note, for example, that if we were given this excerpt without identification of its speaker or date, even though Minow's observation itself is often heard today, we would immediately suspect that the excerpt was from "the old days." Speeches rarely sound like this anymore.

They sound more like what we begin seeing when we fast forward ten years later plus one. Here is Jane Fonda speaking over Radio Hanoi against the Vietnam War in 1972:

> But now, despite the bombs, despite the crimes being created—being committed against them by Richard Nixon, these people own their own land, build their own schools—the children learning, literacy—illiteracy is being wiped out, there is no more prostitution as there was during the time when this was a French colony. In other words, the people have taken power into their own hands, and they are controlling their own lives.
>
> And after 4,000 years of struggling against nature and foreign invaders—and the last twenty-five years, prior to the revolution, of struggling against French colonialism—I don't think that the people of Vietnam are about to compromise in any way, shape or form about the freedom and independence of their country, and I think Richard Nixon would do well to read Vietnamese history, particularly their poetry, and particularly the poetry written by Ho Chi Minh.

Even with clues to period removed, I think most of us would sense this excerpt as "modern," or more to the point, "normal" by our expectations. Part of this is the language style. Fonda largely preferred words used in casual speech, and her sentences are not carefully paced for length and balance the way McCarthy's and Minow's were: There is no sense of making a kind of music. Fonda's statement speech would seem less appropriate as a piece of written prose than McCarthy's or Minow's.

And much of the reason for that is the other clue to its modernity, how front-and-center Fonda places herself as an individual. McCarthy and Minow kept their individual selves all but concealed in their speeches: They largely presented self-standing treatises—they recited a written text. And this was a manifestation of formality—formality suppresses the individual in favor of group norms; informality means letting our uniquenesses hang out. By the seventies, this up-close-and-personal tone becomes a standard modus operandi in public addresses. This means that speeches are as much written talk as spoken writing, which narrows the space for words like *impotency* and phrases like *it has always been thus*, and makes written-style sentence construction less relevant.

Fonda's speaking style is now the going thing for Americans at the podium. That is clear ten more years after her speech above, in 1981 when Mayor Ed Koch makes a speech after reelection:

> Intellectual honesty and fiscal integrity got us elected four years ago, and that is how we ran the city during the past four years, and that's how we will continue to run this city for the next four years. I love this job and I love this city, and I'm proud of what has been accomplished. I told the people the truth. I spelled out what had to be done, and we did it. It wasn't easy—but we *did it*!

This must have been fun to hear live. But compared to McCarthy's or Minow's addresses, Koch's displays essentially no concern for craft at all. It's hard to imagine Koch's speech included in an anthology, especially with all of those references to "I" that render it more a personal statement—talking—than a self-standing essay. Yet, in the recording, vocal clues make it clear that Koch was reading it from a script. Koch wrote up a passage of talking—welcome to our America.

And so it has been since. An address that Disney chairman Michael Eisner made in 1998 to the American Society of Newspaper Editors is a perfect example of the prominence of the "I" in modern speeches, the self-deprecation that informality encourages, and the virtual reluctance to ever sound like a book:

> When we find ourselves on our deathbeds, I don't think we will say to our adoring family hovering nearby, "Do you remember that really salacious nude roller skater I put on the air back in '98? Wasn't that great television?" And I don't think our adoring spouses will smile and say, "Yes, dear, that was—expletive deleted—wonderful." If we keep this in mind, I think we'll all do all right.

Today, as Jimmy Durante used to say, "Them's the conditions that prevail."

Archaeopteryx on Sproul Plaza

Let's zero in even closer. Certainly there was no one day in, say, 1965, when American speechmakers went up to their podiums with elegant texts in hand only to shout "What the hell!" undo their top shirt buttons, and spend the next twenty minutes yammering off the cuff. We would expect transitional figures: people in the mid-1960s whose speaking styles were somewhere between Newton Minow and Jane Fonda. As it happens, the college campus scene provided just such a figure.

The legendary UC Berkeley student activist Mario Savio was born the year after the 1941 congressional speeches on Pearl Harbor. He spearheaded the Free Speech Movement in 1964, protesting the restrictions that the Clark Kerr administration at Berkeley had placed upon students' political protests. Savio was one of the last public figures in America to be regularly described as a gifted orator (Jesse Jackson, I know—we'll get to that shortly). There is a historical irony in this. His silver tongue helped spark a seismic shift in college campus culture that was central to the countercultural revolution—which, in transforming Americans' relationship to their language, pushed rhetorical gifts like Savio's to the margins of our culture.

Savio was more properly a kind of *Archaeopteryx*. *Archaeopteryx* is a long-extinct creature whose fossils helped support Darwin's theory of evolution, being midway between reptile and bird—a sort of crow with teeth and a tail. Savio, in his way, was one part William Jennings Bryan and one part Senator Brownback.

His most famous speech was at a massive sit-in of Berkeley's main administrative building, Sproul Hall, on December 2, 1964. Looking back on the speech, we can see that orator he definitely was. One feels it in the gradual adrenaline rush that comes even from reading it, and in tapes of him delivering it, Savio seduces us with his knack for summoning the theatrical without veering into the shrill. Conveying what so stirred Savio's listeners that day requires quoting a rather generous slice:

> We were told the following: . . . If President Kerr actually tried to get something more liberal out of the Regents, in his telephone conversation, why didn't he make some public statement to that effect? and the answer we received—from a well-meaning liberal—was the following. He said: "Would you ever imagine the manager of a firm

making a statement publicly in opposition to his board of directors?" That's the answer.

Well, I ask you to consider. If this is a firm, and if the Board of Regents are the Board of the Directors, and if President Kerr in fact is the manager, then I tell you something—the faculty are a bunch of employees, and we're the raw materials, but we're a bunch of raw materials that don't mean to be . . . have any process upon us, don't mean to be made into any product, don't mean, don't mean to end up being bought by some clients of the university, be they of government, be they industry, be they organized labor, be they anyone— we're human beings. (applause)

There's a time when the operation of the machine becomes so odious, that you're so sick at heart, that you can't take part, you can't even passively take part,[6] and you've got to put your bodies upon the gears, and upon the wheels, upon the leaders, upon all the apparatus, and you've got to make it stop, and you've got to indicate to the people who run it, to the people who own it, that unless you're free, the machine will be prevented from working at all!

The "I ask you to consider" and "The answer we received" were staples in Savio's speeches, which were couched to teach and convince, in the roots of the old-time rhetorical tradition. Reginald Zelnik in a *New York Times Magazine* tribute caught this well in noting that "the dialogical quality of his speeches engaged students at the level of their own apprehensions; they were not being fed dogma but were invited to a forum"; another commentator called him the Free Speech Movement's "Socratic teacher."

As William Jennings Bryan's pedestrian mind highlights oratory as a discreet muscle rather than a mere symptom of intelligence, Savio stuttered as a child, and according to contemporaries was never exactly a smooth talker in private. Yet, when he got up in front of a crowd, the words just flowed. He had a specific gift, of a sort that technology of the future will probably be able to identify the neurological sources of on CAT scans of the brain. After his death in 1996, one of his wives recalled

---

6. Transcriptions of the speech tend to either have *tacitly* in place of *passively* here, or omit the phrase the word occurs in completely and skip to "you've got to put your bodies upon the gears," suggesting a possible question as to just which word Savio used. However, close and repeated listenings to the videotape make it clear that Savio in fact said *passively*.

him as "in love with language," "rigorous about using language precisely," and a poetry lover.

He clearly thought of himself as "making a speech," as engaged in a brand of performance distinct from casual talking. For example, Savio was of working-class origins. Most people of any class use some nonstandard language in their casual speech: few normal human beings *never* say things like "Penny and me—we haven't been there in twenty years!" over "Penny and I haven't been there in twenty years." However, as ordinary experience suggests and linguistic studies have confirmed, working- and lower-class people tend to use such forms more often than middle-class ones, uneducated people more often than educated, and so on. Savio's background acquainted him well with -*in'* for -*ing* and the like. Yet in his speech he uses only standard English; he had a sense, probably unconscious, that one did not use casual forms when, well, orating. He felt a certain distance between speaking and talking, a sense that public address required more than just mastering stage fright. Neither in this speech nor on other recordings does Savio ever display the more casual, almost deliberately artless approach to speaking that modern young people so often do even in public forums. The times were a-changin' and Savio was in the middle of helping them do so—but he was minted before they had a-changed yet, and it showed in how he made a speech.

But then, there was obviously a sharp contrast between Savio on Sproul's steps and W.E.B. Du Bois making his address on a Harvard lectern. Given how stirring Savio was live, one almost hates to nitpick—but that first paragraph only really makes sense if you imagine it spoken. "We were told the following," Savio said, but then backtracks to a question posed to Clark Kerr that would *yield* the "the following." We *talk* like this all the time, but Du Bois's oration was perfectly linear and reads as smoothly as it sounded.

Savio's second paragraph contains some small patch-ups and hedges—rife in anyone's casual speech but considered a demerit in rhetoric as once conceived. Then in the third paragraph, there is actually a logical inconsistency in the passage that most stirred people then. "You've got to put your bodies upon the gears, and upon the wheels, upon the leaders, upon all the apparatus . . . ," Savio said—but did he really mean that we should "put our bodies upon" the leaders? Almost certainly not. He started out with a clean metaphor about putting bodies on the gears—this, in itself, as good as Bryan's cross of gold—and then reinforces it by adding the wheels. But then he becomes more concerned with a general list of evils—gears, wheels, leaders, apparatus. Good, too, but getting through the list while keeping the rhythm he has set with repeating "upon the . . ." encourages using "upon the . . ." for all four items, even if it doesn't technically make sense with one of them.

You didn't notice this hearing Savio deliver the speech. Persnickety concerns like this only occur to us when reading or writing. Casual speech is too rapid and couched in emotion to submit to this kind of anality—but in that, Savio reveals himself to have been as much talking as speaking. In describing his love of language, his wife specified his sensitivity to the rhythms of speech, him having spent his youth in "fanatic listening" to them to overcome his stutter. Lynne Hollander Savio's tribute strikes a chord of admiration in us today, with the high place that the genuine occupies in the way we assess how our leaders speak to us, how a singer sounds, how a novelist writes prose.

But this is a sign of our own times. A Savio speech never strayed too far from how people actually talk—but Everett or Bryan used casual speech rhythms as a springboard at best. For their audiences, authenticity ranked much lower than a stylized kind of theatricality. The last thing Victorian orators were trying to do was sound like regular fellas. True, long before Savio, populist speakers like Huey Long and preacher Billy Sunday were making speeches in ordinary language aimed at reaching the common man as directly as possible. But until the 1960s, this was but one genre in speechmaking, and not the dominant one. In bringing this style to the middle-class Establishment world of the elite university campus, Savio's addresses were part of a new guard.

Addresses without notes, for instance. One might object that Savio and Du Bois are an apples-and-oranges comparison in that Du Bois was reciting a memorized written essay while Savio was speaking without a net. But in fact, that's just it. In Du Bois's time, when public speeches were usually couched in written language, it was expected that one had "prepared some remarks" beforehand. Du Bois, who lived on throughout most of the twentieth century and died just the year before Savio rose to fame, always read from notes. A mustachioed, gaslight-era Mario Savio, then, would most likely have done so as well. But the actual Bay of Pigs–era Savio made his Berkeley orations extempore, and elsewhere, usually improvised from brief, general notes.

The difference between the two men was a symptom of a new relationship to the use of English in America that was coming to reign in the

1960s. Specifically, a countercultural imperative that scorned the American Establishment as morally corrupt naturally cast adherence to its *formalities*, with the effort, exposure, and risk this had always entailed, as backward. Who are President Johnson or Clark Kerr, with their country clubs and lacquer-haired wives, to shoot bullets at my feet and make me dance? Most of the results of this sentiment were rather clear— changes in conduct, dress, sexual mores, etc. Perhaps less apparent was the linguistic result—a tacit rejection of rigorously stylized English as old-fashioned or false.

Even then, though, Savio did not leave a stammering, word-shy America in his wake as soon as he descended Sproul's steps. As it happens, our opening "Can you tell me where the freshman dorms are at, asshole?" joke was being told at Berkeley right when Savio was turning the campus upside down. That joke still made some kind of sense to those kids in cat's-eye glasses and cardigans dancing the Madison. But how quickly it would cease to. I began college in 1981, seventeen years after the Free Speech Movement, and can attest that by that time, that joke would have gone over like a lead balloon.

"It's the culture, stupid!"

Three refinements are necessary to clarify that culture was the key here. The first two show that educational quality was beside the point.

Exhibit A: I can backdate even further the point at which that joke became a curio, in that it would have been equally antique in the private schools I attended in the seventies—despite our substantial reading assignments and solid compositional training. We wouldn't have found the joke relevant because of the culture we were growing up in, not due to the quality of our education. By the seventies, students and everyone else were living in an America where the distance between casual and formal speaking was smaller than it had ever been until the last sixth of the nation's history.

Exhibit B: We might suppose that the joke no longer works because the preposition rule has actually not been regularly taught in America for several decades, and there has always been a healthy tradition of resistance to it even among the literati (Winston Churchill's dismissal of a copyedit with "This is the kind of thing up with which I shall not put" being a famous example.) But the joke even falls flat if we use a blackboard grammar rule that still reigns supreme, the "Billy and I went to the store" notion. "At Dartmouth, we never say 'Billy and me went to the store'"—see? Even with a rule that most people assume is legitimate, the notion of college education teaching students to use it any more than they did in high school is hopelessly off today.

But the third indication, Exhibit C, pointing to culture is, ironically, the very fact that there is no evidence that Savio deliberately adopted a looser speech style out of fury at the suits. What I mean is that Savio was affected subconsciously by the context he was living in, where a new attitude was blowing in the wind. What suggests this is that radical politics alone had not spelled looser oratorical conventions in America before his era. Politics affected the language only when the radical became chic.

After all, if politics alone was the culprit rather than culture, then we would expect to see funkier speeches much earlier than 1964, since the hard left certainly did not begin with Mario Savio. Emma Goldman, for instance, found the American Establishment a lot more odious than Savio did. But she and Savio would have found that they had different ways of speaking to a crowd. In line with her century-straddling era, Goldman often read from prepared speeches written in the sort of prose we have seen so much of in this chapter that I need not quote it (yet). Like Savio, she was known as an orator—and in the old-fashioned rhetorical sense of being a master of swaying audiences—to such an extent that it made the American Powers That Be distinctly uncomfortable. She serves us well in two ways.

First, note that I wrote that a Victorian Savio would *most likely* have read from prepared speeches. The noteless speech was hardly unknown in the old, old days. But in an era when the public speaker was expected to put the language's best foot forward as a matter of decorum, we would expect that even spontaneous orations would be tidier than Savio's lusty but shaggy ones. And Goldman did occasionally speak without notes, and stenographers' word-for-word transcriptions survive of some of these speeches. They reveal that while at such events Goldman did not couch her thoughts in quite the baroqueness of Edward Everett, she did approximate this style to an extent that Savio and his audiences would have found archaic and pretentious.

On June 4, 1917, Goldman spoke to an audience of ten thousand in New York against men being drafted into what we now know as World War I. And here is a swatch of exactly what she said:

We tonight of the Anti Conscription League raise our voices to the very sky to tell you that you may fight your battles, if you believe in the trenches, but you are representing a losing cause. You represent the past and we represent the future. The Conscription Law has been the means of awakening the people of America. Before the Conscription Law was passed the American people used to think, why, we have freedom, we can do whatever we please, we can go to war if we want to and stay away if we don't want to. My friends, we are grateful to the Government for having passed the Conscription Bill for it will teach the American people that American Liberty has been buried and is dead and is a corpse, and that only our voice is going to raise it up and revive it again, until the American people and all the people living in America will unite in one great mass and will throw out capitalism and Government by militarism.

Nor was it that the transcriber was cleaning up a speech that sounded more like Senator Brownback, because he even got down the predictable soft spots, such as the then colloquial (although today rather quaint) "why . . ." before "we have freedom, we can do whatever we please," or this one, where I use italics to call attention to the flub:

But since that day twenty-seven years almost have passed, and I have come to the conclusion that when the law for conscription *was* passed in the United States the Funeral March of 500,000 American youths *is* going to be celebrated tomorrow, on Registration Day.

Whoops—a composition teacher would sniff out a problem with tenses. This is the kind of sentence someone comes up with speaking off the cuff, but that one would correct, or more likely not even come up with, while writing.

But where this kind of factory defect is rife in Savio's speech, it is rare in Goldman's. In line with her times, she felt more linguistically corseted than him. This comes across beautifully in a newsreel clip of Goldman visiting the United States in 1934 after having been deported in 1919. Asked her opinion of Franklin D. Roosevelt by a reporter, she calmly answers, and I quote: "I'm glad that President Roosevelt has been one of the very few men in the White House who has come to realize the right of the working people to organize and to better their condition by means of their organized power." What a gorgeous, balanced, elegant sentence—and she came up with that on the spur of the moment. As public figures of her era were expected to. Savio was much less likely to toss off lapidary prose like this when answering reporters.

But the main way Emma Goldman helps us here is in the sheer fact of her being an anarchist who nevertheless operated under a working assumption that carefully crafted, maximally concise English was legitimate. She never knew an America where a substantial and influential portion of the populace swooned to her politics. This stands out in the newsreel clip when the announcer opens by chirping "No longer the fiery 'Red Emma,' she seems considerably tamed as she faces the reporters." "Tamed" indeed—Goldman's politics were in fact unchanged, and she looked quietly disgusted at having to endure the reporters' dopey questions. But that was about as good as it got for hard leftists in 1934 America's media. In her time, truly anti-Establishment politics were a fringe phenomenon—elsewhere, the closest equivalent was the more specific economic grievance of the Populist movement, which beyond this sought no back-to-cases overhaul of the American experiment. Goldman spoke largely to an enlightened cohort of square pegs. Savio spoke to what gave all indication of being the future itself. To wit, Goldman was fighting a rising tide, but by the sixties, Savio *was* the tide, representing the culture that would shortly triumph. When culture changes, so does language use, and thus naturally we would see a linguistic shift in Savio—the new wave—rather than Goldman, who died a beleaguered dissenter.

William Jennings Bryan dressed English in a tuxedo. Savio in 1964, tieless in his rumpled blazers, was using button-down English. Just a few years later, college students would be pushing English out onto the stage in a headband and jeans.

Q: Can You Think of a Living Famous Orator?
A: Jesse Jackson!

What Savio was doing, in his way, was preaching. And while I have never seen this documented, this may have been due in part to how he had spent the summer before the Free Speech Movement broke out. The

Savio of that fall's headlines was fresh from the Freedom Summer in Mississippi, where he had participated in the drive to enfranchise black voters that led to the murder of three white volunteers. Surely Savio heard many public addresses by black preachers and speakers, and this may well have influenced his oratorical style.

In any case, the resemblance between Savio's addresses and Baptist or Fundamentalist sermons is clear, and brings us to a point many have likely been waiting to see addressed. Isn't Jesse Jackson an orator? And if he is, isn't any preacher who uses his style an orator as well?

The answer is yes, but. Yes, Jackson, deft at stirring the gut with words, is an orator. And yes, in that countless preachers black and white use this style in their sermons, we can say that oratory rings throughout our land every Sunday morning even today. But—the word *oratory* covers a larger patch of meaning than the one I have been addressing in this chapter.

The particular kind of oratory that once had a solid place in American culture was, recall, a highly planned affair, an oral rendition of language as it can only first exist in writing. Speeches like Everett's or Bryan's were couched in a kind of pristine and elaborate syntax that no humans anywhere use in casual speech. Rhetoric as once understood was an artificial endeavor, where language was filtered through the technology of writing.

Folk preaching, on the other hand, is a highly spontaneous activity, characterizable as a heightened form of *spoken* language. Here, for example, is a transcription of part of a sermon given in 1968 by a black preacher in North Carolina. The sermon had a rousing effect on its audience, and if we imagine it delivered in the ringing, rhythmic cadences of a Jackson, we can see why. Yet the contrast with the mainstream rhetorical fashion of 1900 is clear:

> I'm sayin' to y' this mornin', Jesus said I'm the way. The truth and the light, your ways—glory—your ways is not right. God's ways is all right. I'm sayin' to y', this mornin', Jesus said, "Thank God almighty"— Revelation twenty-two, sixteen and seventeen—he said, "I'm Alpha and Omega—the beginning and the end, the voice in the void, I was here when there was nothing. I was here before the world—and I'm still here." Thank God. This mornin', I'm sayin' to you, in my closin' remarks that if y' hold on, to God's hand, God will make a way, out of no way.

Sermons like this suffer when written out on the page—we can't hear the intonations, feel the pregnant pauses, or hear the congregation's sympathetic responses rising as the sermon builds. But with a little imagination we can see—or better, hear—that this preacher was not simply running his mouth in random fashion. He was delivering a statement just as Du Bois was with his "Jefferson Davis as a Representative of Civilization"; he was engaged in a deliberate, focused activity. The sermon, too, for example, has a set name, "I Am the Way."

But the folk preacher hews much closer to casual speech than a Bryan would. Note the short phrases, reminiscent of spoken rather than written language. And recalling that spoken language is spontaneous while written is planned, it is key that the folk preacher does not chart out his performance as anally as a Bryan. Scholars have studied this preaching style, and find that the preacher starts with a kind of skeletal game plan, but in performance fills it out in an in-the-moment fashion. The folk preacher continually tosses in, for one, assorted set phrases like "I say unto you tonight," "I want you to know this evening," and "You shall know the truth / And the truth shall make you free." In the sermon above, note the set mannerism "over yonder," less likely in modern conversation, but lending a feel of the grand and biblical in a sermon.

A crucial contrast: Du Bois at the commencement wrote out an essay and then declaimed it from memory, but for the folk preacher, even if he does write out the sermon beforehand, in the pulpit he spontaneously translates it into sermonese. Folk-preaching analyst Bruce Rosenberg usefully gives us first what a preacher wrote out, reading not unlike something Bryan might have come up with:

Then was Nebuchanezzer [sic] full of fury, and the form on his face was changed against the three men, so he ordered that they should heat the furnace seven times hotter. And he commanded the most mighty of his army to bind the three men, and cast them into the burning furnace.

and then gives a transcription of what the preacher actually said in church, with the line-by-line format conveying the crucial rhythmic tempo:

I can see the old king when he ordered
That their furnace be heated

Or heated seven times hotter
They tell me that he sent for the three strong men
The strongest men from his army
He'd taken these men in and bound them
Hand and feet

The church version translates written English into something quite different, closer to talking as opposed to speaking.

Of course, this is an art in itself, as is especially clear from a passage from a sermon most of us will be able to hear in our heads as it was delivered, Martin Luther King, Jr.'s "I Have a Dream" speech. Sure, it's highly oral; the sweaty-palmed Princeton student with his hair parted down the middle in a nineteenth-century rhetoric class would find little in it that recalled Aristotle's teachings on the subject. But no one could deny the power of the likes of:

Let freedom ring from the mighty mountains of New York.
Let freedom ring from the heightening Alleghenies of Pennsylvania.
Let freedom ring from the snow-capped Rockies of Colorado.
Let freedom ring from the curvaceous slopes of California.
But not only that.
Let freedom ring from Stone Mountain of Georgia.
Let freedom ring from Lookout Mountain of Tennessee.
Let freedom ring from every hill and molehill of Mississippi, from every mountainside,
let freedom ring.

And indeed the scholarly analyst has taxonomized repetitions like "Let freedom ring from . . ." as a formal compostional technique called "anaphoric parallelism." But Rosenberg is repeatedly a tad perplexed to find that the preachers themselves are not consciously aware that they are using these tools. Of course, the obscure terminology itself would be unknown to them. But scholars have broken such terms down to preachers in common language, hoping the preacher will enthusiastically lay out their rhetorical modus operandi like a car mechanic might expound on the master cylinder if asked how to fix a car's brakes. But even then, folk preachers tend to sit somewhat bemused—they didn't learn this from formal instruction; they watched other preachers, drank in their style, and now they just *do* it. Or God does it—folk preachers tend to insist that when delivering a sermon they are inspired by the Lord. Spontaneity is central in what they do—just as in casual speech.

In contrast, even Bryan, a man of blazing religious conviction, could never have claimed that when on the stump he was passively channeling God—for the simple reason that he had crafted his oration down to the word in pen and ink. Naturally, he may have seen the Lord's hand in his having accomplished that—but then this would be a different kind of allocation of divine power. The Victorian orator recited written English, but the folk preacher, in all of his skill, presents a charismatic refraction of *spoken* language. And the relevant contrast is not only the obvious one with, say, Du Bois's commencement speech, but even the elevated oratory in societies with unwritten languages—the kiva language of the Zuni is not just an animated version of casual Zuni speech decorated with sprinklings from a toolkit of savory terms and phrases, but a sober switching to an alternate set of vocabulary items that must be carefully learned. There are indeed societies where the oratorical type of speech is essentially a performative way of talking—to orate ceremonially among the Mohave in Arizona entailed adopting what was described by observers as an "abrupt, staccato, forced delivery" of ordinary speech. But note that folk preaching resembles this more than a Bryan speech, or the words that "flowed and flowed, so easy, so smooth" from Pomo orators.

And finally, to the extent that preaching beyond the folk style was once rooted in the written, today the art is drifting ever more toward the oral. Dr. Richard Lischer, a professor of preaching at Duke's Divinity School, has identified a decline in the mainstream preaching art over the past two decades. Sermons once tended to be oral presentations firmly rooted in, but not slavishly following, a written, prepared text, perched somewhere between Bryan and Jesse Jackson. But preachers are drifting ever further from preparing their sermons as self-standing essays. Today, seminaries tend to guide divinity students to couch sermons as conversations. In our terms, American preachers, like the rest of the country, are increasingly Doing Their Own Thing.

Modern America, then, is a country where rigorously polished language, of a sort only possible when channeled through the deliberate activity of writing, is considered insincere. And this is not a Yankee keystone, but a trait only a few decades old. And it leaves us culturally and even intellectually deprived.

Any Lack of Delicacy

For one, we have become unusual in the global sense in our deafness to the sheer spiritual, Dionysian pleasure of our language wielded in an artistic way. In 1882, when *Time and Again* takes place, alumni of the Rensselaer Polytechnic Institute had their annual gathering in New York City. Engineer Rossiter W. Raymond was one of those people who, like Edward Everett, was renowned as a "speaker." He gave a toast to acknowledge how significant Washington Roebling's wife, Emily, had been to the construction of the Brooklyn Bridge during Washington's convalescence from a case of the bends he'd contracted working with his men in the underwater caissons. The toast:

> Gentlemen, I know that the name of a woman should not be lightly spoken in a public place, but I believe you will acquit me any lack of delicacy or of reverence when I utter what lies at this moment half articulate upon all your lips, the name of Mrs. Washington Roebling.

Ye Gods! This at a dinner of cigar-chomping men? "Acquit me any lack of delicacy"? Today, no matter how formal the social occasion was, anyone who spoke this way would elicit gales of laughter, and if they kept it up, would be gently escorted to a mental ward. When today's RPI alumni convene, we can be quite sure nobody talks like this before everybody digs in.

Yet in its way that toast was beautiful. Anyone who readily praises Shakespearean language as poetic would be hard pressed to explain why Rossiter's toast—or the speeches of Bryan, Du Bois, Franklin D. Roosevelt, or John F. Kennedy—was not. In our spontaneous sense that this kind of oratory was overdoing it, we contrast with even preliterate peoples worldwide who sit down to a ceremonial occasion warmly anticipating hearing someone speak in a beautiful way. Today, the tiny set who cherish poetry retain an affection for language pushed beyond the mundane. But in 1882, there was a place in American society for one kind of artful language even at jolly, roast-beef occasions—despite America already being every bit the vulgar, materialistic society it is today, if not more. Today, few of us have any desire to speak in a fashion terribly far removed from the way we speak, and few of us have much of a taste for hearing anyone do so.

Reaching Versus Preaching

Moreover, our wariness of the written debases the rhetorical power of our political and cultural discourse. As I noted in the last chapter, written language is couched in the objective rather than the subjective, and is subject to careful revision, and is thus a better vehicle for outlining a sequential or layered point than spoken language. In an America where we have fallen out of the habit of listening to written language spoken, we are less likely to be presented with careful, extended arguments in a speech. We may *think* we hear such speeches, but we have lost a sense of what a truly rhetorically intended speech can be.

In the 1870s, Susan B. Anthony's staple speech was "Women Want Bread, Not the Ballot." In city after city, she presented a careful argument that women must have the vote for the specific reason that it would grant them the leverage to gain fair wages and strike effectively. She even opened not with airy, genial comments, but with a direct indication of her desire to convince her audience of a point:

> My purpose tonight is to demonstrate the great historical fact that disfranchisement is not only political degradation, but also moral, social, educational and industrial degradation; and that it does not matter whether the disfranchised class live under a monarchial or a republican form of government, or whether it be white working men of England, negroes on our southern plantations, serfs of Russia, Chinamen on our Pacific coast, or native born, tax-paying women of this republic. Wherever, on the face of the globe or on the page of history, you show me a disfranchised class, I will show you a degraded class of labor. Disfranchisement means inability to make, shape or control one's own circumstances.

The speech was long, but for a reason: She carefully vanquished reigning counterarguments such as that capital alone determines wages, or that the disenfranchised themselves, in the grip of mundane exigencies, often see sustenance as more important than gaining the vote.

Today, however, it is simply not part of American culture for a person to make a speech putting forth an argument with almost lawyerly care and precision—i.e., rendering an oral version of a use of language only possible when writing exists. Our speeches are mostly symbolic exercises packaging a few large points in short, punchy sentences. State of the

Union addresses are today composed in sequences of sentence packets designed to elicit applause like the chest-beating speeches that pro wrestlers make. The goal is the gut rather than the head. Certainly, there has always been a great deal of sloganeering, shorthand, and sloppiness in America's public discourse. There was never a time when our citizenry glided around informed by a media pitching its reports at the level of university lectures. But there remains a stark contrast in degree with the past.

The current Bush administration, for example, invaded Iraq amidst indignant, despairing outcry from America's intelligentsia and a great many educated "Blue Americans" concentrated in college towns. An hour-long speech by the President that addressed each of the common objections to the invasion point-by-point would have made for a richer and more constructive public debate. Sure, Bush and Secretary of State Powell mentioned the broad-stroke justifications in various speeches— that Saddam Hussein had flouted the United Nations, that there was evidence that he was hiding weapons, that he had gassed his own people, etc. But those opposed to invasion had widely broadcast objections to these points, at the time teeming on editorial pages and regularly heard in countless kitchens and bars across the nation. But then, myriad analysts had counterresponses to these objections, as did, presumably, Bush and his aides. So, why not an extended speech—oration, perhaps—that really got down to cases, addressing sequentially and in pointed fashion the objections of *The Nation*, *Mother Jones*, the *New York Times* editorial page, and Dominique de Villepin? Even though more than a few would have remained unconvinced, a speech of this kind would have narrowed the space for the more apocalyptic suspicions among many that the Bush administration was merely full of thoughtless cowboys intent on dominating the world and shoring up the oil industry. In the end, most can be made to understand that there are cases in which reasonable people will disagree.

But this speech did not, and in our America, could not, have happened. It would no more have occurred to Bush's team to write a speech like this than to putte a Tax on Tea, since in modern America, to present this kind of argument in crafted oral language is as archaic a concept as having to dial the operator to make a phone call. Bush's speechwriters would be stymied trying to compose such a text, and Bush himself, reared in post-oratorical America, would not be up to the task of rendering it as effectively as a Franklin D. Roosevelt could have. It is assumed that in the public sphere, this kind of engagement with an issue takes place largely in small-circulation political journals—which only a sliver of the population have even heard of, much less read.

Compare this with Woodrow Wilson's speech in defense of his League of Nations proposal in 1919. "I have perceived more and more that men have been busy creating an absolutely false impression of what the treaty of peace and the Covenant of the League of Nations contain and mean," he noted, and proceeded to methodically address all of the leading objections to his proposal one by one, covering each point at eloquently pitched length, using English in a fashion derived from its written level. Rather than merely sounding off proclamations, he couched the speech as *rhetoric*: a direct address to listeners' potential objections: "You will say, 'Is the League an absolute guaranty against war?' No; I do not know any absolute guaranty against the errors of human judgment or the violence of human passions but I tell you this: With a cooling space of nine months for human passion, not much of it will keep hot"; or "But, you say, 'We have heard that we might be at a disadvantage in the League of Nations.' Well, whoever told you that either was deliberately falsifying or he had not read the Covenant of the League of Nations," followed by careful explanation as to what he regarded as the proper perspective. The level of policy detail that Wilson dwelled in alone marks his speech off from one imaginable today from a President: "You have heard a great deal—something that was true and a great deal that was false—about that provision of the treaty which hands over to Japan the rights which Germany enjoyed in the Province of Shantung in China," or "But you will say, 'What is the second sentence of article ten? That is what gives very disturbing thoughts.' " Wilson gave ordinary Americans a serious exploration and defense of a policy issue. It didn't work, in the end—but this was because of Wilson's faulty diplomatic skills. His ability to articulately render his point was not one of the things that hindered his mission.

As late as 1965, such speeches remained possible. Lyndon Johnson's "We Shall Overcome" speech carefully argued for the passage of the Voting Rights Act of 1965, outlining the obstacles blacks faced in trying to vote, the fact that previous legislation designed to address the problem had proven ineffective, and appealing at length to the moral fiber of the Congress and the nation to demonstrate the ideals our republic was founded on by giving blacks their due. But this was the end of an era. It is striking to peruse collections of speeches and "rhetoric" over the ages and note the sharp difference in artfulness and substance between those before the mid-sixties and those afterward. The latter usually seem to only fall under the rubric of rhetoric in a formal sense.

Before we move on, a clarification. I hope not to have implied that there was ever a time in the United States when all, or even most, people were capable of giving windy speeches in elevated language. Casual speech has always reigned among people of all classes, although written conventions tend to percolate to some degree into one's speech according to education.

My point is that in an earlier day, there was a certain space in the culture for crafted oratory—one that a representative number of people of letters and influence filled, and that a representative number of people of classes beyond and below this were receptive to. In other words, what strikes me is the simple fact that such a big crowd listened raptly to Edward Everett that day, regardless of how many of them could pull off such speeches themselves. Today, all but *nobody* speaks on this oratorical level, and if anyone ventures to do so, it qualifies as a precious event like sighting a comet.

Think of it this way. Ask an American when they last heard a real "speech": i.e., a complete statement rendered with especial grace and power, that they wouldn't have minded having a printed copy of. Also remind them that Mario Cuomo's "City on a Hill" oration was twenty years ago as you read this—there were no cell phones, sushi was a novelty, and Britney Spears was in diapers. Posed to an American of 1903, the same question would come off as trivially as "When's the last time you washed your car?" would to us. The person would hardly find themselves scratching their heads and gamely popping up with a dandy speech they heard back in the Gilded Age.

After all, speechmakers back then spoke. Today, they just talk.

CHAPTER THREE

"Got Marjoram?"

or

Why I Don't Have Any Poetry

One of my favorite *Seinfeld* scenes is the one in which the snooty executors of George's late fiancée's trust fund ask him who his favorite poet is. George mumbles into his hand "Flavman," obviously neither having a favorite poet nor even able to come up with the name of a poet on a moment's notice.

I laugh as much with as at George in that scene, though, because truth to tell, I'm a great fan of Flavman myself. I own about five thousand books, but until I researched and wrote this chapter, among them was not a single volume of poetry of any kind. The reason is that I have never cottoned much to poetry. Most of it bores me, although I feel a little guilty about this, and in an idealized version of myself in my mind, I spend the occasional evening poring over a book of verse, cat on my lap, and hot cup of tea close at hand.

And poetry is not much more significant to my friends. Literate sorts though they tend to be, very few of them read much if any poetry, nor do books of poetry come up among the books we recommend to one another. One couple I know did once have a party where the gimmick was that everyone was to bring and read their favorite poem. But this was presented as a kind of challenge, a party turn indeed, out of a background assumption that most of us would have to work to come up with a favorite poem. One person ended up reading from a Dr. Suess book.

When Poetry Mattered

I see all of this as another demonstration of how Americans' relationship to elaborated renditions of our language has changed over the past forty years. Corresponding to Americans' skepticism of crafted oratorical language is a lack of interest in poetry that is unusual in the global sense. Yet this, like the dearth of serious oratory, is a recent development. In the first half of the twentieth century, an academic and writer such as myself would likely have had more of a relationship with poetry, and poetry was much less marginal a presence in American life—not only among the literati, but even among ordinary folk. For all one hears about the poetry revival in America, poetry still plays about as significant a role in modern American life as marjoram plays on spice racks (have you got any marjoram right now?). And where poetry does thrive, it tends strongly to read like casual speech.

Certainly my observation about poetry's marj-, I mean, marginality is old news. As far back as 1934 Edmund Wilson was asking "Is Verse a Dying Technique?" But he was recalling the antique tradition in which stories, history, and even science could be couched in verse. In 2003, few of us can get terribly excited that, say, a scientist would not discourse on the origins of syphilis in verse as Fracastoro did in *Morbus Gallicus* in 1530. More apropos would be Joseph Epstein's "Who Killed Poetry?" in 1988, and especially Dana Gioia's landmark *Atlantic* piece of 1991, "Can Poetry Matter?"

Gioia famously argued that poetry has become the fancy of a hermetic community of writing teachers publishing in each other's magazines and anthologies, with the web of professional interdependence discouraging serious criticism. Many in these circles have seen the growth of this little world as a sign that poetry is alive and well in America, but Gioia disagreed:

> The proliferation of literary journals and presses over the past thirty years has been a response less to an increased appetite for poetry among the public than to the desperate need of writing teachers for professional validation. Like subsidized farming that grows food no one wants, a poetry industry has been created to serve the interests of the producers and not the consumers.

But Gioia has recanted in the introduction to the new edition of his book *Can Poetry Matter?* He celebrates the proliferation of poetry festivals and discussion groups, the increased presence of poetry on the radio, and the poetry scene on the Internet as signs that America has taken poetry back into its heart. But then, even though since his essay Gioia has become one of the most celebrated poets and critics in America and is now the head of the National Endowment for the Arts, his book is published by one Graywolf Press based in St. Paul, Minnesota. Whatever poetry revival there has been, the contrast between today and the old days remains striking.

Why Bugs Bunny Read Longfellow

Literally so. Traveling back to America between the wars, various unexpected things would throw us. One would be the absence of plastic. Another would be that young women would often smell like very old ones to us, because women now in their eighties and nineties formed their taste in scents when they were young. And a third thing that would strike us is how much more present poetry was at all levels of American life. Time and again we would find ourselves patiently listening to kids chanting their way through poems, running up against bits of verse in newspapers, and wondering why people we paid to see joke or sing were using recitations as palate cleansers.

For example, in this era, Edna St. Vincent Millay was, of all things, a Celebrity Poet. Her work, despite its dense vocabulary and mannered style, had a solid place in the middlebrow consciousness. In 1927, Millay wrote a poem decrying the impending execution of Sacco and Vanzetti that was immediately printed in newspapers across the country, not tucked away in an anthology. Five years later, she had her own nationally broadcast radio show for eight weeks, from which she recited her work. In 1942, her poem about the razing of Lidice was broadcast nationally—and in a prime venue: Alexander Woollcott's *The Town Crier*, a national staple that was a kind of cross between *Nightline* and *Oprah*. Young women readers recited Millay's poems the way their equivalents today cherish the lyrics of Tori Amos. For example, as an aspiring actress in the thirties, Dorothy McGuire told interviewers that she liked to read Millay in her spare time.

While there are a few poets like U.S. Poet Laureate Billy Collins who can pack the house at readings, they do not remotely fill the public space that Millay occupied in her heyday. What poem are we all aware of about famine in Africa or even 9/11? Surely such poems have been written— but they have not been reprinted in Gannett's newspapers or recited on Leno. Or on that, where is the national radio show featuring not poetry itself, but one poet? Where's *Sailing Alone Around the Room with Billy Collins*,[7] even on NPR? And who is Julia Roberts's favorite poet? I'd put my bets on Flavman.

Today, a few magazines aimed at the kind of people who listen to NPR print poetry. But through the twenties, verse was regularly scattered around even humble daily newspapers. It's one the odder things about trawling through microfilm of dailies of the time. Little of this coy dog-gerel was exactly for the ages, and it was often used just to fill extra space—hungry journalists got paid for it by the yard. But this still meant that poetry was part of John Q. Public's print world in a way that it is not for today's Justin Q. Public. In 1918, Howard Dietz, later a top Broadway lyricist, wrote a review in rhyme of one of H. L. Mencken's early books: "H. L. Mencken will surprise you / With the smartness from his pen: / Read this volume, we advise you— / Read it once and then again."

Of course, to write a book review in rhyme was a joke even then— but we don't joke much in rhyme today. And recall that "'Twas the Night Before Christmas" was introduced in newspapers—and then consider that no such narrative poem could emerge and catch on today. There'd be no public place for it—newspapers wouldn't touch it, nor would any widely heard radio show or hit television show. We preserve "'Twas the Night Before Christmas" out of tradition, and because it is connected with a major holiday. But we create nothing of its sort, and have not for a very long time.

Then there was the tradition of recitations. *Recitation* seems like an ordinary word. But if you think about it, the very concept of a recitation is so foreign to modern American life that a foreigner learning English would no more need to learn the word than we need bother remember-ing words for things like *waistcoat* in other languages. I can pretty confi-dently say that I have never once "recited" anything since 1977, nor can I recall seeing anyone do so except occasionally in a joking vein.

But to the end of his long life, Broadway lyricist Adolph Green, born in 1915, enjoyed reciting Lewis Carroll's "You Are Old, Father William"

[7.] *Sailing Alone Around the Room* is the title of one of Collins's anthologies.

("'You are old, Father William,' the young man said, / 'And your hair has become very white; / And yet you incessantly stand on your head— / Do you think, at your age, is it right?'"). In our era, this looked like a dear eccentricity of an old man—but then Green was reciting this when he was a young man, too. Just as the heavy perfumes of elderly women were once what Thoroughly Modern Millie wore, the old man reciting poetry from memory today grew up in a world where people with straight backs and unlined faces were doing the same thing when the occasion demanded it.

And that's just it—there were occasions that demanded or allowed it that no longer exist for us. Around when Green was born, one of the highlights of Marie Dressler's vaudeville tour was her recitation of "When Baby Souls Sail Away," a sentimental poem about infant death, a common theme in popular culture in the late nineteenth century. The meat of Dressler's act was big, loud songs and slapstick pratfalls. But she and her audiences felt it as ordinary for her to take a breather by reciting this poem, which regularly brought audiences to tears. Edna St. Vincent Millay's mother, whose lifespan closely paralleled Dressler's, would recite Whittier's *Snowbound* from memory to little Edna before bed—despite not having finished high school.

She also read Edna lengthy narrative poems like Longfellow's "The Song of Hiawatha." In 1941, the early Bugs Bunny cartoon *Hiawatha's Rabbit Hunt* frames the usual chase antics ("I'm gonna catch me a rabbit and I'm gonna put him in this pot. Yeah, ye-ah—that's what I'm gonna do") with Bugs reading from the poem while chomping away on his carrot. To me and my friends growing up seeing this cartoon on television, Bugs's reading from this flowery-sounding poem just "was." We enjoyed Mel Blanc's voice acting (Bugs cawing away in his Brooklynese "Sail a-lawng, liddle Hiawadda . . ."), but the activity itself had no meaning in the America we grew up in, where despite solid educations none of us were ever exposed to "The Song of Hiawatha" or much poetry in general. Nor did my mother, who read to me a lot, ever read poems to me. But the men who created the cartoon were of roughly Adolph Green's age, and were mocking what was still a living tradition in 1941.

Nor did having Longfellow on his bookshelf render Bugs Bunny pretentious. Gioia himself noted in his essay that in the thirties and forties, anthologies of Robert Frost, Elinor Wylie, W. H. Auden, Robinson Jeffers, and Millay were brisk sellers, and that Louis Untermeyer's *Modern American Poetry* was a bestseller for years. Untermeyer was almost a middle-class bookshelf cliché in those days. But can you think of a modern equivalent to Untermeyer? "Well, what about the *Norton Anthology?"*—yes, many of us were assigned it in school. But it's a schoolbook. Not only do we not precisely expect to catch it as we browse a literate person's bookshelf, but if we do, we assume they kept it from college, not that they went out and bought it at Borders. Or, which individual poets do we almost expect to find anthologies of in people's living rooms?

In January 2003, the Book of the Month Club was selling just one anthology of a living poet, Billy Collins, and his special status as U.S. Poet Laureate presumably informed that inclusion. There were various other anthologies, all of which I presume are worthy tomes. But the issue is not whether such books are being printed, but what place they occupy in our society, and in that light, I have never heard of any of these anthologies. Certainly this is partly because I don't much like poetry—but in 1940, as an academic I would have known of Untermeyer just as I am aware of Douglas Hofstadter's erudite doorstop *Gödel, Escher, Bach* as a ubiquitous sight in educated people's homes despite my not having gotten around to reading it (and having heard more than a few who own it admit the same!). The closest thing to a living representation of poetry being sold by the Book of the Month Club as I write this is an anthology of the poems that Jackie Onassis liked!

During the Camelot era Onassis presided over as Jackie Kennedy, my mother had the college graduate's middlebrow sense of culture typical of the period: LPs of Van Cliburn, the Swingle Singers, Tchaikovsky's Sixth, *Porgy and Bess, Brigadoon,* and *Kismet;* novels by Katherine Anne Porter, Leon Uris, and James Michener, and a little later on Rod McKuen and *Jonathan Livingston Seagull.* To this day, I successfully predict things she will enjoy by putting myself in the head of a "career girl" circa 1962.[8] This included Untermeyer on her shelf, and I clearly recall, from pawing as a child over the books she amassed before getting married, that this tome was well-thumbed, though Mom was not one for gliding around reciting Frost. I am my mother in many ways, including my sense of "bookshelf"—but this does not include an anthology of poetry, and I doubt I am alone. I would be about as likely to be asked "Where's your poetry?" as "Have you got any flashcubes?"

As with oratory and crafted prose, the change I refer to concerns the status of poetry in society. I hardly claim that there was ever a time in

---

[8.] My mother's Negro *That Girl* stage did not last long, however: She went on to earn a PhD while raising two children and working more than one job.

America when poetry was a mania among all or even most Americans. The national bestseller lists of the twentieth century have included the same kind of sap, smut, swill, and sensationalism decade after decade (although Millay's *Fatal Interview* was an exception in 1931). But the space poetry did occupy was larger before. Appalled at developments in Europe in 1939, renowned pundit Dorothy Thompson made a call for "the intuitive imagination of the great poets, to comprehend in even a small way the nature of the forces that are moving the world." In times just as distressing, none of us are waiting for Maureen Dowd or Thomas Friedman to say anything like this. And as late as the 1960s, Marianne Moore was appearing on Johnny Carson's *Tonight Show*—and *more than once*, not just as a once-off coup to help sell a book. I don't even need to wonder whether Carson spent his evenings puzzling his way through Moore's challenging poetry, nor did most Americans. But nevertheless, she was on the show. The symbolism itself makes that a different world than the one we live in.

The Hidden Costs of Literacy

And in the case of poetry, education did play the decisive role in the difference. To all but a few viewers of *Hiawatha's Rabbit Hunt* today, Bugs is reading some poem for some reason. But to a lot more than a few viewers in 1941, Bugs was reading that poem that he read in school and is revisiting in his spare time (I know he's just a cartoon rabbit, but you take my meaning). Schoolchildren were once required to memorize poetry, and this exposure is why people of modest education so often had a grounding in poetry beyond most college graduates' today. This included the language of Shakespeare: A set of his works was once a treasured feature of even the homeliest bookshelf (even if rarely opened). There is a sweet moment in one of grand old monologuist Ruth Draper's set pieces from between the wars where a rural, uneducated woman in Maine rapturously describes her son's talent for reciting Shakespeare. The character gives no evidence of being a reader or theater fan, but she thrills to hearing language beautifully couched and recited. Draper based her portraits of people like this on life experience, having spent many summers in Maine as a child, and it is hard to imagine one of Draper's descendants—Lily Tomlin comes to mind—depicting a "hick" as liking Shakespeare on any level.

And this is partly because in the old days, even the unlettered person was likely to have been enlightened to the joys of poetry in school, even if they left after eighth grade. The reason this so often took was because it is a universal of human societies to thrill to the poetic use of language. There are no societies without a linguistic activity that falls under the rubric of poetry. Even in our age so fiercely unsentimental, students fed poetry the old-fashioned way tend to respond just as their ancestors did. When Russian emigré poet Joseph Brodsky has insisted that American college students memorize and recite poetry in his classes, they first bridle at the imposition—so foreign has the very concept become—but soon come to enjoy it and acquire a taste for poetry they didn't have before. Recitation can be fun, especially when what's in your mouth is language fashioned well.

But Americans have not been regularly shown this for several decades now. Memorizing poetry was long ago swept away in the revolt against rote learning in education, which had been brewing since before the turn of the century, but became a norm in schooling in the sixties. And at the same time, the skepticism toward the Western inheritance was growing into the commonplace it is today in the education world. In this context, naturally, dear old poems couched in high English strung into sentences that require as much decoding as drinking in were sitting ducks. Too authoritarian, too old, too white, too Western, too removed from the gritty, personal, here-and-now experiences that children must be engaged through. But without close engagement with this kind of poetry at the crucial stage of their formative years, Americans lost their taste for it.

This is especially clear in many foreign countries, where anyone who has been anywhere near a school cherishes national poets to an extent that comes off as distinctly exotic to us. Brodsky was born in a country where schoolchildren have traditionally been drilled in a rich array of Russian poets, required to memorize and recite them. As a result, Russians tend to walk around with reams of poetry memorized. I once asked an undergraduate raised in Russia about this, and she—a thoroughly hip, contemporary person, not a Poindexter singleton sort—immediately started rattling off elegant, baroque strophes of Pushkin. Russians hold Pushkin, in particular, in a sentimental esteem that Americans reserve for John Lennon or Tupac Shakur (no accident, and we'll come back to it). The notion of an American student, even if a product of the toniest suburban school, enthusiastically chanting lines of Lindsay or Frost on command is utterly weird—the closest they could come would be to sing the theme song to *The Brady Bunch* or *Gilligan's Island*. Mihai Eminescu occupies a similar place among Romanians, who even without college educations can often recall whole poems of his. We have our famous poets and our poet laureates, but there is no poet that we hold this close unless we are fans of the form. If there is a single exception, it is Dr. Suess. And as clever as he was, a whole monograph could be written on the fact that *Horton Hears a Who* occupies the same place in our hearts as Pushkin does in Russians'.

Ironically, widespread literacy rendered poetry's place in the American soul more rather than less precarious. Because English is a written language, for centuries elaborate poetic language was crafted, disseminated, and encountered largely on the page. This contrasts with illiterate societies, where high poetry is often passed along orally. The Homeric epics were originally delivered orally in a society in which literacy was but an elite activity. Into the twentieth century, there were still bards in the former Yugoslavia reciting similar epics from memory in song to illiterate peasant audiences—in an elaborate form of language none of them was using while milking their goats:

'Sestro naša, Blažena Marija!

Kakva ti je golema nevolja,

Te ti roniš suze od obraza?'

Al govori Blažena Marija:

'A moj brate, gromovnik Ilija!

Kada neću suze proljevati?'

'Our sister, blessed Mary!

what is your great sorrow

that you weep tears adown your cheeks?'

answered him blessed Mary:

'O my brother, thunderer Elijah!

how may I not pour forth my tears?'

But once there is writing, these feats of memory become less necessary, and the principle of least effort that so deeply impacts human affairs comes into play. Why go to the trouble of keeping it all in your head if you can write it down? But this means that eventually, poetry is engaged exclusively in print. Our inclination is to think of the advantage that permanent documentation lends. But there is a flip side: If we only meet poetry on the page, then an educational establishment that soft-pedals poetry ends up pulling the rug out from under us. One of the main purposes of schooling is to usher children into engaging the un-natural world of written language. If poetry is no longer a main course in schoolchildren's diet, then inevitably society will lose its taste for it.

Poetry Gets Real

But education is only part of the story of poetry in America. The six-ties swept away lofty oratory and marginalized elaborately constructed prose. But poetic language is a hardier thing—it is one of the human traits that Donald Brown documents as a universal. It follows from this that even if no longer taught much poetry, we would predict that as hu-man beings Americans would continue to engage in poetic expression somehow. They did—but the fashions in which they did so corresponded perfectly to the transformation in how Americans relate to linguistic ex-pression.

For example, despite its shrunken audience, poetry has continued to be written since the 1960s—but in a form hewing to the spoken rather than the written variety of English.

Lemonade Out of Lemons: Poetry As a Brain-Teaser Exercise

A poem by Edna St. Vincent Millay, for example, was couched in highly crafted language that no one would ever speak spontaneously, the rhymes exact and the scansion perfect, as we see in one of the verses that college coeds thrilled to:

> I shall forget you presently, my dear,
> So make the most of this, your little day,
> Your little month, your little half a year,
> Ere I forget, or die, or move away,

And that was meat-and-potatoes as Millay went; much of her work was denser in its vocabulary and less immediately infectious in its rhythms. And during her lifetime, mainstream American poetry became even more "written." The New Criticism school's philosophy focused on text for text's sake and richness of allusions. Here is an excerpt from John Berryman's 1953 "Homage to Mistress Bradstreet," obscure even in its reference, America's first poet, Anne Bradstreet, who lived in the seventeenth century. The excerpt describes her giving birth:

> drencht & powerful, I did it with my body!
> One proud tug greens Heaven. Marvelious,
> unforbidding Majesty.
> Swell, imperious bells. I fly.
> Mountainous, woman not breaks and will bend:
> sways God nearby: anguish comes to an end.
> Blossomed Sarah, and I
> blossom. Is that thing alive? I hear a famisht howl.

The occasional archaic spellings summon up Bradstreet's time, but are a purely written affect that would be lost in recitation. "sways God nearby" and "Blossomed Sarah" are similarly archaic, contrasting with the almost colloquial "I did it with my body!" and "Is that thing alive?" Drinking in the kaleidoscope totality of this poem is only possible from the printed page: Talking only peeps out from the cracks. This was not designed for Berryman to be booked to recite at the end of *Your Show of Shows*.

But a poem need not be as willfully dense as this one to fall far beyond the looseness of speech. "Black Girl Shouting" is a poem James Baldwin wrote for the magazine at his high school; here is a selection from it:

> Stomp my feet
> An' clap my han's
> Angels comin'
> To dese far lan's.
>
> *Cut my lover*
> *Off dat tree!*
> Angels comin'
> To set me free.
>
> Glory, glory,
> To de Lamb
> *Blessed Jesus*
> *Where's my man?*

> Black girl, whirl
> Your torn, red dress
> Black girl, hide
> Your bitterness.

The Black English forms recall speech, but they are harnessed to tight craft. Mere words sitting on the page summon a taut drumbeat—hear it?—as well as passion and terror within the strictures of very brief lines and a focus on single-syllable words. Even for those to whom Black English diction, structure, and cadence were most natural, spinning off this crystallized rendition of the dialect while kicking back one night would be impossible even at gunpoint. Baldwin was never one for just talking.

"That's a Poem?"

But since the 1960s, a different kind of poetry has come to reign. Literature scholar David Perkins describes how poets tended to reject the notion of art as "constructed, closed, perfected, and posed"—like written language—"created laboriously through many repeated revisions." Instead, the new tone was "casual, relaxed, conversational." Here, then, was the kind of poem we today associate with the coffeehouse reading. Our nation's current Poet Laureate is a prime example. Mary Jo Salter gets Billy Collins just right:

> You don't go to Billy Collins for complex metrical effects or rhyme schemes, either of which might be usefully mnemonic. His pacing and sense of proportion are rhythmic and graceful, but their effect feels as tossed off and elusive as conversation. Nor can you turn to Collins for much in the way of assonance, alliteration, wordplay, or even for a venturesome vocabulary.

In other words, Collins just talks to an extent that would have baffled a Laura Riding or a Walt Whitman: These poets would not have known quite what to make of a Poet Laureate whom Salter accuses of taking a "vacation from his own language," nor of Salter's affectionate equanimity on the subject despite being a poet herself.

I don't mean to knock Collins here. Beautiful things can come out of this new conception of what poetry is, as in the opening of one of Collins's best-known pieces where a man savors gastronomic afterglow after a meal of Osso Buco accompanied by "cold, exhilarating wine":

> I love the sound of the bone against the plate
> and the fortress-like look of it

Collins goes on to describe the bone sitting in a "moat of risotto", and zeroes in on the marrow, "the invaded privacy of the animal". The poem fairly glows in a cozy, domestic, middle-aged, autumn brown. I like the precise sensual evocations: the clunk of the bone, the prizing out of the marrow, the not just swallowing but swallowing down. I am taken by the novelty of such a specific, even random moment being captured in a poem. Or to continue in the culinary mode, Collins' title "I Chop Some Parsley While Listening to Art Blakey's Version of 'Three Blind Mice' " is "spoken" language with that casual "some", but also reveals an awesome gift for conjuring quirkily immediate sensual images: one pictures the cutting board, the jazz in the air, even certain implications of class and type. The layman can have a hard time seeing "poetry" in work like this: even teacher and reviewer Cristina Nehring dismisses such poetry as mere "humble diction and off-rhymes, at best," grousing of these poets that "too often their poetry sounds like apologetic prose." But that's a nervy opinion that most poets and poetry scholars would dismiss as backward. Longfellow, Whitman, and even Millay would have agreed with Nehring, but poetry like Collins's is very much a norm today.

But the point bears mentioning, for our purposes, that the deftness of this kind of poem is largely in the summoning of images and the choices of words. Collins is unconcerned with pushing the language very far beyond its spoken form in terms of grammar or reaching for lesser-known words to convey particular phenomena. And rhyme and scansion are obviously so irrelevant for him that to even mention them in relation to his work is like wondering when people shaking their booty at a club are going to go up on their toes like ballet dancers.

Of course, if tightness of rhyme and scansion were the only measures of the depth of transformation from spoken to written, then Dr. Suess would be taught in universities. Plenty of poets long before the sixties wrote in freestyle, such as Christina Rossetti or Emily Dickinson. But they did so with vocabulary often foreign to speech, and gave themselves a lot less breathing room in format and sentence structure. Take Dickinson's "Wild Nights":

> Wild nights! Wild nights!
> Were I with thee,
> Wild nights should be
> Our luxury!
>
> Futile the winds
> To a heart in port,—
> Done with the compass,
> Done with the chart.
>
> Rowing in Eden!
> Ah! the sea!
> Might I but moor
> To-night in thee!

God, I like that one! A quest for an orgasm in just forty-three words, honed like flint by candlelight. But though it registers as hot as a lubricious disco lyric, this is not how Dickinson spoke casually. We must not let Dickinson's Civil War hairstyles fool us into thinking that *thee* or *might I but moor* were current speech even in the 1800s. If "Wild Nights" isn't the quintessence of craft then I don't know what is, and if I liked poetry more I would have a book with it on my shelves. (As it stands I know it from having seen it around.)

Literary critic Judith Shulevitz has aptly said that "poetic composition is the art of finding beauty in constraint, of turning limitation into aesthetic opportunity." Comparing Whitman and Millay on one hand with Collins, only with difficulty can we claim that there is no apparent difference in degree of the kind of constraint Shulevitz refers to. The modern American poem is less likely to suggest that writing it involved thinking of the brainteaser kind. Sure, much art lies in making the difficult appear easy, as the endless rehearsing and retakes that Fred Astaire required show. And Collins may well agonize for weeks over word choices and do endless rewrites to get a poem to the point that he feels it as "right" (although more than a few poets since the 1950s have scorned extensive revision as interfering with truth). But Collins dedicates this effort to poems that read a lot like someone running their mouth, and this gives him a waiver on channeling his effort into a great deal of formal constraint that even Dr. Suess considered de rigueur. It also bears mentioning that the poet bound by rhyme and meter is also as concerned with word coloring, choice of image, and flow as the poet who writes in more casual form. Taking away rhyme and scansion leaves the poet with less to attend to. We could say that this means the poet has more space to breathe, but we could just as well see art triumphing over craft.

"Now, That's a Poem!": Verse Among the Preliterate

It's ticklish to many of us modern Americans to venture into ranking Frost and Collins on craft: We prize Collins's relevance, we're taught from an early age that the unadorned likely conceals complexity, and we distrust qualitative rankings.

But sometimes we can see clearest in stepping outside of ourselves. Take another example of oral poetry, one of my favorite examples, Somalian poetry. Somali has only been used as a written language in a meaningful way for about thirty years. But traditionally, the Somali who would probably have become a writer in a literate society engaged in a range of forms of oral poetry with highly constrained formats. Here is an example of one of the various types:

Ilaah baa dabkoodiyo sandahay,   *danabbadoodii ye*

— — _/ —_ _ _/ _ _   _ _ _/ _ _ _/

Dadka ugu ma liitaan e waa,   *diriri waayeen e*

_ _ —_/_ _ _ _/ —   _ _ _/ _ — _

Afartaa sidii Deleb La riday,   *maysu dabo joojay?*

_ _ — _/ —_ _ _/ _ _   —_/ _ _ —_/

Da'daan kaga bilaabiyo miyaan,   *deelka ka habowshay?*

— _ _ _/ —_ _ _/_   _ _/ _ _ — _/

Ma daleeyay deylqaafku waa,   *Kaa dilaa gabay e.*

_ _ _—_/ — — _/ —   — _/ —_ _ _/

God has put out their fire and has dampened (the valor of) their heroes;
They are not the weakest among people and yet they have not fought (at all).
Have I not put these four (points) one after the other, like the (marked)
    sticks in the Deleb game?
Have I lost the alliteration in the letter D with which I began?
Have I not set it out clearly? Errors and prevarication spoil a poem!

Note that the sophistication of the poem extends to self-referential irony—there is nothing remotely quaint or untouched about it.

Somali poetry is based on the feet familiar to students of classical poetry, which I indicate above with slash lines. Each sequence of five syllables can be divided between short (_) and long (__) syllables in one of eight possible patterns. In the particular genre of poem that the one above represents, only four of these patterns, not all eight, can be used (those termed the pentabrach, first paeon, third paeon, and palimbacchiac in classical poetry). Alliteration is also key in these poems: in this one the sound to alliterate is *d*. In this genre, the rule is that whatever sound is chosen must be alliterated in each half line—but in another genre, alliteration must occur within a whole line, while in another the alliterated sound can change from line to line. In all of the genres, however, words next to one another may not alliterate: no getting by with things like "bouncing baby boy." And then, each line in this genre and others must have the pause in the middle that we see above—but then the feet don't just stop at the pause, but straddle it. And this is poetry by preliterates!

The boundedness, the stark, heartless regulation of this form of verse, parallels Millay and at least hearkens to Dickinson. Millay would have recognized Somali poets as kindred souls, perhaps wangling an affair with a local wordsmith to later describe elliptically in a poem. On reaching Somalia, Dickinson would have desperately sought an attic to retreat to, but would still have remarked at the verbal sophistication of the "Ethiopes."

But Somali poetry is so different from Billy Collins's "And you are certainly not the pine-scented air. / There is no way you are the pine-scented air" that one can imagine an alternate-universe America where what the Somalians were doing and what Collins does were referred to with different words altogether, just as many European languages have different words for knowing a fact versus knowing a person (*connaître/savoir, conecer/saber, kennen/wissen*). John Barth once wrote "I'm inclined to prefer the kind of art that not many people can *do*: the kind that requires expertise and artistry as well as bright aesthetic ideas and/or inspiration." In that light, I feel safe in surmising that Barth would prefer Somalian poetry over Collins's.

Poetry by the Bobos in Paradise

But Collins cherishes accessibility, and in this, he is a person of our times. The change in the texture of American poetry was in large part a response to the same sociopolitical sentiments that turned us away from high oratory and cut-glass prose composition. Perkins chronicles that on the 1960s American poetry scene, "Spontaneous immediacy in expression was prized because of its 'truth,' 'sincerity,' or 'naturalness.' " The artifice of older poetic forms came to feel incompatible with democratic commitment: "To impose a form on an experience or a thought is to put it in a context and perspective, and thus to repress other contexts or perspectives that might be no less valid."

Since the 1960s, leading poets have tended to be "deeply alienated from our imperialist, bureaucratic, consumerist, commercially manipulative civilization" as Perkins puts it. His wording makes it sound as if the typical poet is refusing to pay taxes and tearing through the streets breaking windows, when actually he is describing a mindset now dominant among even the most mild-mannered of thinking people. But the prevalence of this kind of position among American poets was clear in early 2003 when First Lady Laura Bush convened a White House poetry symposium only to postpone it when one of the invitees, poet Sam Hamill, solicited 50 friends to submit to him poems decrying the impending war with Iraq to be gathered into an anthology to be presented at the event. The responses Hamill received climbed into the thousands, leading him to create a poetsagainstthewar.org website to handle all the submissions.

Hamill said that the invitation from the White House led him to feel "overcome with a kind of nausea." Because that mindset discourages dressing up to suit reigning norms, to the poet thusly inclined, forms of language associated with empire and oppression may likely seem irrelevant. Bringing poetic language down to earth and taking it from the elite even becomes an artistic act in itself, as willful as earlier poets' quest to draw language away from the everyday to bring it closer to the heavens. To Collins, then, accessibility means returning to the elemental, departing as little from casual speech as possible while still producing crafted work.

And that is a sense of accessibility that marks our era. Millay was impatient with willfully opaque poetry, and considered accessibility one of the hallmarks of her work. But to her there was no contradiction between accessibility and mannered craft of a sort that made her poems require careful perusal. Each year, her humble high school designated a student the Class Poet (this alone shows her America as one in which poetry was more front and center than we can easily imagine today). Much to her chagrin, a classmate won the distinction with a poem that had largely been Millay's work. In making it prizeworthy, she had "rhymed lines that didn't rhyme, balanced the shaky meter of other lines," and had been disgusted with poems he had written her the year before that were "queer rhymeless, meterless things which I suppose he meant for poems." Her Victorian idea of what a poem was doesn't translate today—it'd be like asking a date as she stepped into your car why she had chosen not to wear petticoats tonight. The nut here is our times, when submitting to externally imposed boundaries carries less weight than doing our own thing.

This kind of poetry was hardly unheard of before Kent State, of course. Some might think of the Romantic poets' call for simple language in poetry as far back as the nineteenth century, but the ornate, allusion-laden language these writers were rebelling against was so baroque that their version of simple remains, to us, highly "written." Wordsworth, for instance, presented his *Lyrical Ballads* as "language really used by men," but his English sounds so studied to us that it is almost comical to read his claim to have written in "simple and unelaborated expressions." More pertinently, Elizabeth Bishop was writing poems in the style of one of her best-known, "In the Waiting Room," as far back as the 1950s:

> In Worcester, Massachusetts,
> I went with Aunt Consuelo
> to keep her dentist's appointment
> and sat and waited for her
> in the dentist's waiting room.

And William Carlos Williams was writing poetry that sounded a lot like this as far back as the teens, when early Modernist poets were already rebelling against the archaic diction, classical references, and melodramatic pitch of Victorian-era poetry. And the Beat poets picked up this ball and ran with it, Allen Ginsberg being especially influenced by Williams. Ginsberg's famous *Howl*, with its searingly memorable opening line "I saw the best minds of my generation destroyed by madness, starving hysterical naked, dragging themselves through the negro streets at dawn looking for an angry fix" dates to 1954, not 1968. But in the fifties this kind of writing remained a movement rather than a norm. Respectable critics could still dismiss *Howl* as "formless" and even "barbarian." The climate of the sixties was a perfect one to seize on the Beat aesthetic and make it the order of the day. Surveying some choice poetry from various foreign countries, masterful cultural critic Margo Jefferson has asked "Why does the United States seem to be the only country in which artists still argue about whether politics can coexist with aesthetic complexity?" The reason is because we learned in the sixties to distrust aesthetic complexity as an imposition from the suits and a distraction from a truer, warmer "authenticity."

We speak the language we know. As a result, the young person who tries their hand at poetry today will often dive straight into a free-form style, whether or not they are of countercultural leanings. In college, I once found my quest to "get next to" a certain woman stymied in part by my inability to meaningfully appreciate her poems, which she put so much stock in. She was a sunny person largely at ease with the world. But to me, these poems just looked like random musings couched in a certain ethereal air that seemed to correspond neither to her personality nor the setting we inhabited. I was hip enough to know that I wasn't supposed to feel that way. But realizing that, I could not come up with anything but wan, dutiful praise, that contrasted too sharply with my more passionate opinions about other things for my real sentiment not to be clear.

I imagine a hipper, more sophisticated guy swept her off her feet one day. But I would have had a little more to grab on to in an earlier time, when the reigning wisdom was that poetry was a kind of elaborate trick rather than just saying stuff in touching or passionate ways. Exactly a hundred years before this book was published, when Millay was just twelve, she tossed off some verses like this for her and her sisters to recite while washing dishes:

> I'm the Queen of the Dish-pan.
> My subjects abound.

I can knock them about
And push them around,
And they answer with naught
But a clattering sound;
I'm the Queen of the Dish-pan,
Hooray!

It rhymes, it scans, it uses vocabulary beyond the everyday. This scrap was a little piece of clockwork—chanted by three girls cleaning dirty plates in a little house in a small town in God-Knows-Where, Maine, the year after the first airplane flew at Kitty Hawk. Today, the scene is almost as exotic as preliterate Somali sitting around crafting poems rivaling Catullus in sophistication.

Is "Stairway to Heaven" a Poem?

But what about people beyond the rarefied world of career poets? The days of cartoon characters reading Victorian poetry in their spare time are over, but humans require poetic language nonetheless. Thus we would predict that Americans after the mid-sixties filled the gap left empty by formal, written poetry, and we do. For all but the sliver of poetry fans, over the past forty years popular song lyrics have been the nation's poetry. People of boomer age and younger cherish rock, folk, and pop lyrics with exactly the intimate fervor that poetry lovers focus on poems:

Turn on the VCR, same one I've had for years . . .

I decided long ago never to walk in anyone's shadow . . .

I'm crazy for feelin' so lonely . . .

(or, if you are on the younger and hipper side:)

I hear Brenda's got a baby . . .

Lines like these, deeply imprinted in the American soul, are our poetry. For many readers, merely reading them will go straight to the gut and set you to bopping your head or singing to yourself in communion with what you hold close as an expression of your soul. These are to us what "My candle burns at both ends / It will not last the night" were to many Americans in the twenties.

This first hit me one afternoon in college when I saw two guys sitting under a tree singing Simon and Garfunkel's "The Boxer" as one accompanied on guitar. They sat face-to-face looking into each other's eyes singing the song with a passion, precision, and intensity, including the exact harmonies Simon and Garfunkel sang, that struck me. That kind of sustained intense interaction is unusual in American men outside of athletic activity. These guys were truly entranced by this song, and the alienated plangency of the lyric had a lot to do with it. In the 1940s, even a fine song like "Stardust" was much less likely to elicit this sense of connection and communion between two guys singing it.

Richard Price nicely captures the same thing in his novel *Freedomland*. An emotionally shattered mother finds solace in the sixties soul lyrics she has always loved, listing them almost compulsively in a note she gives the detective working with her. With the later revelation of something horrifying that she has done, we realize that this list was a way of signaling that love and humanity reside inside of her nevertheless. Again, these lyrics are her poetry. She feels them as keystones of her soul in a way that a 1920s version of the character would be less likely to in relation to the pop songs of that era, even if she were quite fond of them.

But in embracing this form of poetry, we take to heart a medium as chary of constraint as so much modern written poetry is. We value pop lyrics for how "real" they are—that is, how charismatically they summon the way we really talk. And again we contrast here with our elders. John Q. Public in the old days expected a degree of artifice and craft in a pop lyric. The last song Lorenz Hart wrote, "To Keep My Love Alive" in 1943, listed the endless procession of husbands that a woman has killed for trivial reasons. The rhymes are exquisite—sixty years later the song still breaks up audiences:

> Sir Paul was frail, he looked a wreck to me
> At night he was a horse's neck to me
> So I performed an appendectomy
> To keep my love alive.

Even theater songs most of us don't think of as exactly quality have nice touches. Here's a lyric from "Put on a Happy Face." Okay, it's a cheesy song in its way (actually from *Bye Bye Birdie*), but how many people do you know who could come up with a rhyming trick like this one?

> Take off the gloomy mask of tragedy
> It's not your style
> You'll look so good that you'll be glad you de-
> cided to smile.

And even throwaway tunes nobody sane knows today often had charmingly close rhymes like this. This is from "The Girlfriend of a Boyfriend of Mine," known only to me, two former roommates, and about eleven other clinically insane obsessives, the lament of a fella who finds out the girl he is wooing has been two-timing him:

> I found that love was just a joke
> and what a broke-
> n heart meant
>
> I even started out to get
> a kitchenette
> apartment

And in all of these cases, the syllables matched the shape of the melody perfectly: There were *rules* to the game. Jerome Kern would write melodies and send them to Oscar Hammerstein expecting him to craft a solid lyric while leaving his melody absolutely inviolate. And yet out of this modus operandi came gems like "Ol' Man River" and "Can't Help Lovin' Dat Man," which sound so natural that we can almost imagine them just emerging fully formed out of thin air (it is not uncommon for people to assume that "Ol' Man River" is a timeless spiritual passed down orally, for example).

My point is not that I would prefer an America in which we went back to lyrics in the old pop style. There were high points, and even the state-of-the-art was often cute. But I also find most of the vintage lyric literature tiresomely sanitized and numbingly general. Audra McDonald is right in valuing the fact that modern musical-theater composers write about things as specific as abortion rather than focusing on romantic love and how marvelous it is to dance. In a way, I see blazing talents like Porter and Hart as having been straitjacketed by the fact that their era funneled so much of their effort into such plastic topics. Lyrics like "Blue Moon" and "Night and Day," for all of their charms, could not become intensely felt watchcries in the way that lyrics by Paul Simon, Carly Simon, Gladys Knight and the Pips, or Tori Amos do.

Yet, while American popular song lyrics have gained in maturity and honesty, they have lost a lot of craft. Take a song that now has classic status, Nirvana's "Smells Like Teen Spirit." Catchy song, this one, although I have never completely understood it. But it also rhymes *entertain us* with *contagious* and implies that *mulatto, albino, mosquito,* and *libido* all "rhyme" in some sense.

It's a kick on the recording. But still, taking the lyric itself, it does not rhyme in any sense a Cole Porter would recognize, its metrical sense is elementary. As it happens, Kurt Cobain's scrapbooks actually show that he worked on this lyric, rejecting first tries, trying out alternatives. But even here, for example, both the rejected and the accepted rhymes tend toward the approximate. This is not intricately crafted language—it's an evocation of just talking, rather like fundamentalist sermons. Old pop lyrics lose less on paper because so much went into putting the words themselves together—Lorenz Hart's lyrics need no qualifiers and apologies when presented without their melodies.

Today, the only popular song lyrics as tightly crafted as his and his colleagues' are written not for the mainstream public, but for musical theater, today a specialty genre. And even there, the tighter the lyric, the less popular the musical will tend to be. We look to a Stephen Sondheim for a lyric from his *A Little Night Music* like this one, in which a middle-aged man considers reading to his teen bride as a way of coaxing her into finally consummating their marriage:

> In view of her penchant for something romantic
> De Sade is too trenchant and Dickens too frantic
> And Stendhal would ruin the plan of attack
> As there isn't much blue in *The Red and the Black.*

That's dazzling—catch that "ruin / blue in" internal rhyme, for example. There is little to none of this kind of thing in the *Evita*'s and *Miss Saigon*'s, but it is they, with more loosely constructed lyrics more like modern pop, that really rake in the bucks and elate more listeners beyond the little coterie of High Musical Theater aficionados.

How new the utter freedom in pop lyric construction is stands out from a random moment in a 1948 episode of Lucille Ball's pre-*Lucy* radio show, *My Favorite Husband*. There's a lot in a joke. The Lucy character and her husband have the boss and his wife over for dinner, and they catch "Bibbidi-Bobbidi-Boo" (the one from the Disney *Cinderella*) on the radio. The boss, a middle-aged man on the stuffy side (played by Gale Gordon, who would later become best known as Mr. Mooney on Ball's second TV show), sniffs "Oh, Gad! That's a popular song?" He prefers old chestnuts like 1914's "When You Wore a Tulip and I Wore a Big Red Rose."

That joke marks the show as a token of its time. The boss perceived a radical difference in craft between:

> When you wore a tulip, a sweet yellow tulip,
> And I wore a big red rose,
> When you caressed me, 'twas then heaven blessed me
> What a blessing, no one knows

and

> Salagadoola menchickaboola,
> Bibbidi-Bobbidi-Boo.
> Put 'em together and what have you got?
> Bibbidi-Bobbidi-Boo!

But even this, with perfect meter and, as the lyric goes on, close rhymes, is Longfellow compared to lyrics like "Lookin' for some *hot stuff* baby this evenin'. Or, to take something more recent and taken more seriously, Beck's "Loser" with its famous line "I'm a loser baby so why don't you kill me," ryhmed with nothing, the rest of the song's lyrics rhyming only optionally and sometimes roughly. Lyrics like these simply did not exist in mainstream pop music in 1948. What would Mr. Mooney have made of them?

But the media were mildly fascinated by "Loser" a little while back, and even the sharpest, most demanding rock critics celebrated Kurt Cobain as having a lyrical gift. In a time when *mulatto* and *albino* rhyme, while we still have our definite senses of what's good and what isn't, it's hard to conceive of any kind of lyric that would move a modern American to ask "That's a song?" Anything can be a lyric now. The stuffy boss on *My Favorite Husband* reflected an assumption that "a song" evidenced a certain amount of craft, artifice, study, sweat in its lyric—even if the result was "When You Wore a Tulip." These days, we wait for lyricists to just write what they feel and make sure to keep it real, and if what they happen to come up with happens to resonate with us on some visceral level, we're satisfied (most especially if the lyric takes an alienated stance). Hip-hop lyrics delight in rhyme and meter more than traditionally white lyrics usually do. But compared to what rhyme meant to even the obscurest Tin Pan Alley hack (who but the obsessed know who wrote "There's nothing sur-er / The rich get rich and the poor get poorer / In the meantime / In between-time / Ain't we got fun?"), much hip-hop rhyme is approximate, with the kick coming as much from the use of a brand name or prominent figure as from how closely the sounds in question actually correspond. Meter is also a sometime thing—now you see it, now you don't. Dynamic in its way—but the contrast in "constraint" with the Sondheim lyric is obvious.

Nor is this taste in lyric a matter of youth culture anymore—it goes back as far as Dylan and the folkies, and today increasing numbers of people old enough to be driving their kids to soccer practice are admitting a fascination with Eminem. The sixties were the dividing line between "That's a song?" and the gray-ponytail sort who warmly recalls how electrified he was when he first heard the Stones and the Dead. Our sense of what constitutes a worthy lyric is a direct outgrowth of a countercultural earthquake that taught us to worship at the shrine of the unadorned—the same one that transformed the poetry world. It is predictable, then, that we only started holding pop lyrics so very close when they came down to earth. Now a lyric is anything the artist wants it to be—the rising influence of World Beat shows that a lot of us no longer even care if we can understand the words at all.

"Then Why Do They Sing It in Italian, Mother?": Why We Don't Mind Reading at the Opera

Johann's Night at the Opera

And that brings us to another indication of our modern American ambivalence toward high poetic language. When I was in college, a friend had us go to a production of Puccini's opera *Manon Lescaut* at the

Metropolitan Opera in New York. Although musical drama has generally stirred me to my depths throughout my life, to the point that I can still recall details of productions I saw thirty years ago (I came away from the animated musical film of *Charlotte's Web* in 1973 ruing the mundaneness of my own life), I recall not a thing about this evening of Puccini. This was 1985, before the Met had given in to supertitles, and so we just watched people singing in Italian for three hours. And as much as I wanted to connect with the piece, I was bored stiff after twenty minutes— for the simple reason that I couldn't understand what the singers were saying. Sure, there was a lengthy summary of the plot of each act in the program. But reading it quickly during the twenty minutes before the curtain went up, I could hardly retain much of anything. I was full of dinner, and besides, usually the people you are with want to talk before the lights go down.

Of course, today we are afforded supertitles in the larger opera houses, and conventional wisdom is that this has solved the comprehension problem. But having to read what the singers are saying requires constant looking away from the stage. According to one estimate, people who attended the Met's 2002 production of Prokofiev's *War and Peace* spent a full one-eighth of the performance reading instead of watching and listening.

American operagoers have become accustomed to this. But imagine spending an eighth of a showing of *Casablanca, The Wizard of Oz*, or *Pulp Fiction* reading. We spontaneously think of people who don't know English watching subtitled versions of these films as having a much less vivid experience than we do—because they do. Reading every ten seconds seems to us a major drag when we're seeing something we know what it's like to feel second-by-second in our bones. Well, just as Quentin Tarantino, waxing eloquent on the commentary tracks of the DVD editions of his films, wants us to savor every frame, Verdi and his librettists wanted us to attend to every moment of their operas.

Let's turn it upside down. I saw the Houston Opera *Porgy and Bess* production on tour in Philadelphia when I was ten, and I still recall when Donnie Ray Albert as crippled Porgy sang "Bess, You Is My Woman Now" to Clamma Dale's Bess. The simple beauty of the lyric—that's exactly how a man like Porgy would feel and exactly what he'd say—and the aching rapturousness of Gershwin's melody just blew me away. I, by no means a cryer, was embarrassed as hot tears ran down my cheeks applauding at the end of the opera.

Now, imagine a production of *Porgy and Bess* in English in Germany. The Porgy launches into "Bess, You Is My Woman Now." The audience member—let's call him Johann—doesn't speak English. So between that and the fact that the distortion of opera diction makes whatever English he does know almost useless, what he hears is about as comprehensible to him as this would be to us:

Ba-a-a-a-zz, lo-o-o-w-eez-na-ay-vo-oh-mah-na-a-a-ah. . . .

But wait—this is the twenty-first century, and so he has *supertitles* (tah-ta-dahhh!) to rescue him. Several yards above the stage, he can read in cold digital print: *Bess, jetzt gehörst du mir* ("Bess, you belong to me now"). But that chilly, inert digital projection is worlds apart from the warm, languid passion on stage, and it is clear to us that Johann is losing a lot. Yes, he has been given the literal content of what the singers are saying (more or less). But there is no comparison between this and us understanding what the singers are saying as it comes out of their mouths, in perfect sync with their actions and expressions—and all night long. We English speakers get a show. Johann, unless he happens to be an opera nut, leaves tired. The ordinary American operagoer foisted with supertitles is Johann. (Here, though, he'd be named John.)

Three Hours of Vowels: Why Johann Just Doesn't Get It

But people in the opera world are staunchly resistant to the idea of translating operas into English except occasionally. No one opposes opera translation utterly, but there is a reigning sense that foreign opera in English is like eating at the Olive Garden—a usually suburban experience hardly worth serious review.

The first argument usually presented is that the lyricists fit the words to particular vowels, in a way that is lost in translation. But the question is how realistic it is to require audiences to savor three hours of beautiful vowels, at the expense of truly connecting with what the characters are saying in often convoluted plots. In any case, the last time anyone checked, all languages have vowels, and few opera translators would force singers to sustain, say, a *th* where the Italian original had an *ah*.

In a related argument, many note that Italian, in particular, sings better than English. And it does—Italian, with its gorgeous open *ah*'s and *oh*'s and *oo*'s, is clearly better suited to project the human voice than many of the world's languages, especially English with its *ih*'s and *uh*'s. But once again the question is whether this admitted beauty can sustain the operagoer meaningfully for three hours. For me, it did not in *Manon Lescaut,* nor did it for the friends I went with, game though they were for the experience, including the friend who had suggested it. The composers and librettists of these operas did not write them to be experienced as processions of vowels set upon pretty melodies.

And arguments like these fall apart given the simple fact that Europeans have often not felt this way about translating opera into their own languages. The prejudice against translating opera lyrics is much lesser in Europe, where it has long been customary or common to give the piece in the local tongue (although somewhat less so today because of—groan—supertitles). When Mozart's works made the rounds of the Continent, audiences were not usually expected to sit through them in a language they did not speak. The French regularly enjoyed *The Marriage of Figaro* in French; after Mozart's death, Vienna audiences enjoyed a German-language version of his *Così Fan Tutte,* and so on.

Opera composers and lyricists fully expected that their work would be translated for people speaking other languages. After all, why would they not be? Sure, Italian is pretty—but three hours?

But in 2002, when Baz Luhrmann brought *La Bohème* to Broadway, he postdated it to France in the 1950s, cast gorgeous young singers, and set it in the roiling red-on-chiaroscuro ambience that made his *Moulin Rouge* so stunning, all to make it accessible to young, modern Americans. Yet the singers were still trilling away in Italian, Luhrmann shrugging: "The language is inherent and fundamental to the music. It just doesn't sound right in English." But then why have so many Europeans felt differently about how operas sounded in their languages—including Germans, whose language most would not find especially beautiful? Is it really that English would sound so ineluctably wrong in *La Bohème,* or is Luhrmann just not used to the idea of grand opera in the language he speaks?

Luhrmann had especially fresh, colloquial subtitles written, to be sure. But this led to another problem: Often supertitles feed the audience a joke several beats before the singer has expressed it. But we depart from wit in laughing at a line we read and then watching it sung. On the cartoon series *South Park*, little Stan has a way of throwing up on encountering a certain girl he likes. One of the posters for the German dub of the *South Park* movie exclaimed "Whenever Stan sees a girl he throws up!" *Nein!*—it's only funny when you experience the joke as it happens, or as time goes on, you savor how the writers vary the formula from one episode to another. Announcing it beforehand dumbs it down, transforming wit into yuks. When you read a singer's joke and then watch him singing syllables that you have been apprised connote the joke in question, you are less laughing at the joke than at the fact that for those few seconds, the incomprehensible stream of sound you have been working to connect with happens to correspond to something as immediate and mundane as that joke. You have been touched less deeply than the creators intended.

And given that Euros have so often considered it beyond question that an opera be in the language that they speak, other objections opera folk level become equally questionable. "Well, hell, I can't even understand what the singers are saying when the opera is in English!" one often hears. And supertitles for English-language operas are hardly useless. I attended the Met's production of William Bolcom's *A View from the Bridge*, and found myself guiltily thankful for the supertitles with the singers' opera diction often making it a challenge to capture what they were saying. But without the supertitles, I would have gotten more than enough to follow the action, and in fact the supertitles ultimately catered to a certain laziness—without them I would have clicked into a certain aural groove that allowed me to translate from an unfamiliar sort of diction. More properly, in English-language opera one misses a certain amount. But any English speaker who sits through a *Porgy and Bess* or a *The Medium* without supertitles who cannot even follow the plot most likely does not speak English as a first language. When I was ten, supertitles were far in the future, and yet I got enough of the *Porgy and Bess* production I saw to walk out embarrassedly wiping my cheeks, and it was definitely not the vowels or the mere passion that moved me. To claim that translating operas isn't worth it because even English can be tricky to make out when sung operatically is like arguing for starving an infant because so much of the food you feed him just falls on his bib anyway.

And finally there is the argument that really good opera singers ought be able to convey meaning through their acting. Lovely notion, but it falls apart in real life. In a summer opera workshop, I once watched two women singers do the "Mira, O Norma" scene at the top of Act II of Bellini's *Norma*. There were no supertitles in the humble university auditorium, nor were there program notes. In the scene, Norma, the heroine, has verged on killing herself and her children because their father, her lover, has fallen for another woman. That woman, Adalgisa, comes upon Norma and promises to go to the lover and convince him to return to Norma. The woman singing Norma, physically resembling a young Leontyne Price with a strikingly rich mezzo, was fantabulous, opening the scene with a facial expression and body language that said to me immediately, at least, that there was something seriously amiss in her love life. The Adalgisa was a deeply committed singer who managed to convey to me in ten minutes that she saw herself as potentially granting Norma something sublime.

But that was all I could get from what was the best-performed scene out of about ten in the afternoon. These two young performers gave their all and were doing everything they were supposed to. But my Italian isn't proficient enough to follow the arch literary variety of the language sung live, on top of this distorted by the requirements of opera singing. For that ten minutes they might as well have been singing in Thai. I left the auditorium wishing I had been able to understand what these two stunning performers had been singing about, and only by doing a little research before writing this have I ever known. These women did the very best anyone could have, period. But not even the most preternaturally talented charades player could convey with body language or diction that they were telling someone they would go consult the father of someone's children to assess whether a reconciliation was possible. If these singers had only sung the scene in English, I would have gotten a lot more out of what they had devoted six weeks of careful rehearsal to, and would have considered my deprivation of some *ah*'s and *oo*'s well worth the enrichment.

And too often, even opera singers—especially young ones—have only an approximate sense of what they're supposed to be saying. In this same workshop, I spent six weeks working on a scene from Mozart's *La Clemenza di Tito* with two people. One of them, who did not happen to be familiar with any foreign language, dutifully scratched in on her score what each of the words she was singing meant. But classical opera lyrics tend to be written in artificial inverted syntax that can be hard to wrap your head around when in a foreign language. Here, for example, are two lines from the beginning of Mozart's *Così Fan Tutte*:

La mia Dorabella capace non è
fedel quanto bella il cielo la fè

Word for word this translates as:

The my Dorabella capable not is
faithful as much as pretty the sky her made

This sort of thing was little help for this singer, especially given that mastering a whole scene requires not just lovingly digesting a couple of lines like these, but making your way through a good twenty or thirty of them. Consequently, this singer never had much but the most general idea of what she was saying—despite being a children's storyteller by trade with a lively narrative impulse. I always wished she could have just sung in the language she spoke so that she could better share her dramatic gift.

Opera You Can Understand: A Guilty Pleasure

Oh, but "It just doesn't sound right in English," we're told. But when smaller opera companies perform English translations, audiences rarely walk out smacking their ears out of discomfort with hearing their native language sung beautifully. For example, in the most widely used English translation of *Così Fan Tutte*, the two lines above are rendered as:

To doubt Dorabella is simply absurd.
She'll always be faithful and true to her word.

Admit it, it's cute. It's even good—more work went into it, matching plausible, singable English to an inviolate musical line, than into jotting down "I'm a loser baby so why don't you kill me." And if it sounds a little stiff to us, then it bears mentioning that no one in Italy is walking around talking in the language of Lorenzo Da Ponte's lyrics either. The English translation parallels not only the content, but the flavor of the original.

But now imagine watching it in Italian with supertitles, where on hearing a singer render the original lyric, we have to avert our eyes to a black screen upon which glows something like "My Dorabella simply could not—the heavens above made her faithful and beautiful." This is an artistic experience? Is this what Da Ponte wanted from us?

Some thought experiments:

1. In the mouths of Italians doing an English-language opera, "High school's never much fun" becomes "Hice cool znehver mahtch fon," and in their heads, the meaning of the sentence is approximately "Post-elementary education is not very amusing." How vital an entertainment will this be to an Italian?

2. Russians, having had warmer and more extended relations with the Japanese than they actually have in actual history, regularly watch and train students in musical dramas in Japanese, because with its vowels much like Italian's, it sings better than Russian with its clusters of consonants and often muddier vowels. We think: "But surely overall they would prefer operas in their own language!"

3. Italians regularly watch and train students in musical dramas in Swedish because of the inherently "musical" quality of Swedish intonation. (That this seems somehow odd shows that part of the acceptance of three-hour evenings in Italian is a certain affection we have for Italian culture, contrasting with our relative indifference to Swedish culture.)

4. Americans regularly watch and train students in musical dramas in Japanese because the vowels sing better. (That is, our tolerance for incomprehension narrows with any lingering sociopolitical ambivalences toward the culture—"What? They already sell us most of their cars and stereos!")

Yet it can be striking how disdainful people in the opera world can be to the notion that an English translation like the one from *Così* above could be suitable for an evening of serious artistic expression. I remember talking to an aspiring opera singer about an English-language production of *The Marriage of Figaro* he had been in. He recalled that where in the original, gardener Antonio at one point indicates that something has happened in the garden, pointing and singing "nel giardino," in English it came out as—Lord forbid—"in the garden"! He considered the very idea of *The Marriage of Figaro* in English as the height of gaucherie.

But at this very time, I was playing Antonio the gardener in a production for this summer workshop, and even though as a linguist I had no problem with the Italian, I could never get past a pressing question: "What in the world am I doing standing up here on stage in California in the year 2000 singing to an American audience in Italian?" A friend of mine who sings opera saw the production. He had previously seen me in a musical-theater production where I played a jolly, butt-pinching senator in 1950. He was honest about my performance as Antonio in telling me that my singing was fine but that while he had seen me make a real connection with the character of the dopey senator, he wondered why I wasn't "inhabiting" the gardener to the same extent. I thought about it for a second and finally said, "Because he doesn't speak English!"

Around the same time in the workshop, I was also doing Frank in *Die Fledermaus*, and thank God we did this one in English instead of the original German (the opera world warms more to translation when pieces are less weighty, as if artistic substance requires incomprehensibility). In this one, I was seen as making that connection with my character—because I could create him using the language I grew up with, with the nuances native to me, and present him to an audience speaking that same language, able to connect immediately with my renditions of the lines without looking away at some digital box every ten seconds. The director encouraged a silly and even raunchy atmosphere (the whole thing was a kind of *Moulin Fledermaus*), and I did Frank's spoken scenes in the voice of old radio and early television comedian Frank Nelson— best known for doing walk-ons as a salesclerk who turns around and says "Yee-ees?" And even while singing, I could know that the audience was fully understanding almost every word I sang the second I sang them. They got me. This is what Johann Strauss and his lyricists Carl Haffner and Richard Genée intended when they wrote the piece. They weren't the emotionless beings that early photography made people look like—they were living, quirky, hearty human beings who wanted to give an evening's pleasure, not an exercise. They wouldn't have cared that in the course of truly enjoying their work, this American audience didn't get to hear the German vowels placed exactly where they happened to set them.

Children can lend us bracing truths. A hundred years ago a child in New York seeing his first opera asked his mother, "Do all these people know Italian?" "Only a few," she answered. "Then why do they sing it in Italian, Mother?" the child asked. The mother answered, "They always do. Stop asking questions." Oscar Hammerstein went on with his recollection of that afternoon:

> I was puzzled and disturbed by the accompanying action on stage. Sometimes the fat lady would look very sad, and there was no way of knowing why. Sometimes she laughed, but I wouldn't know what the joke was and I wished I did. It then seemed clear to me why Grandpa lost money on opera. Listening to people sing words you didn't understand wasn't much fun. That's what I thought then. That's what I think now.

And that's what I think sixty years later, because Oscar was right, and I highly suspect he would have found supertitles cold comfort. Hammerstein did an English version of *Carmen—Carmen Jones—*setting the story among black factory workers. I dare anyone to listen to his smashing version of the Habanera, "Dat's Love," and claim that it "just doesn't sound right" in English, or that after hearing this, you would still prefer to watch it rendered in French while glancing at a chilly translation flashed every two lines somewhere high above the stage.[9]

Interestingly, in the 1950s the sun broke through the clouds on this issue for a brief shining moment. There were delightful television performances of grand operas translated into English in the 1950s, and at the same time, New York's City Opera was presenting translated versions of operas and continued to do so into the 1960s. But not after that. Twenty years later I was sitting politely through *Manon Lescaut* at the Metropolitan Opera listening to vowels, and a while later supertitles came in, conventional wisdom considering any comprehensibility problems thusly resolved.

[9.] Especially useful will be to watch Dorothy Dandridge performing it in the film of *Carmen Jones* because, first, she was dubbed by opera superstar Marilyn Horne, and second, a certain equation of blackness with the "real" perhaps has a way of cutting through some of the resistance many have to opera in the language they speak. But opera fans will find Horne's singing too "musical theater" here—she was clearly instructed to tone down the operatic diction somewhat for the more intimate film medium. But Muriel Smith on the original cast album and Wilhelmina Fernandez on the 1991 London recording render it in operatic style—and still touch the listener more deeply than opera purists tend to admit would be possible.

There is a reason American opera practitioners are so comfortable presenting a passionate form of musical drama in languages neither they nor their audiences speak, and why American audiences have been so tolerant of such a peculiar tradition. As Americans, we do not cherish formal renditions of our language enough to want to hear opera lyrics in it. We don't love English, and thus have no interest in hearing it dressed up, wound up, and let go. We want our language sung to us sounding as much like casual speech as possible, in repetitious song lyrics three minutes long. If we can't have that, then we'd just as well prefer lyrics we cannot understand at all and can only relate to as aural wallpaper. Hence "'. . . in the garden . . .'—it was just . . . Oh, God." High-mannered *English*? Please.

Song Without Words: Telling It Like It Is

Herewith an example of the kind of thing that demonstrates this. One night at a New York piano bar, I had the occasion to hear a massively intoxicated gentleman do a solo rendition of, as it happens, Oscar Hammerstein's "Ol' Man River." (I might add that unlike most men who solo on this one, he was very white—there is nothing ethnic about this anecdote.) Through my eyes, his version of the song was a truly bizarre experience, of the kind that makes one wonder if one has had a little stroke.

The man was so profoundly drunk that he wasn't up to even pretending to render the actual lyric in anything approaching its written version. Instead, he mooed out a kaleidoscopic upchucking of Hammerstein's words, now touching on an isolated phrase placed nowhere near where it belonged in the melody, now filling out the melody with complete gibberish, and all at a lugubrious, lurching tempo. You can get some idea of what this was like by the fact that whereas the written lyric ends with "just keeps rolling along," this man's rendition filled out the same notes with "ol' man ri-iv oh ay."

It was a galumphing, pathological mess of a performance. I had found this alternately funny and frightening. But the small crowd listening to him erupted into hearty applause when he finished, and sincerely wanted him to do an encore! What would have been next? "Supercalifragilisticexpialadocious" without consonants? Nor were they cheering him in an ironic sense; I examined their faces to check for it—they meant it! They had taken in what he did as a kind of art, when the simple fact was that he was very, very drunk, and clearly so, and knew it himself.

I wasn't alive before the late 1960s, and cannot attest to people's reception of performers then from personal experience. But from everything I have read, heard, and seen from "B.C."—before the counterculture—including conversations with people now in their sixties and beyond, I have the strong impression that even those considering themselves bohemians ahead of the curve would not have received a performance like this man's so warmly. Except perhaps on the Beat scene, people would likely have heard a drunken man not singing the words, period. The people heartily cheering this man's jolly, alcoholic destruction of a song in 2003 cherished its very incoherency as summoning something ineffably "true." That is, to them it was *poetry*—in the modern sense indeed. They didn't need him to sing actual sentences.

And then after this, the bar's waitress for the night sang Cole Porter's elegant perennial "Ev'ry Time We Say Good-bye." The first thing one noticed about this woman is that she and her boyfriend, the bartender, looked so uncannily alike that they were the only couple I've met for whom telling either one of them to go perform a certain impossible sexual act upon themselves would have been redundant. But then, one wouldn't have wanted to say such a thing to either of them—not only were they fine people, but the waitress sang the song with a poised precision of articulation reminiscent of the way a woman would likely have put the song across in about 1942. It was neat.

And crucially, she was Australian, a product of the British Commonwealth. The style she chose hewed to the arch formality of Porter's lyrics rather than refracting and fracturing them into communicating her own in-the-moment, idiosyncratic tortures and perplexities. Definitely, people in Britain as well as Australia have thoroughly drunk in the rock aesthetic in general. But if an English-speaking singer decides to go in this by-the-book direction, she is today more likely not to be American. American women who sing that way today are usually youngsters still focused on technique at the expense of what people in the biz often term "taking chances." To the extent that they keep singing that way beyond this tender age, critics start taking them to task for not "revealing themselves." Until about 1965, Melissa Errico and Christine Andreas, today submitting to such criticisms, could have sung as they do until retirement and be consistently toasted as goddesses by the critics (Lillian Russell and Anna Held did not "reveal themselves" in performance).

So, within ten minutes, the person who actually savored the words on the page was a foreigner, while an American who shredded and doused the words into mush was the hit of the night. Poetry hovers at the margins in America because we don't *want* to hear our language stylized beyond the way we use it on the phone. Even in a performer, what we want to hear him do is just talk—or just as well, even less than talk.

But What About Spoken Word?

But there is one phenomenon that has arisen since Dana Gioia's article that could be taken to suggest that poetry is back in America in a major way. During the nineties, the Spoken Word movement arose among young urban poets, beginning in Chicago and acquiring a national profile in venues like the Nuyorican Poets Café and the Brooklyn Moon Café in New York City. Nurtured in a competitive "slam" format in which judges and audiences rate poets for their readings, Spoken Word has been covered in a well-known film documentary (*Slam*), has been anointed with a television show (*Russell Simmons Presents Def Poetry*), and has reached Broadway in Simmons's production *Def Poetry Jam*.

As welcome and interesting as this scene is, however, it does not signal that poetry in general has regained anything approaching its former place in America. Rather, a particular kind of poetry is thriving among a certain sliver of Americans.

Flying High Down to Earth

Poetry it is, however. Although Spoken Word is deeply rooted in hip-hop and its tics and ideologies, outsiders who dismiss it as rap without the rhythm track are missing a bigger picture. Given that the poems are designed to be spoken rather than read, one might assume that the genre would be one more example of writing like you talk. And it is indeed a demotic art, aimed at immediate accessibility by ordinary people. One of its spiritual fathers is Amiri Baraka, who like Allen Ginsberg was especially inspired by William Carlos Williams's work, learning from him "how to write the way I *speak* rather than the way I *think* a poem ought to be written."

But Spoken Word artists stylize the language far beyond casual speech. Here is an excerpt from "One Afro's Blues" by one of the movement's most celebrated poets, Jessica Care Moore:

> Tongues tied to the wet lie licking wounds like
> a good humor bomb pop
> on a hot day when you read an article in a New York magazine
> calling your life-work "that Jessica Care Moore shit"
> when I just arrived 24 months ago
> Two years of a child's life

Since rhyme is not an issue here and there is no ticktock meter visible, on paper there seems to be little difference between this and Billy Collins purring about his dinner. But there are few better demonstrations of how approximately writing represents speech than laying a Spoken Word piece down in print. Live, passages like this are delivered at a rapid pace, with intonational spark, various rhythms that come across through speaking but that cannot be indicated in print, and evocative intonations. Nobody talks anything like that.

And Spoken Word poets are hardly strangers to rhyme, although they are unlikely to use it with the kind of precision and regularity a Wordsworth would assume. Instead, it is often used variably, as a kind of dramatic seasoning, sparking audiences in fits and starts. Here is some of Tracie Morris's "Switchettes (Las Brujitas)"[10]:

> blessed and cursed
> being double handed
> leaning to left
> strands deftly commanded
>
> understudies be understanding
> switchettes fidget digits
> turning dispel, casting
> breaking curses

---

10. *Brujitas* are conjurers who practice West African rituals.

Also, recall that these pieces are delivered from memory—no mean feat given that some of them last as long as twenty minutes. In addition, one does not usually just stand there and recite—the hip-hop aesthetic perfuses the performance style with a range of gestures, moves, and bodily stances associated with urban youth, mostly brown ones. Some performers actually dance throughout a recitation. Many pieces also include interpolated sung lines.

It's quite a meal, and John Barth would be unlikely to dismiss such poetry as not seeming to require much special effort or talent. For my money, there is more energy, in all senses of the word, in five minutes of Spoken Word than in any number of the doggedly flat rainy-day poems one sees in venues like *The Atlantic*—you know the type; the ones that go something like:

> I stare
> out the window
> and just past the hedge
> it comes again
> shimmering
> quiet
> much like the color of
> the
> chamomile tea
> left in your mug
> when
> of an evening
> I pour it
> whirling
> down
> the silver drain.

Getting with the Program: The Message of Spoken Word

And yet, none of this means that Gioia's 1991 essay is now obsolete. This is because in the thematic sense, Spoken Word is highly bounded: the essence of the movement is alienation and scolding. Poetry writ large, on the other hand, can be based on not only this, but a great many other things.

Now, I am aware of how generalizations from outsiders can sound to participants and aficionados. Many will say "All classical music sounds the same" to the horror of people to whom a Mozart string quartet and a Schumann symphony might as well have been written on different planets. As a musical-theater cast-album collector, I am fully aware that to most, all musicals sound like a homogenous kind of drivel. One afternoon when I mentioned that I was about to buy an old musical on CD, my dear sister said, "Oh, I can just imagine: Dick Van Dyke and Sandra Day O'Connor in *Dancing in the Daisies*." As it happened, I was on my way to buy *Promises, Promises*, with music by Burt Bacharach, which to me sounds nothing like the sort of musical Holly was referring to. But to many people, *Promises, Promises* would make the same impression as *Damn Yankees* or *Into the Woods*—that is, *Dancing in the Daisies*. *Chacun à son goût.*

In that light I am aware that beyond the rappy word showers, Spoken Word involves quiet love poems and calm, chuckle-rousing monologues. But I would be stubborn not to admit that despite the exceptions, musical theater is "about" an apple-cheeked conception of love that was getting tired as early as the 1920s. And as much as I cringe when people call theater music bouncy—*110 in the Shade* is "bouncy?"—I know deep down that compared to most other music, the charge is an accurate generalization. If you're coming from Missy Elliott or Weezer, hell, even Stephen Sondheim's reedy, cerebral *Pacific Overtures* bounces across the room.

In that same vein, I present a sympathetic outsider's generalization: cocky Speaking Truth to Power is the essence of Spoken Word.

Let's try this, for example: A slam night during which all of the contestants happened to do love poems and folksy monologues would be felt by most as an off night, while on an evening in which all of the contestants happened to present spiky, kinetic poems, no one would be too terribly upset that no one had done a love poem or a monologue. Or: If Spoken Word only involved the love poems and monologues, the movement would never have exactly caught fire; if it involved only the rapid-fire, cranky, in-your-face showpieces, it would be every bit as popular now as it is.

In the introduction to one of the growing number of Spoken Word anthologies, Yusef Komunyakaa spells out that "These poems are not spoken from an assumption of freedom based on birthright. These young voices have witnessed the voicelessness of loved ones (family and/or community)." He later notes the "rage in these voices," characterizing it as a response to "the backlash against the Civil Rights movement that ushered in the Reagan era." Komunyakaa did not have love poems and puckish little monologues in mind when he wrote that. Even the titles of the anthologies reveal the guiding spirit: *Listen Up!*, *Burning Down the House*, *Aloud*: The theme is people who feel that they have been denied a voice in American life "speaking up" and comin' at ya.

In this, Amiri Baraka's role in the movement is indicative. The Beats' poetry-as-protest electrified him as a young man, when he realized that "poetry could be about some things that I was familiar with, that it did not have to be about suburban birdbaths and Greek mythology." Thus it was *Howl* and its like that turned Baraka on to verse and shaped his style, and consequently, his stature among Spoken Word artists helps channel the Beat poets' philosophy to these new poets. But that was and remains a philosophy with a constrained agenda.

Def Poetry Jam, which premiered on Broadway in the fall of 2002, was a useful demonstration. The night I attended, three things got a rise from the audience most dependably. First, to insert black inflection or slang was a surefire ice breaker. Palestinian-American Suheir Hammad dropped an "ain't" amidst her mainstream-sounding diction and the audience, at first a little cool toward her reserved stage persona, whooped. As I mentioned earlier, it's not that there is anything wrong with *ain't*—and it has always crossed race lines anyway. But "Ebonics" still has a symbolic meaning to blacks and to the increasing numbers of non-blacks who are incorporating it into their verbal toolkit these days. That meaning is down with the people, real; Black English is today the language of protest par excellence—language from below. The second element was profanity: More than once a poem got its first reaction with a cuss word. And then the third was brand names.

The night I went, I took down the words that got the biggest hands of the evening. They were the following, in order: CIA, Lumumba, Hiroshima, Malcolm, Feds, motherfucker, McDonalds, pussy, funky, Goya, Spam, shizzle,[11] fuck, butt, and Katherine Harris. The artistry of the work acknowledged, for more than a few Spoken Word artists, being challenged to write three pieces *that they considered choice ones* that had no

---

[11.] *Fa shizzle* is, at this writing, a slang variant of *for sure* that rapper Snoop Dogg is said to have originated. In fall 2002, the expression was established enough to pop up in a mainstream gum ad.

Ebonics, cussing, or brand names would be like asking a novelist to come up with a coherent page without the letter *t*. And that makes Spoken Word a subset of what poetry is, and actually, a rather small one.

For people who went to *Def Poetry Jam* for a night of verse, it was also a pretty *loud* event. The women poets tended to start quiet and gradually build up to yelling, like rock or gospel singers. And the Chinese-American Beau Sia literally hollered his poems the whole evening. I get it: He was challenging the stereotype of Asians as quiet and docile. And usually what the women were yelling was pretty interesting and artfully rendered (Mayda Del Valle was phenomenal). But the fact remains: Poetry that must be yelled is but one sliver of what poetry is. If you must yell, then there is an awful lot that you can't say.

Here I may seem like the crabby jazz critic who jumps on jazz saxophonist Joshua Redman for whipping up the audience with raging, honking, show-off solos. But these critics are on to something—because Redman is so good, when he resorts to pyrotechnic, rock-star cacophony, he is "cheating," going for the easy score. In the same way, one thing one learns quickly as an actor is that rage is the easiest emotion to portray and one of the surest routes into an audience besides humor. Many a person off the street who had never acted before, perhaps put at ease with a drink, could pull off a decent rendition of an angry scene. It's the more ambiguous, layered, or reflective emotions that are harder, but as Komunyakaa notes casually despite his affection for the form, "there is limited space in these poems for contemplation and meditation."

Part of this is surely due to the sportlike scoring aspect of the slam scene, which means poems' reception hinges on how easily they hit the gut and elicit applause on first exposure. Naturally, sticking it to the man, being black or pretending to be, cussing, and mentioning Chips Ahoy take on a certain cachet. But it also narrows the form.

Protest poetry is healthy, and the rise of Spoken Word is a miraculous thing. Who would have thought in 1975 that twenty years later twenty-somethings of all colors would be gathering in cafés challenging each other in word craft? My point, however, is that this does not signal that poetry itself has returned to its former place. Rather, there is a particular strain of poetry in flower, just as Beat poetry was but one of many branches on the tree in its day. But today, Spoken Word is the only branch on the tree getting remotely this level of attention beyond a cult-level realm—no other form of poetry is remotely as hot in modern America.

Of course many, including Spoken Word poets, assert that protest is the very essence of art. But that idea has always been a truism dearest to artists whose work happens to go in that direction and their followers. The vast weight of human artistic achievement was not created in indignation, and few of us would wish that it had been. What is thriving in America now is a *youth-based* brand of *performed* poetry, specifically a kind that springs from the edgy *hip-hop* aesthetic and its populist political leanings. In an alternate universe, a poetry movement could spring up among people of all ages, could focus on the written rather than the oral, or could have arisen from the grunge crowd, gay people, etc. That is: The Spoken Word movement is a highly specific affair. It does not mean that poetry itself has regained its former position in American culture.

Billy Who?

For that to happen, there would be a national television show airing weekly on a major channel on which poets simply read their works, as much of it quiet as irritated, with no hip-hop in the background and no scorecard ratings. The show would be called something like "Coffeehouse America" and would have a Joyce Carol Oates-ish feel that would eventually elicit a *Saturday Night Live* parody, with the Baraka-esque spirit represented more as garnish than as the main meal. A poet, their name known to most Americans, would have written a poem about the shooting death of Amadou Diallo reprinted in newspapers across the country. That poet would then have been invited to recite their piece on *Letterman* while Paul Shaffer noodled some inspiring strains in the background.

One might ask Gioia: If the situation today is so different from what it was in 1991, what exactly caused this? Gioia is too modest to boast that his article was the catalyst, but if it was, then reality would dictate that one article could accomplish about exactly the minor blip on the radar screen that I detect since the article appeared. Gioia could hardly have done better, because the reason America no longer thrills to the poetic as it once did is founded on irreversible currents in our national linguistic soul. The poetry whose explosion since 1991 Gioia sees as astonishing is the same poetry that, really, I don't much care for anymore than I did in 1991, see no increased interest in among undergraduates, encounter no more affection for among the many educated people I know, hear recited from memory after dinner by no more people than I ever have, and that I see no signs of reviving with anything approaching the energy of the Spoken Word revolution.

In his article, Gioia listed some correlates of a certain 2 percent of the public—his profile boils down roughly to people who like kalamata olives and *The New Yorker*—who once had a place in their lives for poetry and now do not. And I would say that despite poetry's increased presence on-line, on the radio, and at festivals, the set Gioia refers to remain as alienated from poetry as they were fifteen years ago. I also submit that there are no more signs that this is going to change anytime soon than there are that Americans will return to making after-dinner toasts that sound like inaugural addresses.

But Is It Art?

Poetry revival or not, then, this is a country where to the extent that poetry is cherished, it is in how charismatically it reflects spoken language, be this Billy Collins, pop song lyrics, or Spoken Word. Because humans need poetry in some form, Americans hold the pop lyrics especially close. The same basic need also explains something B. R. Myers decries in the book-length version of his notorious screed against modern fiction writers' prose, "A Reader's Manifesto." Myers is unimpressed that critics and fans of writers like Annie Proulx tend to cherish her prose on the level of the poetic deftness of isolated sentences, rather than assessing the throughline and clarity of her prose overall. But this tendency in evaluation is predictable in our America. A people rarely given poetry—at least of a sort that most people will immediately embrace, especially as youngsters—will naturally seek it elsewhere, such as sniffing for it in the prose style of novelists.

But in the meantime, many spontaneously see poetry's move toward the spoken as a genre getting real, past the birdbaths and the *perchance* and the inverted syntax. There is some point here. But artifice has its benefits in a society.

For one, the spoken fetish weakens the rhetorical power of protest poetry. Just as our speeches are usually too come-as-you-are to spark serious thought, modern protest poetry preaches to the converted more than convincing the curious. This hinges on the nature of the spoken/written dichotomy. "Written" language, decoupled from the emotional stream that spoken language floats on, facilitates standing back and taking all sides into account. But the protest strain of poetry, now the most vibrant poetic presence in American society in its Spoken Word guise, tends to assert rather than reflect. As David Perkins notes, in protest poetry "tentativeness, speculativeness, skepticism and humor are frequently short-circuited."

An example would be Amiri Baraka's "Somebody Blew Up America," a poem he presented in his debut as New Jersey's poet laureate in 2002. Because of a few lines, his poem was widely decried as anti-Semitic, but despite the fact that Baraka did express some open sentiments in that vein in his earlier work, the critics misread him on this particular poem. It actually simply condemns everything and everybody, including victimizers of Jews. The villain he addresses would appear to be the elusive bugbear traditionally termed "The Man."

But the problem is that what Baraka presented is more tantrum than argument, as we see from this sample from the body of the poem:

> Who own the oil
> Who do no toil
> Who own the soil
> Who is not a nigger
> Who is so great ain't nobody bigger
> Who own this city
> Who own the air
> Who own the water
> Who own your crib
> Who rob and steal and cheat and murder and make lies the truth

. . . and so on: almost the whole poem consists of dozens upon dozens of brisk lines of this kind piled upon one another, culminating in one long "Whooooooooooooooooooooooo!" This is spoken language: Black English syntax, short phrases strung together. Baraka and his fans consider this an advance on "artificial" poetry, and it is certainly easier to grasp the meaning of quickly than most of what Edna St. Vincent Millay wrote. But in a way, grasping it is *too* easy. For anyone who embraces conspiracy theories and Baraka's hard-left worldview, the poem comes off as telling it like it is—as I write, black college students and their white campus-lefty comrades have been giving Baraka standing ovations for reciting this poem for months now. But for those not sure that this is the way it is, this poem will not nudge them into considering a new view, and eventually comes off more as a verbal drive-by.

Poetry like this has less scope and impact in the polity than it could, helping to ensure the increasing marginalization of leftist (as opposed to liberal) positions from national debate. Millay's protest poetry went over the wire services. Baraka's could not, nor is his kind of poetry what Dorothy Thompson meant in summoning poets to write against World War II. This is not only because of Baraka's stridency, nor is it because he is black—a white poet writing the same way would be no more likely to have his work broadcast nationally. It's because Baraka's poem cannot be said to put forth its argument with ingenuity. The poem is designed less to make the reader think "Hmm—Baraka's poem got me to thinking about the oppression of the many by the few" than "There's Baraka telling it like it is." This is true of any poem that takes facile, shorthand potshots at Dick Cheney, etc. more with the aim of eliciting knowing approval from a certain set than fashioning an actual observation or argument. During a revolution, shouting shakes people up and breaks down barricades. But once the revolution is over, we return to an eternal reality: The louder you shout, the less people listen—even those initially willing to hear you out. Poetry that shouts can only be a sideshow. It cannot inspire a nation.

It can also be argued that for all the beauties of poetry with no meter and irregular rhyming if any, that the less written-style constraint in a poem, the less likely it is to be sincerely cherished by people beyond the eternal coterie of poetry fans. We are taught to distrust the ticktock nature of poetry that rhymes and scans and to suppose that there is something larger and deeper in freer verse, liberated from the old-fashioned confines of structure. But then watch a Russian reciting Pushkin, lighting up as they savor the close rhymes and careful rhythms and the marvelous feat of pulling these off while also communicating a sublime or humorous point. Nothing corny here—and so sad that we Americans have no equivalent experience today.

It's hard to imagine Baraka, for example, sweating unduly over assonances, rhythms, or word colors in "Somebody Blew Up America." Frankly, it just doesn't look like it was difficult enough to produce that I stand in awe of its having come into existence. And Baraka is of course just one example of an established tradition. For a great many people, most modern poetry evokes quiet thoughts of emperors without clothes. We are taught not to say it too loudly, though, as John Barth understands:

. . . the most traditional notion of the artist: the Aristotelian conscious agent who achieves with technique and cunning the artistic effect; in other words, one endowed with uncommon talent, who has moreover developed and disciplined that endowment into virtuosity. It is an aristocratic notion on the face of it, which the democratic West seems eager to have done with; not only the "omniscient" author of older fiction, but the very idea of the controlling artist, has been condemned as politically reactionary, authoritarian, even fascist.

Poetry that tames language into tight structures and yet manages to move us comes off as a feat, paralleling ballet or athletic talent in harnessing craft to beauty. When poetry is based on a less rigorous, more impressionistic definition of craft, its appeal depends more on whether one happens to be individually constituted to "get it" for various reasons. The audience narrows: poetry becomes more like tai chi than baseball.

Got Marjoram?

CHAPTER FOUR

Rather Too Colloquial for Elegance: Written English Takes It Light

If we asked our American of 1903 by mail when they had last heard a crackling good speech, they would likely write back in prose that would remind us of a flowery Hallmark card—even if they were humble sales clerks. The barefoot relationship America developed to its language in the 1960s has also transformed the way we write.

In 1925, George Gershwin dashed off a letter to a female squeeze of his. An excerpt:

> Mr. E. Hutcheson has very kindly given me the use of one of his studios every afternoon and evening, so every day between 2 & 6 and evenings between 8 & 10 you will find me diligently writing notes, playing piano or praying (you've got to pray in Chatauqua) to the God of Melody to please be kind to me and send me some hair-raising "blues" for my second movement.

To us, that passage summons the image of an elderly gent. But Gershwin was only twenty-six, came from humble circumstances and unlettered parents, had been a bad student, left high school after ninth grade, and rarely cracked a book thereafter.

As such, in his casual letters he becomes an alien to us. Like any man of his era, he wouldn't have dreamed of hitting the street without a hat and jacket. In the same way, he approached even casual writing as a craft in a sense that we are much less likely to. E-mail only scratches the surface:

the change had set in before e-mail existed, in the kind of letters we were already writing (or not writing). It is impossible to imagine anyone talking casually in the style of Gershwin's letter, in his times or ours. But in his time, when you sat down to write, you put on a suit, so to speak.

Yet meanwhile in his music, Gershwin was helping plant the seeds for the kind of America we know. The year he wrote that letter, he and his brother, Ira, had written the song "Sweet and Lowdown," a catchy little jag clueing us in on a little dive where "They play nothing classic, oh no!" and "Philosopher or deacon, you simply have to weaken" to the hot jazz. The song embodies the "get down" ethos that would take the throne four decades later, and popular music of the twenties was a harbinger of that future—once infused with that element, Tin Pan Alley never turned back, even if its practitioners were still wearing ties. Gershwin's bluesiness is much of what makes his songs speak to us today, from an era that otherwise strikes us as quaint.

But this very sweetness we find in the lowdown has also transformed our relationship to writing, so much that Gershwin's letters leave us wondering how such an unlearned soul could have even pulled them off. Back in the day, you might play lowdown, and you might even talk lowdown—but to the best of your ability, you wrote high-hat. Today, that is true neither of most of us nor authors and journalists to nearly the extent it once was. These days written American English, like public speaking and poetry, drifts ever more toward the casual. And even where formal language still reigns, black-tie has become dress casual. An exuberance has been lost.

The Old Days: Strutting at Our Own Conceit

Kermie Crawls with the Utmost Rapidity: Epistolary Elegance in "Auld Lang Syne"

Gershwin was merely typical in his natural impulse to write "up" in private correspondence. Perhaps the most famous example today is the almost counterintuitively ornate writing in letters that ordinary soliders wrote from the front during the Civil War. My favorite of these is by a Confederate surgeon in 1863, coyly recounting to his wife the development of their courtship:

In a few instances when she has arrived at about the age of 15 this shyness and reserve seemed to be forgotten, and I would pass an hour or two in the enjoyment of her company with great pleasure to myself and I imagined with at least satisfaction, if not enjoyment, to her. I began to think that my happiness was identified with hers. I began to pay her special visits or at least seek opportunities by which I might be in her company. I sought her society on pleasure rides and thought it not a hardship to ride 65 miles in 24 hours if part of the time might be spent with her. She always exhibited or observed the decorum of modest reserve which might be construed into neither encouragement nor discouragement.

Note that slip in verb tense in the first sentence: "When she has arrived" should be "When she had arrived" if the following phrase is "this shyness and reserve seemed to be forgotten," in the past tense. In other words, he's human! The person writing the letter was a living, fallible human being, penning this letter on his haunches in some damp, chilly tent by the light of a flickering lantern. But even under conditions like that he casually wrote prose sounding like Edward Everett's orations (Everett had, as a matter of fact, given the Gettysburg oration three weeks before the letter was written).

Especially astounding from our vantage point is that many of these Civil War soldiers had modest educations at best. In 1830s New York, the scandal of the decade was the murder of a prostitute named Helen Jewett. The evidence that issued from the case revealed a seeming mismatch between writing ability and educational level so countertuitive to our eyes as to beggar belief. Jewett's murderer, Richard Robinson, was a nineteen-year-old clerk of yeomanly small-town circumstances, who had left school at the age of fourteen. Certainly this was much more common in his day, but the fact remains that he had less than ten years of formal education. Basically, he was just some guy who worked behind a counter. But here is a passage from his first surviving letter to Jewett:

At best we live but one little hour, strut at our own conceit and die. How unhappy must those persons be who cannot enjoy life *as it is*, seize pleasure as it comes floating on like a noble ship, bound for yonder distant port with all sails set. Come will ye embark?—then on we go, gayly, hand in hand, scorning all petty and trivial troubles, eagerly gazing on *our rising* sun, till the warmth of its beams (i.e., love) causes our sparkling blood to o'erflow and mingle in holy delight, as mind and soul perchance some storms arise . . .

"O'erflow"? "Perchance"? This was just some Leonardo DiCaprio bozo—but *gayly* he goes on and on like this in pen and ink, with neither spell check nor a word processing program to allow backtracking and corrections.

We might suppose that what has changed is wooing technique rather than private writing in general. Could it be that fancy writing, like elaborate ballroom dance steps, was once how one paid court to a damsel, but that in writing beyond this, people loosened up and wrote the way we do? But Robinson even wrote like this to himself in his own roiling little diary, despite giving no indication of supposing that he was on his way to fame. A Macaulay Culkin stripling of a lad who would have been stunned to find out that people would be reading his diary excerpts 170 years later wrote things like this:

Most youths at seventeen or eighteen years of age take a pride in boasting of their amours, of their dissipations, and of their wild exploits; I have, however, no taste for such exposures. If I had, I could mention things that would make my old granny, and even wiser folks, stare, notwithstanding that I am young, and look very innocent.

That's someone who never got past eighth grade! And the same kind of writing was de rigueur far beyond the realm of mating and diaries. The correspondence between pioneering feminists Elizabeth Cady Stanton and Susan B. Anthony is couched in similar language, for example— here is Stanton in 1859:

. . . but lo! you did not come. Nor did you soften the rough angles of our disappointment by one solitary line of excuse. And it would do me such great good to see some reformers just now. The death of my father, the worse than death of my dear Cousin Gerritt, the martyrdom of that grand and glorious John Brown—all this conspires to make me regret more than ever my dwarfed womanhood.

Or—Theodore Roosevelt writes to his mother-in-law from his ranch in 1890, about his son:

Kermie crawls with the utmost rapidity; and when he is getting towards some forbidden spot and we call him to stop Ted always joins in officiously and overtaking the small, yellow-haired wanderer seizes him with his chubby hands round the neck and trys to drag him back—while the enraged Kermie endeavors in vain to retaliate.

That's almost sickening today, but also plain bizarre in the language arts formality of the prose, including words like "officious," which I venture would stump more than half of most university student bodies. "Utmost rapidity": really—imagine writing a passage like that to anyone you know today, or imagine anyone writing it to you, or anyone writing it to anyone! And again, a spelling error ("trys") showing that a live, breathing person with bodily functions wrote this.

We might think that especially back then, writing to a mother-in-law may have occasioned a certain special respect. But what about Roosevelt writing in the same kind of language to that same son by the time he had reached eighteen? This time, Roosevelt is writing to a subordinate, and one with whom he presumably had little if any desire to sleep with or marry. The subject is Roosevelt's then-protégé William Howard Taft:

But I believe with all my soul that Taft, far more than any other public man of prominence, represents the principles for which I stand; and, furthermore, I believe in these principles with all my soul; and I should hold myself false to my duty if I sat supine and let the men who have taken such joy in my refusal to run again select some candidate whose success would mean the undoing of what I have sought to achieve.

And into the 1960s, personal letters like this are common in biographies. Here is African-American classical singer Marian Anderson writing to her husband while on tour, in the same style she wrote in even to her mother and sisters:

You have been disappointed, I know, for that I am sorry, but maybe all the blame should not be put at my door, because you, more than any other person I know, being unique as you are, have had opportunities that would not present themselves to other men, and success and failure for either of us should not have to hinge on the last seven years, important as they are.

And we must note: Anderson was not a career intellectual or person of letters, and for the record had only a high school education, and a rather fitful one at that.

From our vantage point, the starchiness of Anderson's language in that letter makes it almost hard to believe that she was writing to someone she loved. For people through the ages, intimacy has required letting one's guard down and getting real. We wonder why Anderson couldn't button down at least a little when writing to her darling. But then even in our come-as-you-are era, we have our customs. If when in the company of our lover the need arises to blow our noses, we are more likely to go to another room—or at least turn away. Certainly: but there was a time when we felt that same impulse to suspend informality in other realms, and writing was one of them.

But today, I doubt that any but a sliver of Americans under about sixty has ever written to intimates in novelistic language like Anderson's. To do so would usually be an outright social gaffe, in fact. In college a friend of mine had a girlfriend to whom the appellation ice queen had been applied. One symptom of her rather singularly aloof manner was the writing style of her letters, couched in a phraseology reminiscent of Jane Austen. Responding to news that he had gotten a plum job in his field, she wrote a letter that included cut-glass sentences like "I'm pleased to hear of your job offer; heartiest congratulations on your good fortune." Elegant in its way, but by the 1980s, a sentence like that conveyed more distance than warmth.

But before the 1960s, that same kind of language could convey genuine intimacy or sincere respect among people at all levels of society. That Civil War soldier is clearly batty about his Mollie. Teddy Roosevelt singularly adored his children, and never really recovered from the death of his son Quentin in World War I. Anderson's husband was the love of her life, and in fact her only known romance. These people lived in an era when formal language occupied a different space in the American soul: It was, like flowers or a caress, one way of demonstrating esteem and affection.

Never Lacking Pluck:
Old-time Journalistic Style

But high writing was a necessity not only in private, but in public—just as we wear clothes around our intimates (usually) as well as while out shopping. Time was that American journalism was couched in a fussy, ornate kind of prose that makes a modern issue of *Newsweek* look almost like it was written by talented foreigners who picked up English in their twenties and mastered basic grammar, but never quite picked up the outer edges of the vocabulary or the more advanced ways of composing sentences.

After Helen Jewett's murder, for instance, the city's journalists tried to piece together the life history of Jewett, whose given first name had been Dorcas. At the *New York Herald*, James Gordon Bennett provided his reconstruction in language of this kind:

> In Augusta, Maine, lived a highly respectable gentleman, Judge Western, by name. Some of the female members of his family pitying the bereaved condition of young Dorcas invited her to live at the Judge's house. At that time Dorcas was young, beautiful, innocent, modest, and ingenuous.

It's hard to even imagine the word *ingenuous* used today in a newspaper story. It has been used thirty-two times in *USA Today* since 1989—but no fewer than thirty of the examples are in film, theater and book reviews, whose writers naturally possess a certain artistic leaning that would make *ingenuous* a more likely choice. But in 1830, the word was fair game even for meat-and-potatoes reporting. And Bennett's casting the content of the second sentence as a single package at all is highly written, as opposed to loosening things up with *and* as in, say, "Some of the female members of his family pitied the bereaved condition of young Dorcas and invited her to live at the Judge's house."

And Bennett wasn't showing off; his prose was typical of the era. Here is part of an editorial in a competing paper, the *New-York Transcript*, on a rumor that Jewett's murderer had also killed another young woman:

> The girl Emma Chancellor—the *chère amie* and protegé of the young miscreant Robinson—has, since the flight of the latter from the city, seduced into actual marriage, an amiable, unsuspicious, and "good natured" young man, with whom she is now living in Brooklyn, of which city he has for a considerable time past been a resident.

Whipped cream in prose, this sounds like a soliloquy written for a play—or better, a play of that period; plays like the *Our American Cousin*

that Lincoln was attending when he was assassinated had characters gliding around sounding a lot like this.

And the style continued through the nineteenth century. Here is a
journalist at the *Brooklyn Eagle* in 1869 describing a railroad trip:

> Slocum, never lacking pluck, had the courage to suggest that nine
> o'clock was, under the circumstances, a barbarous hour. He quickly
> won the majority over to his way of thinking. (. . .) As we retired the
> blessed spring rain was falling against the windowpanes, and after
> the day's fatigue sleep came as gentle as the dew.

The trip was an information-gathering tour of various suspension
bridges, organized by Washington Roebling's father, John, the originator
of the Brooklyn Bridge project. Later that year, John Roebling had his
foot crushed in a freak dockside accident—the ensuing tetanus infection
killed him and left his son to build the bridge. But while he was still
alive, the same *Eagle* reporter describing John after the accident wrote:
"He spoke our language imperfectly, because he had not the advantage
of being born on our soil," and "He thinks and talks of the bridge as incessantly as ever, and seems unwilling to have the conversation of his
professional assistants diverted for a moment to his own accident." In
1869 *He had not* rather than *He didn't have* was already archaic in spoken
English by several centuries. Yet this writer tossed it into a popular newspaper report. Things like this and the "diversion" of the assistants' "conversation" would look thoroughly pretentious in *Newsweek* today.

But for this reporter it was ordinary. The language he wrote in
reminds us of the oratory we saw in Chapter Two, and was indeed the
written manifestation of how people of this age related to English. It was
no accident that the program for the Brooklyn Bridge's opening thirteen
years later would include what was billed as "Principal Orations," a passing detail that actually tells us two things. First, speakers were going to
get up and speak, not talk genially like Michael Eisner did in the speech I
cited earlier. And second, imagine a program on a website today listing
"Principal Orations," as opposed to, say, "Main Speeches." Even on a
humble handbill for a ribbon-cutting ceremony, in 1882 the sense was
that what one put on the page was to be something different from what
one would actually say.

Well into the twentieth century, journalists would have recognized
the writing of their nineteenth-century predecessors as only a tad more

crafted than their own. Here is an anonymous reviewer in Cincinnati in 1909 commenting on a stage musical with the premier black entertainers of the day, Bert Williams and George Walker. The reviewer thought them so good that:

> There are some pointers in the way of enthusiasm and conscientious work by which their white confreres in the profession might profit. And as to singing they are marvels. They tackle the big finales with a vim, a discretion, a judgment as to points and effects, which is a revelation. Attention was called to this same characteristic in these columns last year, but the effect of this aptitude for large choral numbers is equally noticeable this year.

This sounds so unlike modern theater reviews that one almost pictures a shabby-genteel lunatic-savant sitting in the theater with a rumpled drugstore pad scribbling reviews that will never know any eyes but his. But this journalistic style lived on up to the 1960s. One of legendary conductor Arturo Toscanini's "Men Friday" at RCA wrote of him in a magazine article in 1956:

> We took to our hearts the people he liked and looked askance at those he dropped. We loved the music he loved, became skeptical about the music he despised, and accepted without question the music that, having summarily cast out, he as summarily restored to favor.

To speak this way in private would ensure one's being "summarily cast out" of most social intercourse. But as late as the Eisenhower era, the press scribbler felt writing as an occasion to shift to a different "language."

Wildest Extravagances with an Air of Reality: Written Language as the Order of the Day

Or even beyond lovers, this kind of language was a matter of basic courtesy, just as today we still often clean up when company is coming. Americans at this time treated formal writing as a requirement of public discourse. Language that feels prissy to us hung thick in the air and swarmed into the cracks.

For example, it's 1890. W.E.B. Du Bois is taking a composition course at Harvard, and writes a rather bizarre screed against the distaff sex, likely prompted by a romantic disappointment the specifics of which are lost to history. His instructor hands it back with the written comment:

> The taste of this is questionable. Certainly, too, such a method would repel many readers who might by an ironical and duly restrained expression of the same line of thought be brought far towards agreement with you.

Damn, that's good! Not a word wasted. It almost makes you want to recite it just to roll it around in your mouth. Those thirty-seven words are almost as perfectly constructed as the Gettysburg Address—but in a mere jotting that the instructor never expected anyone to see but Du Bois. Can you recall any teacher or professor whose written comments read anything like that? If you can, I congratulate you on having lived a stupendously long life.

In 1905, the young H. L. Mencken has yet to fully crystallize the growling epigrammatic style that would make him famous, and writes his first prose book, on George Bernard Shaw, in a style typified by:

> In all the history of the English language, no man has exceeded him in technical resources nor in nimbleness of wit. Some of his scenes are fairly irresistible, and throughout his plays his avoidance of the old-fashioned machinery of the drama gives even his wildest extravagances an air of reality.

The verdict of *The Nation*? "Rather too colloquial for elegance"! How? This is how vigilantly even the middlebrow of the literati in this era guarded prose from the slightest hint of encroachment by the oral. This reviewer would have a stroke—or as he would put it, suffer a bout of apoplexy—reading just half a page of *Maxim*.

Or, it's 1931 and the director of the Associated Negro Press urges Anderson to beef up her publicity: "I hesitate to suggest the expenditure of any sum of money which might seem to you considerable, and yet if it aids in the securing of larger audiences, it might be considered justified."

A few years later, a booklet of serving ideas that came with a toaster-*cum*-toppings-tray set includes prose like "And here's another thought: The dishes with which both the Hospitality Tray and the Breakfast Tray

are equipped, as well as the Trays themselves, are of course useable sepa-
rately in any one of many ways that will frequently occur to you."

But then—an interesting letter to the editor of the *Village Voice* in
1968. At this time, the integrationist focus of the Civil Rights movement
is shifting to a more separatist one. This writer embodies this in her discomfort with whites' new openness to the very race mixing that blacks
were once violently persecuted for. Her language, however, predates her
politics: The *sisters* was new black argot, but her schoolbook word choices
and crafted syntax could have been written forty years before:

> It certainly seems to many black sisters that the Movement is just an-
> other subterfuge to aid the Negro male in procuring a white woman.
> If this be so, then the black sisters don't need it, for surely we have
> suffered enough humiliation from both white and black men in
> America.

This is another sixties *Archaeopteryx* Moment, like the Smothers
Brothers' television show airing at the time, where two guys dressed like
college glee-club singers took potshots at the Establishment right from
the hippies' playbook. But 1968 was late for this kind of prose, and the
way America wrote was already on the move.

Less Like Arabs Every Day: Talking and Writing Getting It Together

And what was happening is that the space between the oral and
the written was narrowing vastly. This has left American articles, books,
and letters from before the 1960s standing out sharply as tokens of another time.

The space between written and oral can be, and stay, much wider
than we Americans might imagine. We get a useful perspective on ourselves by comparing American English with a language where this gulf
yawns so widely that minding the gap is a clear and present part of
speaking and writing every day. The Arabic that we see in news photos
on banners is a different language entirely from the one that, say, a Palestinian actually uses when talking on an everyday level. Arabic's written
standard is based on the ancient language of the Koran, and is about as
far from Palestinian Arabic as Latin is from Spanish. This is also true of

the other Arabic dialects, which are also as different from one another as the Romance languages: A Moroccan has the same communication barrier with a Saudi as an Italian with a Portuguese. Just as many of us learn to speak written English, the educated Arab elite learn to speak Modern Standard Arabic. But just as few of us could speak "written" all of the time without casual usages popping up as fatigue set in, few Arabs can speak perfect Modern Standard Arabic at any length.

Especially since in their case, they are truly speaking a different language from the one they learned at home. In standard Arabic, *nose* is *'anf*, *he saw* is *ra'aa*, and *what* is *maa*. In Egyptian Arabic, *nose* is *manakhiir*, *he saw* is *šaaf*, and *what* is *'eeh*. No Egyptian would dream of writing *manakhiir* in an essay, even though that is the word they learned at their mother's knee for *nose*. The closest equivalent we have to a gap this wide is the difference between words like *dine* and *eat*, or *children* and *kids*. Now imagine if differences like that applied to most words in the language instead of to just some, and if *dine* was less a possible alternative to writing *eat* than an obligatory choice, with writing *eat* as gauche as writing *whole nother* would be for us.

This, then, is what a real gap between the spoken and the written is like. While American English was never as linguistically schizophrenic as Arabic, James Gordon Bennett, Richard Robinson, and Elizabeth Cady Stanton show that our language once had a wider spoken/written gap than today. You talked one way, but you wrote in another one quite distinct, and mastering that alternate code was central to presenting oneself as a respectable adult. And this was even in an America that Alexis de Tocqueville, H. L. Mencken, and others had long pegged as anti-intellectual, vulgar, and individualistic, right up through and beyond the onset and triumph of the pop culture behemoth.

But over the past few decades, our writing has become more and more like the way we talk. That is, we have eased prose out of the class of activities that we *decorate* out of a basic sense of exuberance in living. Like our elders, we put our hearts into, say, the culinary: Cookbooks sell furiously, newspapers run food sections, and we still put our best foot forward when feeding company. But we do not see English as worthy of that kind of loving, artful attention. Just as an after-dinner "speaker" like Rossiter Raymond would have no social capital today, a journalist who insisted on couching his prose in the mannered style of James Gordon Bennett would rarely have the wherewithal to eat at all, at least not from his writing.

Mannered that style was—but the skepticism that this very concept arouses in us today is local to our times. Mannerism of the language means pushing it beyond its natural state, and to our forebears, nothing seemed more pleasing or appropriate. Reading that old style of prose, a modern American can barely help wishing from time to time that those people had gotten real. But that would have made no more sense to James Gordon Bennett than heating up frozen pizzas for a dinner party would to us. To us, the frozen pizzas would be egregious because preparing them took no effort and they only get so good (most of them literally taste no better than the box they come in). But public decorum in the old days put language in the same space. Writing like you talked, or more generally without decoration, would take no effort, while dressing up the language on the page was a way of giving delight, of paying respect, of showing that you were alive.

But in our moment formality remains a force in cooking while not in language, and this is no accident. There are few more specific, personal, and deeply felt expressions of ourselves than language. Gourmet or not, food is something different: one does not break down and proclaim that "Those crabcakes are . . . just . . . [sob] . . . well, they're *me*! Do you hear? *Me!*" But we vent our hearts through language. The accent we grow up with is extremely hard to break. The slang we adopt as teenagers expresses who we decide to be (that week). Many of us can hardly bear hearing our own voices on answering machines because hearing a voice is an intimate act, and psychologists make a healthy living off of the discomfort that intimacy with our deeper self creates in us. Language is our soul.

And it was in the 1960s that soul came in as a synonym for authenticity. Authenticity stirs us more than ever before in American history. Obviously individualism has defined being American for centuries. But just as obviously, the 1960s focused this to an unprecedented degree, in response to thinking people's recasting of the American Establishment as a mistake in need of correcting, unworthy of personal allegiance. The result was a new cultural norm elevating the natural to an extreme that would have shocked the nineteenth-century Transcendentalists and Romantics who had made their version of the same argument. Thoreau would have been baffled by Woodstock.

Sparked in a subset especially concerned with sociopolitical issues, this cult of the informal easily spread in waves throughout the less tuned in realms of the culture. It was carried partly on its charisma, and partly on its sheer comfort—the principle of least effort entices us all, and few revolutions have asked less of their adherents than the one that called for us to shed starchy formalities, scoff at authority, and have more sex. Thus what began as rebellion mellowed into reflex; indignation among a committed minority conventionalized into fashion among a game majority.

Berkeley's Free Speech Movement provides a window on this devolution as it was happening. Just a year after the 1964 rallies, with most of the movement's original leaders having graduated, a bunch of students initiated the "Filthy Speech Movement," which entailed shouting dirty words in public places and wearing "Fuck" signs, deliberately courting arrest. Savio and his comrades had specific political goals; this new guard took advantage of the mood this created to party and defy authority just for the thrill of it. Always the *Archaeopteryx*, Savio himself, returning to campus and referring to the "Fuck" sign in a speech, could only bear to refer to it by calling it the "Sexual Intercourse" sign. Revolutionary though he was, he remained a product of an era that assumed a certain linguistic decorum that now seems almost weird to us. The "Filthy Speech Movement," then, symbolized a transition from the political to the attitudinal. Enter David Brooks's Bobos in Paradise and everyone else in America who harbor a reflexive anti-Establishment sentiment reflected more in accoutrements and voting patterns than lifestyle or career choices.

What would have been surprising is if the old-fashioned writing style had *not* quickly begun melting away in the late 1960s. That style entailed mastering a tricky craft in observance of an enforced public norm. Recall H. L. Mencken working in a culture where reviewers were looking over his shoulder sniffing that even his crafted prose was "rather too colloquial for elegance." When Booker T. Washington was marveling at the quality of Charles Eliot's English in 1896, Mencken was already a teenager, and as a man of this linguistic culture, he would in 1921 gleefully pan Warren G. Harding as writing "the worst English that I have ever encountered." Up in New York five years before, Edna St. Vincent Millay had written a letter to her sister asking "Don't you suppose mother could get a job editing some dum [sic] page in some newspaper?—she might. She writes such beautiful English and she's so funny." Today, we would put it as "she writes so well"; to point to a person's English in particular signals a sense of our own language as a particular piece of work, which Americans have a responsibility to dress in its best.

In this era, one also heard English referred to this way in speech. Recall the elderly Mississippi Delta woman at the opening of Chapter One who said, "Seems like most folks, they speak pretty good *English*," rather than just "they talk pretty good." In one volume of Maya Angelou's autobiographical series, a black woman says to Angelou, "You speak such good English, you must have a diploma," rather than the "you speak so well" that would be more natural to Americans black and white today. Of course, we can't know if the woman put it just that way, since Angelou was quoting decades later, in an account fashioned to read as much like a novel as like reportage. But then Angelou herself did write the "line," and thus we can take it as reflecting the living language of someone born in 1928—who participated in oratory contests as a schoolgirl (and who was also, as it happens, made to memorize "The Song of Hiawatha").

Obviously, there is now less room for comments like this under what Louis Menand deftly terms "the fetish of the unconditioned."

The New Days:
Leave Your Coat with the Door Bitch

"Pre–Writing–What–You–Say":
The Entertainment Press from Talkie to DVD

Another example: While we can bury ourselves in the print sources of yesteryear and get only occasional hints of how people were actually talking casually in the real world, when people fifty years from now want to know how Americans were talking at what they will be calling the turn of the century, they will find themselves almost overwhelmed by the data just leafing through our magazines, newspapers, and books.

The entertainment press will be a fertile lode. In the December 2002 issue of *Premiere* magazine, an interview article on actress Natascha McElhone is written in prose like this: "Her name still doesn't really ring a bell does it? Good: That's just the way this classically trained, classically chiseled knockout likes it." "Classically trained, classically chiseled" is indeed rather *Entertainment Tonight*, but the passage still rings with the flavor of spoken English. That "really" in the first sentence is one of those indicators of personal attitude like *just* that I mentioned in Chapter One. It connotes "If you think about it . . ." as if you were saying it to

someone on the phone. A *New York Times* article might state "After assorted inquiries, no source consulted could provide details on the case,"
but with the addition of that one word *really*, suddenly it sounds like
something you'd only read in *The Onion*: "After assorted inquiries, no
source consulted could really provide details on the case." Or, in the current issue of *The Onion* itself as I write, one headline reads "Punk Band
Has Something Against Newscaster for Some Reason"—that's funny because it conveys the dismissively perplexed "Whatever . . ." stance typical
of conversation rather than formal prose.

Then, the "Good: That's just the way . . ." in the *Premiere* passage. We
say "Good: . . ." that way, but again, the *Times* does not describe a congressional session with "Good: The Senate will not adjourn until they
have passed the bill." *Premiere* is talking here rather than writing. The article continues with "Not that she's ungrateful for Hollywood's attention—
for this is a woman who, she says, doesn't remember 'pre–wanting-to-act.' "
This is the sort of jolly made-up language that we all indulge in in real
life and that characters indulge in on sitcoms: *Seinfeld*'s "close talker,"
Sex in the City's "Up-the-butt girl." Judge Reinhold's interviewer asks him
"Who today inspires you to play a little five-on-one? And don't say your
wife. I realize you don't want to sleep on the sofa, but please." The
onanistic reference itself reveals formality as the driving factor, of course.
But that informality extends to the very structure of the language: "And
don't say your wife." "But please." This is language as finger food.

But isn't this just mass culture having its way with the language?
Doesn't communicating with the lowest-common-denominator sub-
scriber base a *Premiere* aims at require loosening the language up for the
receptionist and the truck driver? Actually, no—because mass culture is
hardly new. Let's rewind to how the entertainment press read back in the
thirties.

One of the most popular movie fanzines in the 1930s and 1940s was
Photoplay. And aimed at the masses though it was, *Photoplay* was couched
in written English, with the casual only sprinkled in lightly as an arch
touch. In a 1935 interview, the writer visits Bette Davis when she was
married to a musician named Harmon Nelson:

> But it just happens that the Nelsons live on a budget predicated both
> on Bette's income and Harmon's income, which last, of course, is
> not movie money. When she's not working, she lives on his pay-

check, and, I might truthfully add—loves it. "Ham," as she calls him, heads an orchestra in a nearby night club, and Bette has a quaint conviction that a wife's place is with her husband. She greeted me wearing slacks, and the worried look of a lady whose Scottie is a surgical problem.[12]

There was a little bit of the Arab in the writer, pushing the language beyond its ordinary spoken version with formal vocabulary and long sentences no one would ever use in a conversation.[13] And yet *Photoplay*, even with its "predicated" and "which last," was aimed at shopgirls and milkmen. The magazine's "Answer Man" plugged rising star Robert Taylor that same year:

Another tall, dark and handsome hero has been acclaimed. The girls have just gone crazy about Robert Taylor, one of the outstanding of the new leading men. (. . .) Most of his leisure hours Bob spends playing tennis. When not thus engaged he likes to take in movies. He says his hobby is clothes, so girls, get out your knitting needles.

Premiere does not "acclaim" Eminem or Owen Wilson, and gives tidbits of their "spare time" rather than their "leisure hours." Also germane is that at this writing, *Esquire*'s column soliciting questions from readers is called not "Answer Man" but "Answer Fella."

I Was Like, "Did She Really Say, 'Otherwise seemingly sensible people'?": Talking with the Stars

We also see the triumph of the oral in the fact that celebrities' language is no longer translated into formal English for print.

For a brief shining moment in the early 1930s, the most popular film star in America was hefty, homely Marie Dressler, my all-time favorite old-movie performer. Dressler's film career was actually a brief coda in a

---

12. What on God's green earth did that last line mean?

13. I might add (but only down here) that the marriage was short-lived, in part because Nelson had a hard time making the transition from "five-on-one" to the conjugal. But then *Photoplay* would never have mentioned this, or "five-on-one" in general.

career she had mainly spent as a stage star, and during that part of her life in 1911, a newspaper interview article quoted her as saying:

> Only the other day I was invited to the home of some well-to-do and otherwise seemingly sensible people and when I was introduced it was like this: 'This is Marie Dressler.' Then, turning to me, my hostess said, 'Now say something funny.' "

Now, I cannot claim to have been present when Dressler gave this interview during the Taft administration, but I am quite confident that this statement did not come out of her mouth in those words. "Some well-to-do and otherwise seemingly sensible people."? "Then, turning to me, my hostess said . . ."? Try to imagine anyone you know, no matter how educated or articulate, actually mouthing sentences like that—this is novelistic prose. Most likely Dressler said something like "Some people who were well-to-do, and seemed sensible enough," and "Then the hostess turned to me and said . . ." But in 1911, journalists operated under a guiding sense that in print, ordinary speech was to be translated into the written, that to simply throw onto the page precisely what Dressler had said word-for-word would have been as inappropriate in the public sphere as First Lady Helen Taft serving hot dogs at a White House banquet (although they would likely have been designated "Frankfurter Sandwiches" on the menu cards).

It was the same in Dressler's memoirs. Like Richard Robinson, she left school at fourteen and never returned, and in *her* personal letters, it shows: they were short and, as her gifted biographer Matthew Kennedy puts it, "unpoetic," reading almost like e-mails. This letter thanks the writers of a hit movie she had done with costar Polly Moran: "You are just too nice and I do want you to know how much I appreciate it—Polly and self are just delighted re *Dangerous Females* and wish you had another like it." Those two *and*'s, just like speech; Dressler wrote like people talk. But in her *The Life Story of an Ugly Duckling*, suddenly she sounds like Virginia Woolf, and it was because her ghost writers made sure she did:

> A time comes when people cannot or may not make the same money as previously and the fact should be accepted as gracefully as possible. When such a situation arises, people off the stage as well as

on should be ready to resort to some other means of livelihood. If an artist or a poet starves because the world does not appreciate his talent in dollars, why should some other occupation be scorned?

But today, *Premiere* feels no compunction to write stars' statements "up." An interview in the same December 2002 issue with Kirk Douglas includes him describing working with his son Michael for the first time in *A Few Good Years*:

> I loved working with him; he really was a good actor—in spite of the fact that after the first thing he did in college, I went backstage, and he asked, "How was I?" and I said "You were awful!" I thought, "That will cure him, and he'll go be a lawyer." But two months later he said, "I'm in another play." I said "Oh my God," and I went to see him, and this time, when he said, "How was I?" I had to say [*resignedly*], "You were very good."

All of that direct quotation of what Michael and Kirk actually said, complete with spontaneous little dramatic imitations (such as what the *Premiere* writer indicates with "[*resignedly*]"), are how humans talk "online." Think of casual English speakers with their "So I said 'Tell me what I should do,' and she's like 'Well, I don't even know,' and I'm all 'Well, I can't go in there with nothing!' and she goes 'Oh—you always say that when it's really that you didn't do your job,' and I'm like 'What*ever*!'" That kind of direct quotation is oral language 101: Remember how J. K. Rowling in the Harry Potter books often *describes* what someone said while a Saramaccan speaker would actually depict someone making the statement "live."

Along those lines, in 1911 Kirk Douglas's equivalent (roughly, silent-film matinee idol Francis X. Bushman) would have been rendered in print something like:

> I loved working with him because he was truly a fine actor. But in point of fact, when I went backstage to meet him after the first play he performed in when he was in college, upon his asking me my impression of his performance, I told him he was awful! I supposed that this would cure him of his acting bug and that he would go on to be a lawyer. But two months later he told me that he was in yet

another play, and despite my reservations, I attended the performance. And this time, when he asked me my opinion of how well he had done, I could not help but tell him that he had been very good.

But today, the *New York Times* quotes Julianna Margulies on the subject of kissing Pierce Brosnan in a film: "Both Pierce and I, when the director went like, 'Great, cut, O.K., let's move on,' we were like, 'Hang on, we've been waiting the entire film.'" *Ecce* talking: Whereas back in the day, to the best of my knowledge, *never* were Hollywood stars ever quoted this directly, even those who were most willfully lowbrow in their off-stage personas, such as Clara Bow, Mae West, or Wallace Beery.

When You Get It, You Get It: Madison Avenue Talks to Us

Print ads also now read more like we talk every year. The *Premiere* issue is full of ads blaring with punchy, slangy phrases. In reference to a DVD set of James Bond movies, we are urged to "Own it. Live it. Give it." Subaru entices us with the rather gnomic "When you get it, you get it." Get what? Maybe Cuervo's tequila ad can help us, slapping "Ready. Set. Let Go." above a picture of distinctly gettable-looking people wet and semiclothed.

In contrast, well into the age of mass marketing, advertising copy did not read like this. Take a look at this exquisite Lifebuoy ad from *Photoplay* in 1929. What first strikes us is its utter bizarreness, of course. Just what has Celia stopped doing that is leaving her "even . . . even . . ." only lately? Why were people indoors "so much now" in 1929—especially when the issue ran in July, when air-conditioning was rare? If I were beamed back to someone's living room in July 1929, the first thing I would ask is whether we could step outside for some air.

But once we get past these concerns, we can also see that the people are written "up"—in the first panel, *quarrel* is a print word; in real life we say *argue* or *fight*. One also wonders whether even in 1929 ordinary people were walking around using the word *dainty* like this, or whether a woman musing over whether her husband thinks she reeks would use *perhaps* instead of *maybe* or *could be*.[14] And even the title of the ad, "A

---

14. Another question that arises is: Did Americans use deodorant in 1929? One never sees ads for it. It's a well-established factoid that people in the Middle Ages stank. But I sometimes wonder—were Americans even as recently as the 1920s and

Quarrel Averted" has the puffed-up air of "Frankfurter Sandwiches" or the Brooklyn Bridge program's "Principal Orations." The America that produced this Lifebuoy ad seems almost a different country from the one that today has it that at this writing, upon leaving a French Connection clothing store, one is greeted with a basket of samples of "Eau de Fuck"—or if one looks more closely, "Eau de Fcuk" (i.e., French Connection United Kingdom), but we get the joke.

Talking Books

The shift to the oral is also creeping upon us in less immediately apparent ways. I have already touched upon B. R. Myers's controversial piece in *The Atlantic Monthly* where he charged that the prose style of various prominent modern authors is glaringly short on technique, and that to celebrate these authors is either to eschew standards or to mistake the incomprehensible for the profound. Though as I noted before, I find Myers's assumptions as to what constitutes aesthetic worth on the arbitrary side, the article was cogently argued and a great read. But one thing Myers missed is that much of the difference between the grand old writers he prefers and modern ones is that the latter are simply more prone to imitate speech in narrative passages.

Myers aims his scorn at excerpts like this one from Cormac McCarthy's *The Crossing* (1994) "He ate the last of the eggs and wiped the plate with the tortilla and ate the tortilla and drank the last of the coffee and wiped his mouth and looked up and thanked her," for example. In the book version of the article Myers facetiously terms this technique the "andelope." But the telegraphic nature of this passage is so obviously deliberate that it's almost too easy to reject it as "bad writing." The "andelope" is a fundamental of spoken language. McCarthy is writing a spoken description here, attempting to convey the sequence of actions as we actually perceive them in our own heads in real time in order to elicit a sense of immediacy and reality.

Myers is similarly dismissive of David Guterson's work on the basis of passages like this one from *Snow Falling on Cedars* (1994):

1930s a little funky by our modern standards? Would we have detected a queer mélange of perfume and pungency even in the first-class dining room of the *Titanic*? Talcum powder and bath soap can only do so much. There still survive people old enough to remember—we should ask them.

He didn't like very many people anymore or very many things, either. He preferred not to be this way, but there it was, he was like that. His cynicism—a veteran's cynicism—was a thing that disturbed him all the time . . . It was not even a thing you could explain to anybody, why it was that everything was folly.

Small phrases follow one another one by one, with rather loose connection ("but there it was, he was like that"). We all recognize this from how we and others talk casually, but Myers is thrown by seeing the oral spread so thick on the page.

The very rules of the game in written English are changing fast, such that dismissing writing like McCarthy's and Guterson's as "bad writing" is like Theodore Roosevelt listening to Elvis Costello and scorning him for not singing with the operatic techniques of Caruso and for not having oboes in his band. One study even shows that in texts from the 1980s, the average length of a sentence is more than half as short as it was in texts from around 1900. Today, the literary critic's job will increasingly be to assess how well a writer has summoned spoken English on the page.

To resist this is to fall out of step with a new cultural reality in which we write what we say to an extent that would have perplexed a Victorian as much as it would an Arab today. It's not that this came to be overnight sometime in 1967. Just as American oratory took it down a notch starting in the twenties, we all know that good spoken American was acquainted with the printed page long before love-ins. Mark Twain and others reveled in writing in dialect in the nineteenth century. And more to the point, between the wars, much of the power of H. L. Mencken's prose came from his fusion of the formal with the colloquial, while Ring Lardner excelled at eliminating the formal altogether. Good authors, too, who once knew better words now only used four-letter words writing prose, Cole Porter told us in 1934, referring to the occasional cussing in Hemingway or the whole evening of gutbucket swearing in Laurence Stallings and Maxwell Anderson's World War I play *What Price Glory?* of 1924.

But degree is key here. The prose of Twain and Lardner stood out as a stunt in their eras. Twain's contrasted with a norm typified by the doily prose of his era's superstar novelist William Dean Howells. Lardner competed with authors like Mary Roberts Rinehart, Gene Stratton Porter, and

Harold Bell Wright, whose novels, written in the full-bore post-Victorian prose that their triple-barrel names suggest, were as common on coffeetables at the time as Danielle Steele is now. *What Price Glory?* popped the monocles off of theatergoers who could be assured that the following weekend they could sleep through a nice piffly play where honeymooning couples pranced around talking like books. And in Mencken, the colloquial was but a garnish. The range of his vocabulary often sends even readaholics to their dictionaries, and his sentence construction was, in all of its muscular pacing, thoroughly "written."

The change I refer to was one that none of these people could have predicted. Case in point: At a mah-velous warehouse party in Brooklyn I recently attended, one of the many featured amusements was an inflated bubble into which one ventured at the peril of assorted debaucheries. I, of course, didn't get around to entering, but I did note that the woman at the door was wearing a sign around her neck that read "Door Bitch." Now, people did get down in their way as early as the 1920s—Clara Bow stripped naked at parties, Babe Ruth was known for shouting at a certain point in a shindig that any woman who was not amenable to certain conclusive intimacies was requested to take her leave right away. But no matter how randy those parties got that Joan Crawford danced the Charleston at in her silent films of the late twenties, we can be quite sure that "Door Bitch" signs would have been regarded as a bit *de trop*.

Make no mistake—I'm enough of a person of my time to have found "Door Bitch" every bit as funny as the party organizers intended it. All the same, it also drags English down to the cold, hard ground. There may be a sense of play in "Door Bitch," but it would be hard to say that there is any love of the English language in it. The very concept was, of course, utterly beside the point for the woman in her leopard-skin coat and sunglasses. Or better, "leopard-skin coat and sunglasses"—she was performing, and the subject of the show was dismissing authority and propriety.

The Love Is Gone: Teaching English Then and Now

So far I have shown the contrast between then and now. Since my argument is that a cultural shift created American English's now, it is certainly indicative that the manifestations of that now that we have seen are deeply entwined with the larger "fetish of the unconditioned": the Judge Reinhold piece referring to self-eroticization, the "Door Bitch" woman hostessing an inflatable den of iniquity. But then correlation and cause are not always equatable. We have yet to zoom in closer to see language use actually transforming in direct response to a new cultural imperative.

The education world gives us a window on this. Its highly politicized nature makes the countercultural roots of the development easy to view, and also brings out the general sense of English as less a treasure than as inherited old furniture we'd just as soon keep in the spare room.

Something to Say and Saying It Well:
Composition Teaching in a Different Day

The teaching of reading and writing over the past one hundred years-and-change shows us getting here from there in living color. Let us return to W.E.B. Du Bois taking that composition class at Harvard in 1890. The first assignment, as in many such classes even today, was to write something about himself. He came up with:

> For the usual purposes of identification I have been labelled in this life: William Edward Burghardt Du Bois, born in Great Barrington, Massachusetts, on the day after Washington's birthday, in 1868. I shall room during the present twelve-month at number twenty Flagg Street, Cambridge. As to who I really am, I am much in doubt, and can consequently give little reliable information from casual hints and observations. I doubt not that there are many who could supply better data than the writer. In the midst then of personal uncertainty I can only supply a few alleged facts from memory according to the usual way.

And despite this elevated level of composition that he was already capable of, he closed with what is today a truly astounding sentence:

> I have something to say to the world and I have taken English twelve in order to say it well.

In other words, despite a level of writing whose easy grace would be beyond most of today's undergraduates at even the best of our schools, a man who thought himself bound for greater things felt compositionally unfinished!

This neatly shows that refined craft in writing had a cultural currency at this time that seems almost otherworldly to us now. A crucial point: There exists no composition class in America that could do anything for Du Bois today. Modern composition classes are designed to teach students the very rudiments of written versus oral expression, and structuring their thoughts on paper. The kind of high-level rhetorical burnishing Du Bois matter-of-factly sought in Harvard's English 12 of 1890 is now something one would have to teach one's self—and only to find it of no use.

"I have something to say to the world and I have taken English twelve in order to say it well"—clearly we are not in Kansas anymore. But for someone who did happen to live in Kansas five years after Du Bois's spell in English twelve and wanted to become a schoolteacher, they had to pass an examination requiring this level of writing ability:

Grammar
1. Give nine rules for the use of Capital Letters.
2. Name the Parts of Speech and define those that have no modifications.
3. Define Verse, Stanza and Paragraph.
4. What are the Principal Parts of a verb? Give Principal Parts of do, lie, lay and run.
5. Define Case, Illustrate each Case.
6. What is Punctuation? Give rules for principal marks of Punctuation.
7.–10. Write a composition of about 150 words and show therein that you understand the practical use of the rules of grammar.

Orthography
1. What is meant by the following: Alphabet, phonetic orthography, etymology, syllabication?
2. What are elementary sounds? How classified?
3. What are the following, and give examples of each: Trigraph, subvocals, diphthong, cognate letters, linguals?
4. Give four substitutes for caret 'u.'
5. Give two rules for spelling words with final 'e.' Name two exceptions under each rule.

6. Give two uses of silent letters in spelling. Illustrate each.
7. Define the following prefixes and use in connection with a word: Bi, dis, mis, pre, semi, post, non, inter, mono, super.
8. Mark diacritically and divide into syllables the following, and name the sign that indicates the sound: Card, ball, mercy, sir, odd, cell, rise, blood, fare, last.
9. Use the following correctly in sentences, Cite, site, sight, fane, fain, feign, vane, vain, vein, raze, raise, rays.
10. Write 10 words frequently mispronounced and indicate pronunciation by use of diacritical marks and by syllabication.

And get this: it was expected that a person could pass this exam with only an eighth grade education![15] Now, as we have gotten a hint of from Richard Robinson and Marie Dressler, in those days it was common to leave school at that point: Twelfth grade was not yet the standard expectation it is now. Yet there is still a striking contrast with today, in that a representative number of people in their mid-teens—gangling, pimply adolescents—were expected to be able to handle a test like this. And it makes you think, as they say, that most aspiring teachers today would be flummoxed by a test like this even with a B.A. from a top-ranked university. Nor do I note that from on high—even as a linguist, I'm not completely sure what the examination writers meant by "caret 'u,' " and thus would be of little use in proposing what four of its "substitutes" might be, nor have I ever encountered the word *fane*. In our America, we would never think of expecting this kind of magisterial command of the mechanics of language from, well, anybody.

At the very time this test was being administered, just across the state line in Independence, Missouri, future President Harry Truman was going to school. And as a grown man in the army in 1912, he wrote to his beloved and future wife:

> Say, it sure is a grand thing that I have a high-school dictionary handy.
> I even had to look on the back to see how to spell the book itself. The
> English language so far as spelling goes was created by Satan I am sure.

[15.] In its wide discussion in the press and on the Internet, this test is almost always presented as having been for eighth grade *students*. However, the actual document reveals that it was almost certainly intended for aspiring teachers. (I found *www.truthorfiction.com* especially convincing on this point.)

So, he did have to use the dictionary to spell words right—but crucially, he used it, and felt this orthographic vigilance as necessary in writing a woman he wanted (for some reason) to marry. Truman's letters are low on spelling errors because he came up in a culture whose schools inculcated a sense that spelling things right was as crucial as putting a napkin in your lap while eating. Now, as we all know, English spelling was indeed created by Satan. But it's not going away, and arbitrariness is the nature of formality. We clip our nails in private, most of us who are not men wear bras (as late as the 1930s, most women did not; it's a thoroughly random fashion), and we spell it *parallel* instead of *paralell*.

And in that, Truman's particular dedication to spelling marks him as a figure from the past: Today, we are much more comfortable just letting spelling errors sit and laughing them off. The passage from the letter is hard to plausibly translate in our time, even between college-student lovers. If anything, we imagine that a milk-drinking, old-school, and probably devoutly Christian sort of person might write something like that—and wouldn't you know, McGuffey readers are still used these days by home-schooling parents, who tend to be deeply religious.

From Henry James to *Hop on Pop*:
Changes in Reading Passages As Time Goes By

Truman's letter fit right into its era: American schools were still operating under a sense that on the page, one dressed the language up, and that no citizen was to escape schooling without learning at least the rudiments of the pertinent *comme il faut*. But that would not last forever. In her book *Losing our Language*, Sandra Stotsky shows how striking the decline was. The fourth McGuffey reader was used as late as the 1920s, and typical reading passages for middle school (i.e., gangling and pimply) students were pitched at a level exemplified by an excerpt from Joseph Addison's "Reflections in Westminster Abbey":

> When I am in a serious humor, I very often walk by myself in Westminster Abbey, where the gloominess of the place and the use to which it is applied, with the solemnity of the building and the condition of the people who lie in it, are apt to fill the mind with a kind of melancholy, or rather thoughtfulness, that is not disagreeable.

By the 1950s and 1960s, the level had already sunk a good couple of notches, as in this excerpt from *Stories from the Arabian Nights* from a textbook last distributed in the early 1960s:

> I decided, after my first voyage, to spend the rest of my days at Bagdad. But it was not long before I tired of a lazy life, and I put to sea a second time, in the company of other merchants. We boarded a good ship and set sail. We traded from island to island, exchanging goods. One day we landed on an island covered with several kinds of fruit trees, but we could see neither man nor animal.

The vocabulary here is less rococo than in the 1920s excerpt with its "solemnity" and "melancholy," and the syntax avoids written tricks like "the use to which it is applied" and the interlude of "... or rather thoughtfulness ..." But now look at a passage from the same sixth grade textbook's 1996 edition:

> Tahcawin had packed the parfleche cases with clothing and food and strapped them to a travois made of two trailing poles with a skin net stretched between them. Another travois lay on the ground ready for the new tipi. Chano was very happy when Tasinagi suggested the three of them ride up to their favorite hills for the last time.

This sounds like something from a Golden Book—we read it thankful that we are too old to have to bother with text so dingdong dull. The passage does present one challenge in the unfamiliar Native American words. But these are actually key to the reason behind the change in the texture of these passages.

Textbook editors now include more and more such foreign-language terms in readings, out of an imperative to introduce students to cultures other than their own. And this in turn operates alongside a tendency to focus on the injustices and tragedies of American imperialism past and present. But as Stotsky argues, the emphasis on these foreign terms has the downside of distracting from students' acquiring advanced, written words in the English language. The number of such words taught in middle school textbooks has declined steadily since the 1960s.

That is, anti-Establishment ideology is incompatible with texts on the level of "Reflections in Westminster Abbey." Say what we might about these editors' intentions, the result of those intentions signals a devaluation of our native language itself. To get a sense of what students learn of English from the 1996 passage as compared to the 1962 one, we could "translate" it (with the assumption that *teepee* is now essentially an English word):

> Justin had packed the leather cases with clothing and food and strapped them to two trailing poles with a skin net stretched between them. Another set of poles with a net lay on the ground ready for the new teepee. Michelle was very happy when Jennifer suggested the three of them ride up to their favorite hills for the last time.

This is the level of reading we expect from twelve-year-olds? Especially the sharp-tongued, precociously sophisticated creatures they tend to be today? Historian Henry Steele Commager once noted about the McGuffey readers that:

> What is striking about the Readers—it was probably not so much a product of policy as of habit—was that they made so few conscious concessions to immaturity. There was no nonsense about limiting the vocabulary to familiar words, for example. (. . .) They did draw generously on modern English classics, and on such American books as might supposed to be classics, and they took for granted that the young would understand them, or that teachers would explain them—something publishers never appear to think of today!

Indeed, there was no need for McGuffey to assert raising the bar high as a policy because it was an assumption of the culture he lived in. But there is no sense of challenge or tutelage in the Tahcawin passage. Its *primum mobile* is not to expose students to a level of English beyond the natural and effortless oral one, but to alert them to the existence of cultures and languages beyond their own. And that means that sixth graders today are not being offered the English language dressed in its Sunday best. This is no longer a priority for the editors in practice, even if their public statements suggest otherwise. And this is because these editors exist in a culture of language teaching in which, since the late sixties, to celebrate English would be morally backward.

"A Conversation About Language Arts but Not About English":
Anti-Americanism in the Ed World

Progressive educational philosophy had cherished the individual "learning how to learn"—take a page from Natasha McElhone and call it "proto–Doing Your Own Thing"—over rote memorization as early as the late nineteenth century. But in the education world, a watershed was the Dartmouth conference of 1966, which overtly decried a focus on grammar, analysis, and writing self-standing essays, instead elevating learning through informal classroom talk—the oral over the written. Since then, composition teachers have embraced the social-dialogic model of the teaching of writing, in which students evaluate one another's work under a model of writing as conversation among equals.

Writing has always been a way of participating in a larger conversation, to be sure. But as we have seen, crafted, elaborate writing allows an *idealized* form of conversation, more precise and substantial than telegraphic, jumpy speech easily achieves. But because writing is an idealization, it does not come naturally to most: It must be imposed, and some will be better at it than others. And that kind of competition goes against the grain of an educational culture focused on shielding students from the evils of The Machine.

That overtly political strain lives on today in the ed world. In 1993, Donald A. McAndrew and C. Mark Hurlbert made a splash with their proposal for a "big, smart English," in which:

> Writers should be encouraged to make intentional errors in standard form and usage. Attacking the demand for standard English is the only way to end its oppression of linguistic minorities and learning writers. We believe this frontal assault is necessary for two reasons: (1) it affords experienced writers, who can choose or not choose to write standard English, a chance to publicly demonstrate against its tryanny [sic] and (2) if enough writers do it regularly, our cultures [sic] view of what is standard and acceptable may widen just enough to include a more diverse surface representation of language . . .

The spelling errors were, believe it or not, deliberate; this article appeared not in some photocopied rag, but the house organ of the National Council of Teachers of English. The editors singled it out for praise in the issue it appeared in, while the Conference on English Leadership judged it the best education article of the year. And at the NCTE's annual conference two years later, a motion was discussed to eliminate the word *English* from the organization's name, on the grounds that it appeared to dismiss people of other cultural heritages: As one member put it "If we are to offer diversity, there can be a conversation about language arts, but not about English."

The people in favor of this motion's multicultural goals were surely sincere. But wherever one's politics takes one in response to their position, a simple fact remains: Under their paradigm, artfully pushing written English prose beyond its bread-and-butter level cannot, in any logical sense, be a priority. Educators in the past could not have imagined any question as to whether we would venture a "conversation about" language arts. But a powerful strain in modern ed-school culture distrusts English as an imperial language, and that essentially means that you do not like it—you certainly don't love it. And if you don't, the notion of students drilled in its intricacies and nuances becomes vaguely distasteful and ultimately beside the point in a new world where freeing students to unlock their inner genius by Doing Their Own Thing is a moral imperative.

Not that the situation in the 1890s was ideal. The difference between the 1921 and 1962 passages above shows that there had already been a sea change in reading textbook passages long before the sixties. Specifically, this happened in the thirties, when star education researcher and psychologist Edward Lee Thorndike published a list of the most frequently occurring words in newspapers and books, and called for textbooks to restrict themselves to these words. And this was a response to what would later be called diversity. Waves of immigrant children over the past few decades, often coming from bookless homes and semiliterate parents, had found the level of vocabulary in turn-of-the-century textbooks almost crippling. The level of failure and dropping out in schools of that era was much higher than we usually know today, given that the semiliterate dropout rarely had the ability or occasion to write about their lives later on. And one cannot help but wonder just how useful many of the things Gilded Age kids had to plow through were to their edification or future success. Take this cloying swatch of preening prose from the fifth McGuffey:

> The quail is peculiarly a domestic bird, and is attached to his birthplace and the home of his forefathers. The various members of the aquatic families educate their children in the cool summer of the far

north, and bathe their warm bosoms in July in the iced waters of Hudson Bay; but when Boreas scatters the rushes where they had builded their bedchambers, they desert their fatherland, and fly to disport in the sunny waters of the south.

This may have made a little more sense in an America where most people still lived on the land. But the only quail I have ever seen have been on dinner plates, and besides the deadeningly treacly tone, I cringe to imagine a child of Sicilian immigrants—or even a little white girl in Salina, Kansas—having to grapple with words like "Boreas" and "disport." There were those who harrumphed at Thorndike's influence. It was what Henry Steele Commager was referring to, for example, in his grousing about "limiting the vocabulary to familiar words," which he wrote as early as 1962, not in our era. But Commager was almost a senior citizen by then, his predilections having jelled in the rich but elitist print culture of the teens and twenties. To me, making primer texts more streamlined and relevant than verbose, sacharrine exhortations about game birds was an advance.

Big Words: The New Threat to Learning

But since then the pendulum has swung further in this direction than Thorndike had intended. He sought to spare students the arcane; today, his descendants seek to spare students even the formal. An example of this shift is, of all people, former University of California President Richard Atkinson.

In 2001, Atkinson made a stir in the media with his proposal that the UC system discontinue requiring applicants to take the SAT I, which includes tests of students' mastery of advanced vocabulary. Atkinson preferred that admissions committees use the SAT II, which measures mastery of actual course content, seeing this as a fairer metric for evaluating students' ability to perform at the university level.

Granted, Atkinson commissioned a study that showed that performance on the SAT I did not factor significantly in students' performance in college after their first year. But what drove him in his gut to even initiate such a study? Human ingenuity generally begins with the visceral experience, the hunch, the bias—and in itself, *honi soit qui mal y pense.* Yet, what situates Atkinson into today's America was the sight that spurred him into action:

For many years, I have worried about the use of the SAT but last year my concerns coalesced. I visited an upscale private school and observed a class of twelve-year-old students studying verbal analogies in anticipation of the SAT. I learned that they spend hours each month—directly and indirectly—preparing for the SAT, studying long lists of verbal analogies such as "untruthful is to mendaciousness" as "circumspect is to caution." The time involved was not aimed at developing the students' reading and writing abilities but rather their test-taking skills.

That passage got around in the media, intended to make people shake their heads at such a sad sight. And there is a point at which "teaching to the test" works against actually engaging or nurturing a young mind. But still, sixty years ago, a newsreel would have presented Atkinson's same tableau as, well, school. Within the context of this book, it is telling that it spontaneously struck Atkinson as so sad, so beside the point of education, that twelve-year-olds were being taught the meanings of written words. There is a short step from this to the saplessness of the Tahcahwin passage—which was written for students at this very age. Words like *mendacious* and *circumspect* are rare in casual speech, and as such, these students were being taught a different layer of this language known as English.

Atkinson, like many critics of standardized testing, assumes that learning these words is unrelated to developing students' reading abilities. But this is hardly as self-evident as he claims. Amidst the highly politicized debates over the value of the SAT, too seldom do analysts actually get down to brass tacks and address at length actual SAT exams and what they require. An article by William Dowling, Rutgers English professor, is an exception, and he elegantly makes a case that—as most of us would suspect—mastery of advanced vocabulary is vital to understanding the texts that college education presents students with.

The weakness of a curriculum-wide correlation between SAT I scores and freshman grades is one thing, but Dowling still found that:

When a departmental task (. . .) gave me an opportunity to compare the grades of my English 219 students over several years with their incoming SATV [verbal portion of the SAT] scores, I compiled a simple statistical chart. What I found was that the SATV scores had an extraordinarily high correlation with final grades, and that neither, in the many cases where I had come to know my students' personal backgrounds, seemed to correlate very well with socio-economic status.

Dowling presents an actual SAT question answered correctly most often by students who score 700 or higher on the SAT I:

The traditional process of producing an oil painting requires so many steps that it seems _____ to artists who prefer to work quickly.

(A) provocative (B) consummate (C) interminable (D) facile (E) prolific

Dowling notes that students who know one of these words are likely to know the others, and that knowing that the correct answer is "interminable" is obviously a strong indication that a student is able to easily process prose at this level. A similar question:

querulous: complain

Which pair of words exists in the same relation?

(A) silent: talk (B) humorous: laugh (C) dangerous: risk
(D) deceitful: cheat (E) gracious: accept

Assessing whether a student can quickly see that the answer is (D) is less a random or elitist hoop to force students through than a sane way of seeing whether they can handle substantial texts in our language.

Atkinson is no partisan zealot. He is an awesomely accomplished, erudite, and civil man, one of whose specialties has been classroom learning. But his discomfort at seeing twelve-year-olds drilled on words like this marks him as a man of our times, for whom learned levels of English are less a main course than a garnish in an education.

After all, there is no theoretical reason that a "progressive" position on education frame learning high vocabulary as an imposition. The same Charles Eliot who championed Progressive Education also complained that "Bad spelling, incorrectness as well as inelegance of expression in writing, ignorance of the simplest rules of punctuation, and almost entire want of familiarity with English literature, are far from rare among young men of eighteen otherwise well prepared for college studies." With all due and sincere respect to Atkinson, I find it hard to imagine him ever saying or writing that—because to rue the problem it addresses implies that students should have been given exactly the kind of tutelage that he considers a detour from "real" education.

To be sure, Dowling and other commentators stress that at the end of the day, what makes a student ace the verbal portion of the SAT is having always been a heavy reader. It has certainly been my observation that undergraduates with an effortless facility with "big words" are bookworms. As such, Atkinson, and people more stridently opposed to the SAT, may feel that the SAT I is discriminatory against students whose backgrounds made becoming a bookworm less likely. But then—aren't classroom drills in the meanings of these words a societally provisioned way to help level the playing field? I have seen students drilling themselves on such words with flash cards enhance their performance on standardized tests decently. I can also testify that having been taught the meanings of words like *expiate, expatiate,* and *arrogate* in language arts classes in middle school has served me well in engaging adult nonfiction prose.

In general, there will always be young people who, by virtue of genes, background, or their combination, are kick-ass readers. Yes, there will be more in Scarsdale, but they will emerge as well in Detroit, East L.A., and Appalachia—they always have, still do, and always will. In all of his good intentions, however, in the grand scheme of things, Atkinson devalues the mastery of vocabulary that this bent lends. To the extent that it does not predict the grades that students make in their first—and only their first of four—years of college, he loses interest. And in this, he reveals that he, as an American of our times, does not cherish or respect expression in English the way his earlier equivalents like Charles Eliot did. After all, there are various things that Atkinson and his peers consider unnegotiably central to an education even though they are tangential to test scores or even scholarly performance. Take, for instance, the workshops and classes devoted to diversity and multiculturalism that undergraduates are constantly exposed to, and never mind the college sports industry (*mens sana in corpore sano*).

But mastery of written English is no longer classed this way. It is considered more important for an undergraduate to understand that racism can be subtle as well as overt than than to know the meanings of the words *provocative, consummate, interminable, facile,* and *prolific.* Literally— most college administrators would have to agree with that statement after a few hems and haws. And that is an American university that has only existed for the past thirty-five years.

Time Marches On:
Just Writing

Obviously all written English in America is not devolving into graffiti. Even in our take-it-light era, there still exists a healthy space for prose whose vocabulary and syntax are more artificially crafted than speech could ever be. But even that prose has changed in particular ways since the 1960s. Written English survives, but in a *Moderato* guise contrasting with the *Allegro con brio* once more common. In arenas where the old-time writer once gilded the lily and considered it part of their job, the modern writer is often more inclined to just get the job done.

For example, in the old days, non-fiction prose in books was often cast at the same level as high literary language. One of the grand old New York music critics of the turn of the last century, Henry Krehbiel, wrote a survey book in 1919 in a tone typified by:

> During the period of which I am writing, even in journals of dignity and scholarly repute the gossip of the foyer and the dressing rooms of the chorus and ballet stood in higher esteem with the news editors than the comments of conscientious critics. (. . .) The phenomenon, inasmuch as it marked the operatic history of the decade of which I am writing more emphatically than any period within a generation, is deserving of study.

Krehbiel meant that; he wasn't writing tongue-in-cheek. And this style, too, lasted to an extent through the middle decades of the century. Here is another comment on Toscanini by RCA record producer Charles O'Connell in 1947, with a feel that immediately marks it as having been written "in the old days":

> I believe that Toscanini's obsession with *energy*, with *force*, his pride in possessing them in so full a measure, his idolatrous worship of these qualities, and his relentless application of them in his artistic and personal life, provide a possible key not only to the magical

effect he has had upon his audiences and his consequent successes, but to the character of the maestro himself as man and musician.

We can see this kind of compositional verve leaching out of mainstream non-fiction prose after the 1960s in *Time* magazine. When I was fifteen, a cocky fellow at school crowed during an argument with someone over current events "I read *Time* magazine, so I know all about that kind of thing." Naif that I was, that struck me as a pretty damaging blow to the opponent, and I decided that to make sure I never got caught short in an argument like that, I would start reading the issues of *Time* that my parents subscribed to.

But it was always something of a chore. To this day, the prose of *Time* in the early eighties remains some of the most determinedly gray, faceless writing I have ever encountered. (It has become somewhat zingier since, in the face of competition from *Newsweek*, cable, and the Internet.) But I wouldn't have felt that way if I had started reading *Time* in the 1930s.

Time is especially illustrative for us, because in its early decades under Henry Luce, it was notorious for a certain idiosyncratic writing style, arch yet snappy. To show the change over the decades, I chose one of the few features of the magazine that has persisted throughout its history, its annual designation of a figure as "Man of the Year." Specifically, I have chosen the place in the magazine where that figure and his impact on the previous year was first officially announced, this place itself varying over the decades (sometimes in a letter from the publisher, sometimes in an article, etc.).

In 1935, Man of the Year was Franklin D. Roosevelt:

> In Chapter 1934 of the great visitors book which men call History many a potent human being scrawled his name the twelvemonth past. But no man, however long his arm, could write his name so big as the name written by the longer arm of mankind. Neither micrometer nor yardstick was necessary to determine that the name of Franklin Delano Roosevelt was written bigger, blacker, bolder than all the rest.

Now, that's prose—the writer sat down and crafted a piece of Writing. When you toss in words like "twelvemonth" and "micrometer," you're singing. *Time* was written not only to inform but to engage. Fifteen years later in 1950, here is the announcement that Winston Churchill had been chosen:

> As the 20th Century plunged on, long-familiar bearings were lost in the mists of change. Some of the age's great leaders called for more & more speed ahead; some tried to reverse the course. Winston Churchill had a different function: his chief contribution was to warn of rocks ahead, and to lead the rescue parties. He was not the man who designed the ship; what he did was to launch the lifeboats. That a free world survived in 1950, with a hope of more progress and less calamity, was due in large measure to his exertions.

Not quite as showy as fifteen years before, but still very much a piece of written oratory, as it were, summoning grand, theatrical images with words like "bearings, mists, course, calamity," and "exertions." And note that clever way of introducing Churchill. This was the first time his name was mentioned in the piece; that year, the announcement was tucked into a long article surveying the first fifty years of the century. No "And the winner is . . ." fanfare; the writer slips Churchill in from the wings while the audience is engaged in action happening stage center. Whether this does it for you or not, one thing *Time* was not in 1950 was dull reading. The writer who just turned in a sober report had not earned his keep—he was expected to craft lively prose.

And this was true right up through the era when Newton Minow gave his "vast wasteland" speech, with Mario Savio's speeches four years in the future. In 1960, the announcement of Dwight D. Eisenhower's selection began with another theatrical—or by this time, cinematic—image of people in foreign lands attending Eisenhower appearances "thirsty" for what modernity offered:

> That thirsting, as many of their slogans and leaders made clear, was less for the things themselves than for the kind of life where the good things could be attained. In 1959, after years of hostile Communist propaganda, spectacular Russian successes in space, threats of missiles and atomic war, the throngs of Europe, Asia and Africa cast a durable vote for freedom and liberty. The faces were turned to the U.S. and to the man who had become the nation's image in one of the grand plebiscites of history—Dwight David Eisenhower, President of the U.S., and Man of the Year.

But how *Times* change. Let's let the sixties happen. *Time*, in tune with its rightward-leaning inclinations in the era, resisted the new America for a little while. An especially poignant issue is their 1970 Man of Year one, giving the designation to "The Middle Americans" for their purported resistance to the counterculture, still hoping the late sixties were a mere fad. But the writers at *Time* were human beings living in their moment like everyone else, and by 1975, the magazine's prose was the kind that would be stultifying me five years later. Even the choice of Man of the Year that year was kind of dull: Saudi Arabia's King Faisal. Here was the announcement.

> As a crucial decision maker and a symbol of Arab petropower, Saudi Arabia's King Faisal is TIME's Man of the Year. Throughout 1974, Faisal's actions about oil prices and related matters touched, in various degrees, the lives and pocketbooks of virtually every human being on earth. Politically, too, 1974 was marked by the increasing cohesion and power of the Arab world, a surging strength fueled by the largest transfer of capital in history. In all this, the shrewd and dedicated King has played a key role.

And that's starting from the top, not snipped from the middle: Faisal is just plopped in like a an egg cracked into a frying pan. And the prose is merely competent—the writer felt no impulse to whip up an engaging piece. "Actions about oil prices" gives no indication of searching for the *mot juste* or euphonious expression. The earlier passages declared cleanly; this writer feels it more important to insert the mediating *in various degrees*.

Five years later, during the Iranian hostage crisis, the Man of the Year was Ayatollah Khomeini. The editors assure us that the award is given to people who have most affected the world not only positively but negatively:

> There have been designees very plainly in the latter category—Adolf Hitler (1938), Joseph Stalin (1939)—but selection has never necessarily connoted either the magazine's, or the world's, approval of the subject. Thus the editors had little difficulty naming Ayatullah Ruhollah Khomeini, intransigent leader of the Iranian revolution, as TIME's Man of the Year for 1979. "The impact of the Ayatullah on world

events is far greater than merely the hostage crisis," says World Editor John Elson, who edited the opening story . . .

Again, this is thoroughly decent, but juiceless writing. And typically of latter-day Man of the Year announcements, instead of crafting a self-standing piece of prose, the editors give much attention to the people who wrote the article on the designee. This authorship angle, pulling back the curtain, sets a passage off from the performances-in-prose of earlier times. In 1940 the *Time* writer danced for all he was worth and went off with a flourish stage right, leaving us wanting more. The *Time* writer of the 1980s executed some steps, stopped to tell us he had just done so, and sat down to rest.

Overall, we see a crucial difference between before and after in reading the pieces aloud. The earlier pieces seem to almost beg for recital, if you can keep from chuckling at the purpleness we perceive now in phraseology like "bigger, blacker, bolder than all the rest." The Churchill passage, with its economical, well-crafted phrases rolling one after the other, almost feels like one of Churchill's speeches. But someone reading the Faisal or Khomeini passages would sound like a modern newscaster— flat and to the point. Indeed, *Time*'s prose was a tad zestier than the average news magazine in the old days, but that itself feeds back to the point: Just why is it that a mainstream news weekly would not put that much pluck into its writing today? Why is it that so much more than way back when, today's journalist just writes?

There are a few passing moments in early episodes of *Mary Tyler Moore* that show why, in a way. It's 1970, and anchorman Ted Baxter is depicted as a fan of the President of the United States: "I always like to agree with the President," he says at one point, and is later miffed that he sent the President a Christmas card but didn't get one back. Baxter's faith in the President was simply meant to show his inflated ego; the writers intended no comment at Ted's politics or sense of morality.

This was in line with how Mr. President was depicted in popular entertainment in the old days. Of course in the real America, citizens have always had a roiling variety of political stances on their administration. The adulation of "President Rooh-zevelt" from characters in old radio shows contrasts sharply with the ample proportion of hate mail FDR got in response to his Fireside Chats. Yet H. L. Mencken's ceaseless barrage of nakedly derisive broadsides at the nation's rulers was, in his day, a peculiarity that occasioned celebrity. The people grumbling about Roosevelt in 1938 were outraged at what they regarded as a perversion of a national endeavor they saw as legitimate in itself. They were shocked thirty years later at their grandchildren's utter contempt for the very worth of America as a country. This sea change rendered the Baxter character's openhearted fetish for Mr. President impossible in television shortly thereafter. Since the 1970s we assume that any intelligent person at least views the current administration with deep skepticism. And Mencken would not be a celebrity today, because his professional acridness would come off as stating the obvious.

The earlier *Time* writers, then, worked in an era when Americans still felt that we had a communal story to tell. Anarchists and skeptics have always had their place in this country, but Hendrik Hertzberg's comment that "To say something worthwhile, you'd probably have to say something that not everyone would agree with" reflects an America more fragmented than ever before, with an intelligentsia and media establishment unusually united in a bone-deep distrust of the American experiment.

The *Time* of 1935 was written for a populace who could be expected to thrill to the story of their nation told with the energy that good storytelling requires. But most journalists and educators, especially given the strong leftist tilt of their professions' politics, cannot connect with that story now. They have no story to tell—and thus no use for performing in the language we would use to tell it. And with language as with so much else: Use it or lose it.

The Joys of the Grapholect

From our vantage point, it can be hard to read the prose of journalists before the wars, the letters people like Elizabeth Cady Stanton or Theodore Roosevelt wrote, or the textbook samples from the early twentieth century, without thinking that our *sans façon* tendency is a breath of fresh air. Maybe there was something a little mindlessly ceremonial in journalists regularly recasting people's statements to make them sound like Mr. Darcy.

But then I suspect that most of us feel that there is something amiss in the dumbing down of textbook passages over the decades, or how readily our educational establishment, of all bodies, has concurred with

Richard Atkinson's dismay at seeing American children being taught big words. Okay, the McGuffey's passage about quail was a bit much, like the mile-high wigs women wore in Louis IV's court. But when a guiding cultural imperative casts the elaborated written layer of English as a meaningless falsity, we risk drifting away from an aspect of language that is part of being human.

Written language, after all, has its advantages. A written standard variety, taking advantage of the permanent treasure-box of vocabulary over the centuries termed the dictionary, allows a degree of precision and nuance that spoken language usually does not—or only can via long-winded specification that written language can pull off in a few strokes. Take the range of synonyms for *help*: *aid, assist, abet, succor, relieve, support, accommodate*. These words convey shadings of a core meaning that are useful to careful expression. It's not that spoken language cannot convey some nuances of its own—think of the difference between *help* and *help out*, the latter connoting a certain intimacy between the participants and/or carrying an implication that the helpee is in an inferior, mendicant position ("Come on, can't you help me out?"). But a written variety surpasses the spoken one on this score because writing allows the preservation of any word that happens to make it into the language. Construct a sentence with *abet* and then try recasting the sentence without using that word, relying on *help* plus modifiers and descriptives. To insert *abet*'s connotation of helping someone in a malevolent activity, one must resort to more verbiage—as the listener taps his foot waiting to interrupt. That's the messiness inherent to speaking; writing gets past this.

To the extent that we sense the ample use of big words in speeches as pretentious, largely relegate their printed use to small-circulation journals and academic prose, spare them to schoolchildren out of a sense that doing so is unengaging or that black kids' and immigrants' histories ought give them a pass on learning any more than necessary of the language of a nation that gives them less-than-perfect lives, and discourage their use in poetry in favor of accessibility, we marginalize the outer layers of our language's vocabulary. In this we risk essentially losing much of our language. Culture lives by the generation, and words that live only in the dictionary or on word-a-day calendars are, in essence, dead.

It isn't hard to sense the fusty and the elitist in such a concern. But let's pull the camera back. French Revolutionary writers, drilled the old-fashioned way in the art of rhetoric, wrote gorgeous prose in quill and ink, the original pages often devoid of cross outs. For all we sense the drilling as an antique imposition, few of us can resist a twinge of envy and wonder at this kind of writing culture compared to ours. Or let's pull the camera back further. We warmly cheer the indigenous tribesman who, taught to write, diligently goes about working to preserve as many of the "old words" as possible—even if the language was under no threat of extinction. He is burnishing his articulateness, flexing the muscles of his humanity.

And, he is preserving his culture. We also sense the French Revolutionary writers as not only wielding verbiage, but communicating significant ideas, singing to the world rich, deathless arguments that, in that case, served as a foundation for the political ideals that, though never realized ideally, continue to shape our own American lives for the better. Written language is an artifice uniquely well suited to imparting substantial concepts. We dilute and narrow their transmission down the generations to the extent that we treat literary words and sentence constructions as square and irrelevant. We leave open the space for fantasies such as the current one that the visceral, staccato, theatrical musings of rap music constitute the rhetorical basis for a vaguely conceived sociopolitical revolution. Neither the French Revolutionary writers nor our Founding Fathers would have been able to understand how a sincere quest for political reform could scorn painstakingly wielded language beyond the level of talking.

And in that vein, what about our *old* words? Even after Thomas Jefferson's writings about black people while sleeping with Sally Hemmings, even after the Haymarket Riots, even after Henry Kissinger, the English language remains as rich a cultural token as the tribesman's obscure language. Americans' native language is draped in two thousand years of history, during which it has drunk in hundreds of thousands of words from countless languages, assigned them a majestic array of bracingly specific and subtle meanings, and served as the vehicle for arguments that resonate worldwide as advances for humanity, from the Magna Carta to the Bill of Rights to Martin Luther King, Jr.'s "I Have a Dream" speech. We genuflect to Shakespeare as our bard. But if we really mean this, then we must realize that our chariness of reveling in the possibilities of English beyond the spoken sets us off sharply from Shakespeare himself and the linguistic culture he lived in.

Turgenev's poetic line *velikiy, mogučiy russkiy jazyk* "great, mighty Russian language" is as well known among Russians as "Honey, I'm home!"

is to Americans. Sure, we might read someone writing "I know in my heart that the English language is the finest instrument the human race has ever devised to express its thoughts and feelings." But then, the writer Princeton Orientalist Bernard Lewis was born and raised in London.

CHAPTER FIVE

What Happened to Us?

or

Play That Funky Music, White Folks

I hope to have shown that we live in an America with a distinctly different relationship to the English language than an America still within living memory. To return to Bugs Bunny, anyone who remembers *Hiawatha's Rabbit Hunt* will also recall the other cartoon when a portly store clerk corners Bugs and says, "Kind of outsmarted ya', ay, little chum? Hee hee hee-eh!" and Bugs says "Hey! You sound just like dat guy on da radio—da Great Gildersneeze!"[16]

Bugs was referring to Hal Peary's Throckmorton P. Gildersleeve character, whose radio show *The Great Gildersleeve* was as big a hit in the 1940s as *Everybody Loves Raymond* has been since the mid-1990s. In one episode, Gildy (as we fans of the show know him) is smitten with a lady and writes her love poems, such as:

> Two eyes of blue,
> cheeks soft as silk,
> a skin as white as Grade A milk,
> a neck as graceful as a swan,
> a step as dainty as a fawn,
> the girl I mean is quite a looker,
> her name is Miss Amelia Hooker.

[16.] This one is *Hare Conditioned* (1945).

The audience laughs warmly.

The significance of this scene requires fast-forwarding for a bit to the late eighties. The *Saturday Night Live* routines where Jan Hooks and Nora Dunn played the Sweeney sisters doing cheesy, desperate medley duets registered at a time when performers like Steve and Eydie Gormé were memories just twenty years old—too far back to be relevant, but recent enough for a parody to hit home. If you think about it, no one would create such a skit today because the target of the parody is now ancient history. Today's young people never knew the glitzy variety shows where people did these medleys straight—nor would many even quite know what *medley* even meant.

In the same way, even in 1942 the poetry sequence mocked Gildersleeve for being a tad cornball, as it would have been put at the time. Yet today the joke would make no sense at all—Ross on *Friends* would never write love poems to a woman he was dating. But the joke made sense in 1942 because this was a world where carefully structured verse still had a certain presence and value in society. Four months after this episode aired, the same network *The Great Gildersleeve* appeared on would broadcast Edna St. Vincent Millay's poem on Lidice.

Or to return to prose: Later in that decade, publicity photos for the radio series *Our Miss Brooks*, featuring Eve Arden as a small-town schoolteacher, would show Miss Brooks in front of a blackboard plastered with grammatical terms. It was assumed that a schoolteacher taught her charges how to create prose in a form beyond the level of the spoken, whose mastery required careful tutelage. *Our Miss Brooks* was a solid hit and went on to further success as a television show. But today, a television series about a teacher would never have publicity photos with the teacher standing in front of a blackboard full of sentence diagrams. Showing a teacher foisting rigorous, abstract rules upon her students' self-expression would be seen as imperiling the character's likeability and "relevance." For a good while, the UC Berkeley website's homepage featured a photo of a teacher standing before a classroom, smiling warmly. Crucially, in the shot she filled the frame, blocking the blackboard itself. The message seemed to be that her personal approachability—very much real in my friend Jane Stanley—was more important in Berkeley's public image than showing her actually imparting mechanical skills.

Or back to oratory: In George S. Kaufman's and Morrie Ryskind's script for the musical *Let 'Em Eat Cake* in 1933, an airheaded, opportunistic general runs for president against the show's protagonist. At one point, he makes a speech, which goes like this:

> On the Fourth of July exactly one hundred and . . . More! . . . exactly *more* than one hundred years ago, Christopher Columbus and his sturdy little band of Pilgrim fathers . . . and mothers . . . landed on Bunker Hill. In the words of the immortal James M. Beck, it cannot be said that if we are advancing from an old order to a new that such a fate was not within the anticipation of the fathers. Washington, in his farewell Address, furthermore said . . .

But what kind of speech is being parodied here? There is no modern equivalent. In 1933, presidential candidates really did deliver speeches pitched like dramatic soliloquies. But today, we would never parody a campaign speech in language of this kind—because no public figure who wanted to get elected could use it.

The Onion brilliantly parodies the difference between then and now in an item from a mock issue of November 5, 1908, subtitled "Public Attention, When Directed to Republican's Mid-Section, Provides Humorous Diversion," describing a comedian pioneering the tradition of making jokes at the president's expense:

> As 400 theatergoers struggled to rein in the enthusiasm of their amusement, Mr. Dugan noted that Mr. Taft "might very well resolve the Italo-Turkish imbroglio were it not for his tendency to employ his time in more gastronomic endeavors." The ribald Dugan added that he was "concerned that our beloved leader may perhaps be violating his own strict policy of deploring trusts of all kinds—for I have heard that at formal banquets, he is known to seek monopolies on many of the delectables." Again, the audience in attendance erupted in merriment.

The exquisite thing about this parody is that it is barely an exaggeration. Even in 1908 no comedian talked like that, but as we have seen, journalists regularly wrote people's statements up to sound not unlike this man's "jests and japes," as the parody has it. And as for the newspaper's writing style, someone at *The Onion* has clearly spent some long afternoons browsing microfilm of newspapers of this era, as the parody beautifully summons the prose feel.

I have argued that the change traces to the triumph of the counter-culture in the 1960s. But there are other explanations that tempt us that I believe are red herrings.

Plus Ça Change?

It is important to always ask, for example, whether or not a phenome-non someone locates in recent memory is actually just old news. It can look as if until the pill, couples having sex before marriage was a rare and unspeakable practice. This is what the public sense of propriety dic-tated, and most of what an era left us before the sixties was the official: movies written under decency codes, stern laws on the books, things the relatives just "don't talk about," etc. But if we open our eyes we learn the truth. We compare the wedding anniversaries of quite a few elderly cou-ples with the birthday of their first child and do the math. When people about my age (thirty-seven as I write) are able to talk to their parents adult-to-adult, we often find out that not only Dad but also Mom had more than one lover before getting married despite being B.C. products, and that this was not considered extraordinary at the time. We learn that more than a few Puritan women were not exactly virgins on their wed-ding day and still fell within the classification as respectable ladies. It's certainly less risky to have premarital sex nowadays, and it's safe to say that the typical middle-class newlywed is likely to have more notches al-ready on their bedpost than they would have fifty years ago. But the dif-ference between then and now is not as stark as we might think.

But I hope to have shown that the change I refer to in this book is a real one. It is true that the linguistic America of 1900 did not thrive un-changed until one day in 1964. By then, oratory no longer sounded like high-dudgeon theatrical performance, the fussy journalistic prose of the teens already sounded archaic, and no poets were singing their verses on CBS. And in general, since the 1600s there has even been a statistical drift in English toward more spoken writing in fiction, essays, and letters, as the numbers of middle-class readers swelled and drew written English away from its initial function as a confection for the educated elite.[17] Thus the change I am charting is typical in showing that history rarely

---

[17.] The article showing this actually treats British English, but gives all indication that the facts are the same for American.

provides us with maximally clean before-and-after cases; we can always identify groundwork being laid long before the break in the dam.

In this case, that commonplace opens the door for counteranalyses referring to well-explored developments in intellectual history writ large that held sway long before 1965. For example, an academic perspective might trace the change to the Enlightenment itself, which encouraged individualism and self-expression in human communications to a new degree.

But the Enlightenment transformed the entire Western world. Yet in Italy today, the norm for public speeches remains elaborated to an extent that would sound archaic in America; written German remains practically a different language from the spoken version; and Russians rattle off tightly metered poetry like auctioneers. Plus, in expressing one's self, simplification and vernacular flavor are but one of many possible choices. There was a time when Flaubert, very much a product of the Enlightenment, could casually intone that "One must not always think that feeling is everything. Art is nothing without form." Many of us immediately think "But what's 'form'? Who are we to say that 'Kum Ba Ya' has less 'form' than Tchaikovsky's Sixth?" But Flaubert would not have considered that a viable question, and in that, we reveal that the Enlightenment can serve as but a bare beginning of an explanation of our particularity.

And Flaubert also shows us that our version of the "preference for the primitive," as E. H. Gombrich termed it in reference to art history, only links to Romanticism in a distant, academic sense. Romanticism was about seeking the natural and the true by searching more widely—which translates for us as multiculturalism—and more deeply within the soul—which we recognize as individualism. But the Romantics were not seeking an escape from elaboration or coherency.

Surely the Romantics lustily broke the rules, and there were times when this meant relaxing the old strictures somewhat. In 1830, Victor Hugo's play *Hernani* infuriated its Parisian audience by allowing rhyming syllables to occur after the pause at the end of the line, off into the next line. But rhyme it remained. Elizabeth Bishop and Amiri Baraka this was not, and meanwhile Berlioz was writing symphonies in richer harmonic language and with lengthier, less four-square sequences than a Mozart would have quite understood, often leaving audiences and critics frustrated. The magisterial historian and cultural analyst Jacques Barzun parses the Romantics' works as leaving unchanged "the permanent condition of artistic creation: hours of solitary, painstaking work, much

acquired knowledge, long reflection and revision, which together increase mastery." Overall, it is hard to recognize meaningful precedents to
our modern American sense of language in Romantics like Pushkin,
Emerson, Wagner, or Wordsworth.

For instance, champion essayist William Hazlitt wrote an essay in
1822 he called "On familiar style," but his sense of "familiar" was actually a highly formal one, based on an idealized conception of speech:

> To write a genuine familiar or truly English style, is to write as
> any one would speak in common conversation, who had a thor-
> ough command and choice of words, or who could discourse with
> ease, force, and perspicuity, setting aside all pedantic and oratorical
> flourishes.

Hazlitt, then, was not calling for us to simply write more like we talk
casually, specifying of his conception of familiar style that "there is nothing that requires more precision." Even his argument itself is couched in
highly written language that hardly gives off the essence of a living,
snorting individual yanking at the ties that bind. It also bears mentioning that the American Transcendentalist brand of Romantic, such as Emerson and Thoreau, for all their concern with the natural evinced little
interest in the folk. The elevation of the masses over the classes was not
their issue. The Romantics sought to get real, but not to get down.

Thus Melville will be of little use to us in figuring out what has happened to American English. The 1960s witnessed a unique phase shift in
Americans' relationship to their language, a seismic lurch that leaves a
question as to just why, just then. It'd be a highly subtle business to distinguish a McCarthy speech from the fifties and Newton Minow's "vast
wasteland" speech from ten years later; and an issue of *Time* from 1950
reads just like one from 1960. But why is it that we can immediately
recognize Minow's speech or an issue of *Time* from 1960 as from the
old days, while if contemporary references were edited out, a Jane
Fonda speech or an issue of *Time* from the 1970s would be much harder
to place more precisely than sometime between the late sixties and
last week?

Pop Culture: Pop Goes the Language?

A ready answer might be that mass culture dumbed down public language in the interests of reaching the pockets of as wide a swath of the audience as possible. But the timing is off.

Pop Culture Did Not Start with the Boob Tube

By the late 1920s, movies were already a multimillion-dollar industry in America. Silent films can seem remote and ineffectual to us now, with the cartoonish acting passed down to us in prints often faded and flickering. But they registered as strongly to their audiences as our movies do to us now. They were shown at normal speed, not speeded up the way we often see them in clips on television, and in pristine, often color-tinted prints, accompanied by a swelling organ or even a full orchestra. The movies at this time were already very much a mass-culture phenomenon.

Yet when sound beset this thoroughly popcorn industry, the studios set a squadron of "elocution" teachers upon the actors. The idea was that performing effectively for the public required learning how to speak clearly and "properly"—that is, in an unnatural way—and not just on the stage, but in Mr.-and-Mrs.-America movies equivalent to our *Sleepless in Seattle*s and *Titanic*s. A staple book on "elocution" from this time casually counsels Americans to speak in what reveals itself as a pure British accent.

And for the next forty years, American movie actors playing prominent roles, unless playing more vernacular sorts (comedians, gangsters, third bananas), tended to speak with an artificial diction derived from stage traditions of the era. One of the women in *Letter to Three Wives* (1949) grew up in a dump-water flat on the other side of the tracks. Yet despite her mother and the mother's friend speaking with good working-class accents, we are asked to believe that for some reason Linda Darnell talks like a Vassar graduate of the period.

Radio was also very much a mass-culture medium from the late twenties on. Throughout the thirties down to the end of the fifties, on the radio America delighted to versions of most of the genres now familiar from television. And yet radio maintained the same gulf between how people were presented speaking English versus how it was actually "spoke" casually. This was especially true in the twenties and thirties. In shows from this era, one of the oddest contrasts to a modern listener is between the minstrel dialect of Freeman Gosden and Charles Correll performing episodes of *Amos 'n' Andy* and the plummy tones of the show's announcer, Bill Hay. Hay, trilling the occasional *r* and reading from copy reminiscent of the kind of English used in magazines of the era, was so staid and starchy that his voice is the perfect aural summation of a tuxedo.[18]

That even against plausibility, the American pop industry insisted on linguistic corsetting so consistently for so long weakens any simple equation between McCulture and a change in linguistic norms.

But Still, My God, Television!

This also applies to the easy score of blaming television. This explanation appeals to us in view of the CNN newscasters I have mentioned, or the chintzy vulgarity of the *Survivors*, *Jerry Springers*, and *The Gong Shows*. But first, as Marshall McLuhan told us, television is a "cool" medium. It's a boxy screen across the room that we can't talk to and that can't talk to us. The coolness is especially obvious in its lack of effect on beings just a few rungs below our level of consciousness: Even looking straight at the screen, dogs and cats don't perceive its mirroring of life as we know it. Though the effects of television on our society are profound, can we really say that anything we have seen on the tube has affected the way we construct sentences in a speech or the way we write?

And in addition, it's easy to forget that from the early fifties through the mid-sixties, television was already a staple in American life. The couch potato was settled in by the mid-fifties. The tube had already become an electronic babysitter for children. Television shows and personalities were already deeply ensconced enough in the nation's consciousness by the fifties to be sentimentally and lucratively celebrated in the nostalgia craze of the 1970s. The Baby Boomers are regularly designated the first generation raised on television.

[18.] Most who have heard the show are likely to know it from its half-hour sitcom version, which did not include Hay. Hay announced on the show's original incarnation as a fifteen-minute daily serial, the version that went down in legend as mesmerizing George Bernard Shaw and forcing cinema owners to pipe it into their theaters to avoid losing business when the show aired.

But this era's television was a highly buttoned-up medium, both culturally and linguistically. The television culture that would only tape Elvis Presley from the waist up was one where, beyond self-consciously proletarian personae like comedians, people did not talk like real people to nearly the extent modern television characters do. This was a TV world of Wonder Bread couples in pristine houses speaking an English straight out of reading primers, of cowboys who used "proper grammar" except for the occasional Westernism, hyperbland newscasters speaking a faceless "Midwestern" English, and hour-long drama shows presenting primmish, WASPy playlets. Yet even this early, it was mass culture indeed, all about money. From day one, network television was essentially entertainment between commercials, many of which hold up today better than the shows themselves.

From Elvis's Hips to America's Lips?

Nor can we blame the focus of advertisers and the media on youth culture since the sixties.

Not that this shift is not real. In 1955, Noel Coward and Mary Martin performed a twee ninety-minute musical TV special called *Together with Music*. Coward was fifty-five in a tux and Martin was forty-one in a gown. This was two middle-aged people (forty-one was older then than it is now) performing coy, twinkly music with no sex, no nose-thumbing at President Eisenhower and his Cold War, no putting it out there. Yet it was a huge hit; you could buy an LP of the special in stores a few weeks later. This kind of thing was ordinary then—only in the seventies would the equation between celebrity and youth become default (Marie Dressler was America's top star for two years in the early thirties, when she was not only in her sixties, but looking and acting like it!). Television has little time for such geriatric affairs these days.

We see the transition in the two versions of Rodgers and Hammerstein's one made-for-film musical, *State Fair*. The original of 1945 is an apple-cheeked, sexless thing, all sugar and prize pigs and sunshine and Dick Haymes. The remake in 1962, however, winks at the youth market that had been eating up Elvis Presley's musicals, and has Ann-Margret tossing her hair around, gyrating in her tight pants, on her way to costarring with The King himself two years later in *Viva Las Vegas*.

But this remake also shows why for our purposes, the youth market alone is less an explanation than a symptom. Sexy pants is about all the action you get in the *State Fair* remake, which is overall an anodyne piece of work, pairing Ann-Margret with, well, Pat Boone. The youth culture that Madison Avenue first fetishized did not contrast with the preceding generation nearly as starkly as it would just ten years later. Ann-Margret's project between *State Fair* and *Viva Las Vegas* was the film version of *Bye Bye Birdie* (1963), which indeed depicted adults exasperated at "Kids" nowadays, including their language ("Kids! Who can understand anything they say?"). But this referred to cute slang, used within the same basic language the adults were speaking. The teens in *Bye Bye Birdie* were not James Deans; they were just "going through a phase," and grew up to become the Brady parents ten years later.

And this was how teenagers had long been depicted in the entertainment media. Only in the late sixties did we start seeing a generation talking in a radically different way than the previous one. Negative evidence can be striking: One episode of the radio show *Dr. Christian* in 1939 (closest equivalent within memory: *Marcus Welby, M.D.*) dwells on what would later be called the generation gap between a mother and her tomboy daughter. Yet the daughter is portrayed as speaking the same crisp, schoolbook kind of English as her mother, despite that it would have been dramatically effective to toss in a linguistic sign of the conflict—especially in a purely aural medium. And crazy teens on old radio always sounded like this: maybe a little hopped-up, a little "Daddy-O," but basically well on their way to sounding like Marcus Welby when they get older. There was a numbing procession of radio shows featuring such adolescents: Older readers will recall *The Aldrich Family*, *Meet Corliss Archer*, *A Date with Judy*, *Junior Miss*, etc. Most of us can get an idea of what the teenaged girl sounded like on radio in this period via Judy Jetson, voiced by Janet Waldo in the same voice she had used for Corliss Archer.

Only in the fifties did we see Marlon Brando and James Dean talking in the alienated, slurring way we associate with the young today, flouting the rules of standard grammar. But even then, they, like the Beat poets of the era, were odd ducks; most teens on TV, radio, and cinema screen at the time were still talking like their parents. Brando romanced the crisply spoken Eva Marie Saint in *On the Waterfront* in 1954. The following year *Rebel Without a Cause* paired James Dean (whose sulky slur has a lot to do with how effectively Dean speaks to contemporary young people) with patent-leather-perfect Natalie Wood, and asked us to accept him as the child of Jim Backus, whose round, showy, vocal tone later made him so natural as patrician Thurston Howell on *Gilligan's*

Island. And *Gilligan's Island*'s star Bob Denver had made his mark earlier in the sixties as beatnik Maynard G. Krebs on the marvelous sitcom *The Many Loves of Dobie Gillis*. But Maynard was depicted not as having the inside track on reality à la Jack Kerouac, but as a lovably confused singleton—and his speech, while bedecked with beat slang, was crisply enunciated and usually dutifully grammatical.

It was not until the late sixties that we started seeing the entertainment media regularly depict teens out-and-out rejecting the way their parents spoke. The tune-in-drop-out speaking style and slumped posture of the laggard teenaged son Francis in Mel Lazarus's comic strip *Momma* in the seventies was an emblem of the new reality. The scene was set for especially resonant depictions such as the speaking style of Sean Penn's Spicoli in *Fast Times at Ridgemont High* (1982).

Thus it is less that Madison Avenue zeroed in on youth already speaking in a new way than that youth started speaking in a new way afterward; the change took place later. Of course we might ask whether perhaps teens in the thirties, forties, and fifties were already talking like we know they were by Woodstock, but that public norms discouraged depicting this in dramatic representations. And it is true that fictional representations can deceive, especially those from an era when the gap between the public and the private was so much vaster. But this only brings us back to a question. If teens were already talking like Dennis Hopper before the sixties—and all evidence suggests that they weren't, but still—just why was it considered so beyond the pale to render their actual ways of speaking more faithfully until about 1967? What changed was the culture and its public norms.

Immigrant Nation, Cultural Degradation?

Jacques Barzun has opined that what caused the eclipse of high cultural forms in America was our status as an immigrant country. He proposes that our history has meant that by definition, our peoples are all uprooted from the kind of indigenous, eternally passed-down traditions that preserve, for example, Russians' relationship to their poetry. But ingenious as this analysis is, when it comes to the specific issue of what happened to English in America, again, timing. We have been a melting pot of strays from square one, and this was especially visible at the turn of the twentieth century after waves of immigrants had poured in from Southern Europe for decades and Manhattan was as polyglot a town as it is now. Yet at this very time, a ruling class, themselves descended from erstwhile immigrants uprooted from Northern European folkways, maintained a public linguistic standard that seems almost otherworldly to us.

Thus mass culture, even aimed at the young, can coexist with an elevation of "written" English. Clearly both television and movies began changing profoundly in the late sixties—but this only brings us back to the fact that the driving factor was something larger than them.

Other Garden Paths

Schools Are Beside the Point

But of all the explanations that tempt us, none are more misleading than the education crisis. The fact that American schooling no longer stresses refined language skills is a symptom of a cultural shift, not its cause. Despite my association with education issues because of topics treated in some of my writings, I would be dismayed if this book were read as a tract on education.

For one thing, to locate the change in education leaves an explanatory gap. To identify conditions that created a national mood swing and then place education as a symptom presents a causal sequence. But to simply trace the change to language-arts teaching going to pieces leaves the question as to just why it did so in the sixties—while the obvious cultural sea change at the same time sits staring us in the face as an explanation. The nut of this book, then, is the American soul, not classroom pedagogy. We can only address the latter within an awareness that it is nested in something larger, and will not change significantly—if we want it to—without an awareness of the full nature of the issue. We must maintain a holistic perspective, as it were.

Certainly the education problem is real. We're all familiar with the usual complaints: "For a long time I have noted with regret the almost entire neglect of the art of original composition in our common schools . . . hundreds graduate from our common schools with no well-defined ideas of the construction of our language." But then that observation was made in 1841, by a county superintendent of schools. And then thirty years later, Harvard president Charles Eliot's crusade to reform the English program was a response to the observation that "Bad spelling, incorrectness as well as inelegance of expression in writing, ignorance of the simplest rules of punctuation, and almost entire want of familiarity with English literature, are far from rare among young men of eighteen otherwise well prepared for college studies." In 1917, a schoolteacher in Connecticut, sounding much like someone writing a letter to the editor of a local newspaper today, noted "From every college in the country goes up the cry, 'Our freshmen can't spell, can't punctuate.' Every high school is in despair because its pupils are so ignorant of the merest rudiments." And then the year after the *Together with Music* TV special in 1955, an English professor at a small college was ruing: "College teachers are suffering increasing frustrations from the astonishing ignorance of entering classes, whose members often know little or nothing of the fundamentals of all education . . . many do not know the alphabet or multiplication table, cannot write grammatically, and seem to have been trained to hate mental exercise . . . often they cannot read intelligently, and dislike any reading."

Thus the first problem with treating education as the culprit is the *plus ça change* issue—people across America have been shaking their heads about the condition of our schools forever. But then on top of this, even these comments give hints of cultural changes larger than education itself. Eliot's disparagement of "inelegance of expression" barely translates into modern pedagogical terms—imagine a college president daring to express such a naked judgment today. In Eliot's America, the crafting of the languge was still valued as a matter of course. Or, catch the 1841 writer's "the construction of *our* language," with its sense of English as a national possession. The contrast is sharp with the modern educators in Chapter Four questioning the very priority of the English language in American curricula, and casting a gimlet eye on "imposing" upon students the nuances of the standard variety of the language. These modern teachers didn't pull this ideology out the thin air; they are products of a national zeitgeist.

In any case, to attribute this change to education would have required that the phase shift happen twenty years after it did. America started speechifying and writing in a different way in the sixties—but the ringleaders of the change were, if in their mid-twenties at the time, educated in the forties and fifties. And the Beat poets were educated as far back as the thirties. If the decline in classroom standards in the sixties was the cause, then technically we would expect the change to have first become noticeable in the eighties when students educated under the new regime came of age.

Nor will the school funding crises that increased in the sixties serve as an explanation in themselves. A comprehensive international survey of schoolchildren's performance in various areas including language skills recently revealed that Finland's education system is one of the most effective in the world. Yet Finland is not a wealthy country. One of the factors analyzed as crucial to their sterling showing is cultural homogeneity. Partly because heavy immigration has been relatively recent and partly because Finland has had minimal geopolitical influence, Finns' esteem of their nation is much less ambivalent than ours. Thus, there is less of a sense that to teach Finnish rigorously is to impose or restrict. On the contrary, Finns treat their language as a national treasure, like most smaller nations. Culture matters in Finland, just as it does here.

And finally we return to the fact that in any case, formal language does not require formal schooling—people who say *dog* and only picture one instead of imagining the written word quite often break out high-flying varieties of their languages on special occasions. Meanwhile, literate cultures often cherish high language, as we once did, and as, for example, Italy still does. Our leeriness of elaborate language is less about teacher's unions and property taxes than about us.

English-Only Versus Loving English

Two other false leads. We might see a contradiction to my claim that Americans do not love their language in the English-Only movement's opposition to bilingual education, dismayed at the prospect of massive numbers of immigrants coming to our shores without ever learning English. We could even bring in the less mannered claims one often hears from certain Americans that anyone who doesn't want to learn English should just "get the f**k outta da country!"

But the latter sentiment is more xenophobia than any particular affection for the English language. Many read the same motivation in the English-Only movement. But a more tempered interpretation, more consistent with representatives' actual statements, is that these people are worried that immigrants are hobbled from success in American society if they do not learn English. It is unlikely that the Chilean immigrant

Mauro Mujica, multilingual head of the U.S. English lobbying organization, is secretly moved by an animus toward Mexicans and Puerto Ricans or the fact that they speak a language other than English.

The English-Only position has its problems. Those worried about large numbers of people passing on foreign languages to their children in the United States are misled by the fact that English alone has long been so widely spoken in this country. We tend to sense second languages as impinging on a natural state somehow, whereas most people elsewhere in the world are bilingual or multilingual. Two or more languages in one brain is not analogous to cramming two or more families into one apartment. And contrary to what one often hears, bilingual education is in fact an effective concept in itself. Most defenses are too caught up in identity politics to speak beyond the already converted, but see Stephen Krashen's *Condemned Without a Trial: Bogus Arguments Against Bilingual Education* for a short, informed (and inexpensive) explanation that keeps the sociopolitics on the back burner. In practice, many such programs in America have been too poorly run to usher students into English effectively—but this hardly gainsays the solid successes of well-run bilingual education programs around the world.

But overall, the English-Only crowd do not contradict my claim that to be American is to not love one's language. One detects no impassioned defenses of the marvels of the English language in this movement's statements, of the kind that bedeck the literature of language-revival movements in Ireland, Wales, or New Zealand, or that speakers of foreign languages often present. English-Only sentiments, however one feels about them, are one part linguistic naïveté and one part age-old ed debates. They are not about language love.

Can a Superpower Love Its Language?

Then a final cause we might look to is our country's geopolitical dominance. Typically, language love thrives most in countries that have lived under threat from others. Just as our life passes before our eyes in dire situations, the threat of erasure leads a country to enumerate and cherish the traits unique to it. Naturally language, so idiosyncratically indigenous to a particular group, takes pride of place—no one speaks anything remotely like Albanian anywhere but in Albania. Americans obviously sense no such threat (or at least did not until recently), and perhaps we could take this as an explanation for why we just don't give a fig for our language. One support for this analysis would be that before America had achieved its current station, many thinkers devoted themselves to fashioning a uniquely American language to set us off from Great Britain. Noah Webster's spelling reforms and dictionary were driven by such a sentiment, for example.

But there are two problems. One, America began bestriding the world under Theodore Roosevelt's militaristic watch in the aughts, and yet as we have seen, America's attitude toward English only changed sixty years later. Even acknowledging historical lags, six decades is a long time—especially when in the sixties there was, after all, a salient transformation of societal ideology, quite opposite to jingoism, that would seem to have had at least something to do with the change.

Two, during the Cold War our country doggedly defined itself against what was presented as a mighty foe ever poised to blow us into outer space. And yet if anything, this was when the cracks in the plaster emerged on the language scene in America. It's hard to see a link between our blasé attitude toward English and our sense of invulnerability when Allen Ginsberg wrote *Howl* within a few years of Nikita Krushchev's being shown in living rooms across the nation pounding his shoe on a podium growling "We will bury you" (or actually, "We will be present at your burial.").

Talking—About My Generation

It has become something of a cliché these days to blame cultural phenomena on the sixties. Yet the evidence in this case convinces me that this is indeed the locus of a profound transformation in how Americans relate to the language they speak. I might note that having known no life before the late sixties and having no substantial memories before about 1970, I did not pass through the sixties set in the ways of another time and set on edge by my world's turning upside down. As fascinated as I am by the past in a fetishistic way—I'd clean out my bank account to spend just one week in New York in 1936—I am too much a product of my times to reject the countercultural revolution out of hand as a regrettable aberrance. Without it, after all, my life would not have lent me the wherewithal to write, much less publish, this book. For example, I'd take out a loan on top of cleaning out my bank account to make it so that I spent my week in 1936 as a white, middle-class WASP.

All the same, I am intrigued by the fact that if we were to insist on pegging a single year as the one when America lost its love for its language, it would be precisely the year I was born, 1965. It just happens that this is around when color became default on television and in films, such that a childish part of me sees America before 1965 in black and white and America afterward in a whole new world of Kodacolor. I often half-want to ask people older than me what it was like when they woke up one morning and the world was in color.

And I also kind of want to ask them whether they noticed that America used language differently once color was invented. Of course no one did notice; it was a gradual change. But once there was color, a new way of relating to our country and our lives started edging out the Camelot consensus. Louis Menand eloquently sums up the new ethos:

> We longed for an expressive form that would combine the urgency and excitement of a musical concert with the cool detachment of an art without illusions. We wished for energy and imagination without pretension, for entertainment that did not pander and art that was not antagonistic to commercialism, merely indifferent to it. I suppose we hoped to strike such a balance in our own lives.

Detachment, no pretension, indifference to commercialism, striking a balance between this and the reality of having children and putting them through college: This is us. Here, for example, is born the current connotation of the word *attitude* and the hoops modern English has put it through. *Bad attitude* is a positive, or at least titillating trait, indicating that one is hip enough to reject the models foisted upon us from the suits upstairs. When I was in college, a petite woman dancing in feisty hip-hop style in a musical production was affectionately labeled "pigtails with an attitude" by the cast. And here, then, is the reflexive distrust of the legitimacy of our nation now considered a mark of sophistication in educated circles: "Question Authority" bumperstickers proliferated in the late 1980s, but would have stuck out like a sore thumb on the back of a Chevy Bel Air.

Certainly this isn't altogether new. Reading the thirty thinkers trashing the United States as far back as 1922 in Harold Stearns's anthology

Civilization in the United States: An Inquiry by Thirty Americans, one sees an early prototype of the "tenured radical" in Stearns's excoriation of our:

> emotional and aesthetic starvation, of which the mania for petty regulation, the driving, regimentating, and drilling, the secret society and its grotesque regalia, the firm grasp on the unessentials of material organization of our pleasures and gaieties are all eloquent stigmata.

But then note that Stearns wrote that in a kind of English that sounds like it was translated from academic German. Stearns still felt legitimately bound by stringent linguistic standards that we have long since rejected as oppressive and even distasteful. The anti-American literati of Stearns's America were more taking America to task for its lapses from an ideal than condemning it conclusively as a moral monstrosity in its very origins. George Jean Nathan, Van Wyck Brooks, Ring Lardner, and other contributors to Stearns's book were not ashamed to be American. Brought to life, they would strike most modern intellectuals as insufficiently hip to the multiculti groove we now take as default.

And in 1922, even the temperate anti-Americanism of these writers had yet to penetrate the national spirit. Menand writes of an era when ordinary Americans' trust in their government began its plummet from 76 percent in 1964 to just 44 percent in 2000, according to the University of Michigan National Election Studies project. On September 12, 2001, I could not imagine blithely traipsing through my lecture; the injury was still raw, and according to what was known in the days immediately after the terrorist attack, not just three thousand but *ten* thousand people had died in New York. So I devoted my class to discussing the tragedy. I will never forget one student casually saying "I just wish that if they were going to kill all those people they could have gotten that *idiot* in the White House too . . ." She was no Sproul-Plaza-placard-waving firebrand sort, just a modern undergraduate hip to the signs o' our times, and half the class applauded her.

That's our America. When William McKinley was shot in Buffalo in 1901, a healthy mob wanted to lynch Leon Czolgosz for his crime. If anyone shot George W. Bush under similar circumstances, while mores have evolved such that no one would want to hang the assassin from a tree, would a cluster of men even crowd in to beat the man up? Even at a Republican event? One just might object that such a scenario is plausible, and I see the point. Open-hearted patriotism runs high among Republicans, given that they have been on the ideological defensive for so long. But it's by no means a no-brainer point, and then—would a crowd of Democratic voters have done the same if Bill Clinton had been shot? Here, I would confidently say no. And the sum total of the two hypothetical scenarios shows that our feelings about our leaders are cooler, more layered today. We don't feel them in our gut—or if we do, it is only on the basis of their foibles and shortcomings (Clinton the ho', GW the moron, etc.).

And this distance from our leaders signals an alienation from public norms, which naturally elevates the informal as the true. On *I Love Lucy*, the announcer gave the names of an episode's guest stars as the credits rolled: "Freddie Fillmore was played by Mister Frank Nelson," he would say. "*Mister*"!—it sounds like something from the *Titanic*. But fifty years later, characters on *Friends* would be casually referring to peeing, and never do we hear of "Mister David Schwimmer."

Living Color

We're in an America in color—literally. The falling away of the color line since the sixties has also fed into our new sense of language. Of all of the spoken varieties of English in our country, African-Americans' falls further from mainstream standard English than any other. African slaves brought to America stirred together West Indian patois and the English dialects of white indentured servants from Britain and Ireland into a linguistic gumbo of their own, now called Black English. Today, their great-great-great-great-grandchildren glide between this and standard English in the way they render our language.

Amidst the rise of the counterculture, as interracial contact increased and deepened, inevitably this way of speaking took on a powerful mystique. Black American culture emerged in poverty and segregation, and it became a more immediate presence in mainstream life within a context of strident and justified protest by whites and blacks alike. Once a quorum of whites no longer processed blacks as a world apart, this dialect was easily incorporated into the new ideological toolkit—no dialect in America was more readily interpreted as a charismatic gesture of alienation from the reigning culture. Naturally, many white Americans began seeing Black English as where it's at rather than as a mere, quaint,

Southern dialect. As a result, whites who in 1997 chuckled at the Oakland school board's claims that Ebonics is a separate language were at the same time singing the songs they held dearest with vowels, cadence, and even grammar straight from the Ebonics playbook.

Yes, they were. Sing to yourself one of the lyrics I presented as our true national poetry in the last chapter: "Please allow me to introduce myself, I'm a man of wealth and taste." It is unlikely that you sang it in the crisp articulation of a librarian. You sang "mah-self" rather than "migh-self," and "ahm a may-in" rather than "aym a man." In other words, you sang it like one of my Southern relatives, although you are more likely white than black and would never say "ahm a may-in" at the office or to a friend or even to a lover. Edith Piaf sang songs in the French she spoke; Astrud Gilberto sings in the Brazilian Portuguese she grew up with. Why are white Americans so given to suddenly shifting to a dialect they don't speak, of a race they don't belong to, when they sing pop music?

You think, well, that's the way Mick Jagger *sings* it, and that's the way I heard it, so how else could I sing it? But then why, really, does the English Mick Jagger sing like a black laborer from Mississippi? Or to bring it home, why do most white American rock and pop singers sing in a dialect they weren't brought up in? Donald Fagen was born in Passaic, New Jersey—what's with "Ah seen yaw pick-chuh / Yaw name in lahts abuhv it" (i.e., "I seen your picture / Your name in lights above it") in Steely Dan's "Peg"? Nobody white talks like that in Passaic (or black, for that matter, but you take my point).

Or—as you sang the Stones lyric or recalled the so-right jam of "Peg," you may well have started bouncing your head to the beat—but not in nodding style, but more in "chicken-walk" style, pushing your head forward from the neck. But white people in silent films do not bounce their heads to music this way, nor does your grandmother. Where did you get that groovy nod? White people picked this up from black people in the sixties (although a keyed-in few had already caught it as far back as the swing era of the thirties). Recall the inevitable guy down the hall in the dorm, given to going barefoot, who plays the guitar and writes his own songs. He was a white guy with long blond hair, probably named Todd. Recall that although Todd's English was typical white-guy white-bread Whatever, the second he started singing, all of sudden *going* was *goin'*, *you* was *yih-oo*, *isn't* was *ain't*, double negatives were okay. Where did this come from? It is not a given that humans switch to a dialect they didn't grow up with when they sing, and this was not the usual case among musical undergrads in America in the twenties, thirties, forties, or fifties . . . or even early sixties . . . just where might I be going here?[19]

And hence, "Play That Funky Music, White Boy," with all that lyric means to us. It's almost staggering how deeply idiosyncratic to the modern American sensibility those six words are. Every single word is full to bursting with subtle shadings that only we can fully drink in. *Play*—here we mean not just execute, like a Julliard piano student, but *play* it—"do it justice," "play it out." And why such a particular request? Well, *funky* is one of the keys to the puzzle—this is an urgent concept, the locus of our hearts; you're going into our *funkiness*. How would you explain to a foreigner what *funky* means? It conveys "down," "honest" with a dash of pungent scent and a sprinkle of sex. *Music*—certainly neither Mozart nor Dean Martin; the music we want the white boy to play is music we can dance to, and we mean *dance*, in a "Hell, it's Friday and I don't give a damn" way, raunch with poise. And now, even the little *that*, as in *That Funky Music*. The *that* conveys that it's *that* music that we folks in the know understand; it indexes that we, rather than the lame-o's and Republicans, are in on what the lyric means—we in our get-down, honest, "real" little home away from home. *White*—the nut is that we are game to watch him venture to produce and touch us with this music even though he's not of the race we associate the music with, and that we're all aware of the looming assumption that whites are at a disadvantage in channeling the spirit that makes the music live. We are cheering him on in getting in with the White Negro groove that Norman Mailer sang of, because in doing so he becomes real, that is, what we modern Americans consider "the shit." Then *boy*—a kind of diminishment, getting on the record that we see the fellow as operating at a disadvantage because he wasn't born with it, getting him back for the eons during which black

---

[19]. I think I may have witnessed the very last of the B.C. versions of Todd. His name actually was Todd, and he was a ninth grader at my school in Philadelphia in about 1980. He was a good guitar player, but leaned toward calm folk music and sang in his own, native, white-bread accent. A girl listening started asking him if he knew various current rock songs (skirtchasing is one of The Todd's main motivations), and I will never forget his response: "I don't know any of those *vulgar* songs!" He was a sunny guy and said this with a laugh—it didn't come off as haughty; he was no Mr. Mooney. But still, what an odd-duck judgment for anyone fifteen by then.

men were called "boy" by white bigots; now it's okay to tap *you* on the back of the head, White Boy, because the times have changed and now *we're* where it's at, so prove yourself, White Boy—but you know that we're only calling you "boy" in the same vein of affectionate diminishment that we call each other "nigger."

That was not some random Nick Tosches–style digression—all that really *is* tied up in that one phrase if you think about it. Imagine translating "Play That Funky Music, White Boy" into any other language. Obviously, "Perform with spiritual dedication the bewitchingly vernacular songs familiar to us, young Caucasian male" doesn't quite do the trick. "Play That Funky Music, White Boy" conveys a relationship to personal expression profoundly local to our country, with our history, in our times. The American modern gets down, on the pain of being marginalized as a reactionary irrelevance. "Play That Funky Music, White Boy" sums up modern American self-expression. In a way that would surprise an America before 1965, "Play That Funky Music, White Boy" is *us*.

Now, Black English is not "bad grammar"—but nor is it William Jennings Bryan's oratorical language, the language of Marian Anderson's letters to her husband, or the poetry of Edna St. Vincent Millay. It is at heart a *spoken* kind of English. Black English *can* be harnessed to elaboration—recall that James Baldwin poem, or the best of Spoken Word, or attend any of August Wilson's plays. But in its live, spontaneous, unadorned form, it is, in all its magnificence, a handy *alternative to* standard English. Cloaked as it is in the horrifically unjust history of the people raised in it, one can choose to hear every vibrant, melodious syllable uttered in Black English as Speaking Truth to Power. And in that, what would be strange is if this dialect had *not* made its way into the heart of mainstream America.

An American Tale or the Story of English?

Something making it especially clear that the issue here is American culture is the fact that the same language that we speak occupies a different place in the English soul. There is a perceptible contrast in language love between America and Britain. One could start with an oddly untranslatable statement. On a BBC radio show, the late conservative Parliament member Enoch Powell was once heard in a debate with rival Parliamentarian Michael Foot, ex-leader of the Labour Party, crowing "I don't agree with what he's saying, but I love him because he speaks perfect English!"

There are any number of backhanded compliments Bill Frist might give Tom Daschle in Washington, DC, but that is certainly not one of them. Now, Powell did bring a certain baggage along with that comment: He was a former classics scholar, and more to the point, was a notorious racist in the Archie Bunker vein, whose nativist views sat immobile as conventional wisdom moved forward. But then that meant that Powell had an old-fashioned, unreconstructed patriotism for his country—whose eclipse among most of today's thinking Americans, take it or leave it, is just what I believe has relegated our language love to the margins.

British sitcoms give another clue. The cream of them are festivals of verbiage in a way that American ones are not. To the American ear, one of the first impressions even of the second tier of them—say, *The Liver Birds*—is that the people *talk* so bloody much. *Fawlty Towers* scripts, for example, came in with almost twice the sheer text of a typical American sitcom script. Although some of the difference traces to American shows' timing out to only twenty-two minutes with commercials, *Fawlty Towers* and other British shows like *Are You Being Served?* and *To the Manor Born* were as relentlessly wordy as plays, overflowing with epigrams, wordplay, and virtual soliloquys. One can watch *Friends* while preparing dinner; try that with any of these three shows and notice that you can barely keep up with the plot. *To the Manor Born* was so resolutely verbal that sets and costumes seemed almost unnecessary, and there actually were radio performances of it after the television run ended.

Of course, most British sitcoms are not besotted with the joy of language to this degree—but then American sitcoms almost *never* are. *All in the Family*, wordy though it was, sailed on its performances and its topicality. I am aware of no one praising it for its writing per se, and minus the topicality it does not hold up very well. Its spin-off, *Maude*, featured Archie's strident liberal cousin, and its witty arguments over issues of the day were deft enough that a radio version may have made a certain sense—*Maude*'s star Bea Arthur is in every way the American equivalent of *To the Manor Born*'s Penelope Keith, for instance. But then the show is rarely syndicated today, and even when new, never made its way into Americans' hearts as Arthur's fluffier next hit *The Golden Girls* did.

I am aware of a single American sitcom that truly paralleled the high

Britcoms in reveling in charismatic wielding of the tongue. *Filthy Rich* of the 1982–83 season was a parody of then-popular prime-time soap operas like *Dallas*, and gave theatrically sized actors deliciously eloquent, festively bitchy scripts week after week. The show's campy bon mot sensibility was reminiscent of what makes Britcom fans out of many Americans, as well as what seduces the crowd who thrill to movies like *All About Eve* and *The Women* (both of which, note, are now ancient tokens of an America that had yet to take off its linguistic girdle). I will never forget my college roommate at the time, very much a member of said crowd, cherishing audiocassette tapes he had made of the shows from the TV speaker (in 1982 VCRs were still something of a novelty). But maybe two and a half readers will recall *Filthy Rich*—it was a quiet fizzle. Americans don't cotton to that kind of thing. Sure, one can venture a case for the occasional show—*Moonlighting* (though actually a "dramedy") and *Designing Women* come to mind (as it happens, both Delta Burke and Dixie Carter of this latter show had been in *Filthy Rich*). But will any cult admirers be quoting lines from these as the decades march on? Words for words' sake just isn't what any American television writer (who wanted to eat) would devote their energy to; it isn't what we are about. Another exception might be *The Simpsons*, whose scripts are eloquent enough to require attention as close as a top Britcom does. But then it's a cartoon. Try imagining a live sitcom so besotted with The Word: To Americans, language for its own sake resides in quotation marks.

But then there is a generation issue here. Enoch Powell was born in 1912, and thus his statement was that of a man of another time. And not only did *Fawlty Towers, Are You Being Served?*, and *To the Manor Born* run awhile ago now, but they all turned to some extent on the bafflement with a changing world of people who had reached middle age by the 1970s. In the Britain of today, "Wow, I love the way she uses English!" does not translate much more gracefully than it does in America.

The cult of the informal spread quite rapidly across the Atlantic to Britain, and is raging about as strongly there as here, with a similar impact on language. Gone are the days when class and education automatically meant using the classic Received Pronunciation of the BBC and Merchant-Ivory films. Estuary English, with its goodly helping of Cockney sounds and expressions, has penetrated British speech so deeply that not only members of the House of Commons but even the younger royals are now using it. One gets a glimpse of this as early as *Are You Being Served?*, a show where the class/language tension was especially front and center. Young staffers like Mr. Lucas and Mr. Spooner spoke what by the 1990s would be called Estuary English, and had no interest in speaking "up," where their equivalents in, say, the 1930s would have spoken at least a decent approximation of Received Pronunciation. But meanwhile middle-aged Mrs. Slocombe, born circa 1920, ranged self-consciously between Northern and posh according to mood. Edina and Patsy on *Absolutely Fabulous* speak perfect Estuary, while Edina's coiffed sixty-something mother sounds like the Queen Mum.

In this "Oh, behave!" atmosphere where posh speech is suspect, we would expect that general interest in English as an art would decline. Naturally, then, British cultural commentator Theodore Dalrymple tells me that to his ear, "Wow, I love the way she uses English!" is imaginable from a British person over fifty, but would be bizarre from anyone under forty.

But even so, if I may be so bold as someone who has never lived in Britain, I detect a remaining shade of difference between us and the British regarding how we view our language. One thing that tips me off is the radio show there called *Just a Minute*, where regulars and celebrity guests are challenged to speak on a topic—"Speaking in Tongues," "What I Was Like at Thirty-five"—for sixty seconds with no hesitations or repetitions. This is old-time American rhetoric training 101, and yet the show began in 1968, though Britain was then undergoing its own countercultural revolution, and has run continuously since. Even on our National Public Radio, nothing like this exists in the United States and I highly suspect could not: We just don't find wordplay and spontaneous articulateness as cute as the British do.

In this light, I did an experiment with this marvelous tool called the Internet. I typed "admire 'command of the English language' " into the Google search engine and looked at what it dredged up. I wanted to see if there was a greater tendency in Britain than in America to praise people for their facility in English. The result neatly revealed the difference I refer to, and shed some light on what has happened in America in the bargain.

As a sample, I used the first eight pages—eighty-two entries. I subtracted:

1. References to people who speak English as a second language.

2. Statements made in irony, such as a controversial commentator who reproduces an invective-laced missive she was sent and compliments him on his "command of the English language."

3. Entries that would not open for one reason or another.

In the end this left fourteen cases, a nice, processible set for our purposes.

Two of the fourteen entailed British people evaluating other British people. An evaluation of a reading course praises the command of the English language that it lent children; a British person praises the language in a book written by British people. I personally find both quotes hard to imagine as said by someone from Michigan.

Three others entailed Americans praising British English speakers, and this exemplifies the American sense that English with a British accent, especially spiked with trademark British reserve, is somehow better than American English. But this is just a random, culturally conditioned response to certain vowels, intonations, and word choices. It has no more *logical* basis than the fact that the color teal was modish on cars, appliances, and clothing in the United States in the early '90s but is not now. And this affection for British English—which I harbor as much as any American—is not, properly speaking, love of one's own language. To love your language as you heard it growing up is to nest; to prefer it rendered differently by people of another land is to travel. We cannot process the British accent as our language in the way that counts when we certainly do not think of Britain as home. We would not see French Canadians as loving their language if they preferred the Parisian accent to their own.

In the same way, then, we cannot see love of one's own language in the American in my survey who praises Patrick Stewart's "command of the English language," or in a reviewer who loves the prose of British Dorothy Sayers. Or, there is a writer on golf commentators in America who says:

> Ben Wright is best known in the golfing world for his many years of golf commentary with CBS. He and good friend Gary McCord livened up golf coverage with their incredible command of the English language—Wright's was more on the Shakespearean order while McCord's was closer to the "good ol' boy" dialect.

I found this so odd that I could not help doing some extra digging. The "Shakespearean" comment got my antennas up and, wouldn't you know it, Ben Wright is British, elsewhere described as having a "silky British" accent. And the comment on McCord is meant as ironic.

Then stateside, a book reviewer praises the "gorgeous" prose of Donald McCaig's Civil War novel *Jacob's Ladder*—but refers actually to McCaig's having couched much of the dialogue in "the cadences of the last century." That is, the reviewer is taken with the English style of a distant era—naturally, given how sharply that style contrasts with ours. This is an American marveling at a rendition of his tongue now virtually foreign, not at what a modern American would do with the language's current manifestation.

What about "command of the English language" as used in America and today? There are eight cases.

Two involve the elderly referring to the elderly—comments reflecting the orientation toward English of another time. In an obituary for former University of Michigan President Harlan Hatcher, economist Paul McCracken praises his "command of the English language." But Hatcher was born in 1898 and McCracken in 1915—both were raised and educated in a pre–Kent State America where elevated oratory still reigned. Sci-fi illustrator Edd Cartier says in an interview about L. Ron Hubbard that "To me it was fantastic that he had such a command of the English language that I didn't." But Cartier was born in 1914, educated thus in the twenties and thirties—the post–Pearl Harbor congressional speeches were still almost ten years in the future when he graduated from high school.

Another case is unclear: A certain educational lobbyist in Sacramento named Ed Silverbrand elicits a testimonial letter praising his English language skills—but Silverbrand's biography (serving in World War II) places his birth around 1920. The age of the testimonial writer is unrecoverable—but I wouldn't be surprised if it was a fellow World War II vet.

Elsewhere, a youngish reporter notes the articulateness of current Secretary of Defense Donald Rumsfeld—and rightly so; I have often noticed how gifted he is with language—but Rumsfeld was born in 1932, his language skills honed in the forties and fifties, long before the age of *Easy Rider*. That the reporter would even notice this is an exception, but then it also highlights that the public speaker minted before the 1960s is more likely to switch to a different, more written level of English.

What about praise of "command of English" for people whose lives have taken place largely after 1960s? There are four cases. One of many tributes to a deceased schoolteacher born in 1947 mentions his "command of English" on the basis of his facility with crossword puzzles and the large vocabulary he used in writing business letters. But this is a weak example—one can both love crosswords and know a lot of ten-dollar words without being a deft speaker or writer. This schoolteacher may well have had a true facility for self-expression, but this one comment about his more mechanical skills cannot let us know if he did.

In another example, someone on a chat list praises someone for his "command of English" for having posted a distinctly pedantic message highlighting certain aspects of blackboard grammar. But by "English," the person would appear to mean formal grammar rules rather than the more aesthetic kind of evaluation that interests us here.

A third is solid, though: a testimonial letter from one Austin, Texas, real estate agent on another praises the man writing that "His appearance, dress, demeanor, and command of the English language was always exemplary." This sounded so odd to me that I expected the subject of the praise to be either ninety or from Tibet. But he is in fact a white-guy American whose biography suggests he was born sometime in the 1950s. And the man who wrote the testimonial is not a whole lot older, from what his biography suggests. So there you go—It Can Happen Here. And even more than once: In the fourth and final example an American compliments a (Canadian) erotica writer for "a exemplary command of the English language." Even if the same could not be said of the writer, his statement still qualifies.[20] (Ironic, though, that *both* of the solid counterexamples are rendered in prose with what most would regard as compositional mistakes: The real estate agent says that in his subject, appearance, dress, demeanor, and command of the English language *was* always exemplary instead of *were*.)

But this means that out of a random sample of eighty-two Internet entries containing "admire" and "command of the English language," of fourteen that qualified as addressing the issue, a mere three entailed an American person enchanted with a living American's facility for squeezing the most out of the language in running, vivid use (as opposed to crossword puzzles), and only two referred to the speech of an American raised in the America we know, rather than one raised in a computerless,

---

[20.] It would be perfect Black or rural Southern English, actually. But the writer does not seem to be striking that kind of note—it looks more like a simple mistake.

Oldsmobile America when over 70 percent of the populace trusted the government.

And thus, it cannot surprise us that in England, rigorous formalism in poetry held on through the sixties much more than here, or that one of England's opera companies, the English National Opera, has always had a strict policy of performing all operas in translation, while some other big companies there have at least indulged their audiences with their own language on a variable basis. The Brits like English more than we do.

It is an especially American trait, then that, to quote Norman Podhoretz's once-controversial critique of the Beat movement, "To be articulate is to admit that you have no feelings."

CHAPTER SIX

La La La Through a New Lens:
Music Talks to America

A few years ago, a team of American paleontologists spent a few months in Egypt unearthing dinosaur skeletons. One night they attended a local tent concert. Two of them happened to be professional drummers on the side, and one sat in with the Egyptian drummers and fell in with their traditional beat. After a while he started embellishing here, slipping in a backbeat there. But each time, the Egyptian drummers would sweetly say *La, la, la!*—"No, no, no" in Arabic. The custom in Egypt is to stick to the format, its immutability felt as a symbol of communal heritage and survival—"We do it like this." But the drummer, as an American, felt a natural impulse in musicmaking to assert *"I do it like this."* He was a young man, suckled in an America that teaches the performer to channel the personal, Doing His Own Thing.

This is so natural to us today that we tend to think of it less as a choice than as a fundamental. But the little cultural conflict this drummer experienced in the very different culture of Egypt neatly illustrated a part of what it is to be American today.

"Spoken" Music and "Written" Music

Over the past two chapters as we have addressed poetry and lyrics, the discussion has touched increasingly on music over language. Naturally so, as music, a form of human expression, is a kind of language, and in this, it serves a purpose for this argument. I have claimed that the United States has undergone a shift in its relationship to self-expression that has had an effect beyond anything traceable to education or larger currents of intellectual history. If I am correct, then I should predict that this shift would include not only spoken and written language, but also music. Thusly predict I do, and the prediction is borne out. The musical sensibility of most Americans of Boomer age and younger parallels their sense of language, preferring the visceral, spontaneous, and elementary over the objective, planned, and elaborated.

After all, there is, in the terms we have used in this book, spoken music and written music, as it were. Like language, music of some kind is a human universal—all peoples have songs and instruments. And as with language, music in its pure state exists without notation; written music is a historical artifice. And it has its downsides: Musical notation systems are every bit as clumsy and approximate as writing systems. The Western musical notation system, for example, is a hidebound, often arbitrary peculiarity that we are stuck with like the QWERTY keyboard. And just as writing cannot convey intonation, music notation leaves out nuances that one can only learn to insert when necessary by listening to musicians render the texts.

But as with language, the writing of music lends advantages. There are places music can only go when there is writing, freeing the musician from the requirements of memory.

In the Western world, the prime example would be classical music. The orally transmitted folk song will have a simple melody that sits easily in the memory, with lots of "And now, everybody!"-style repetition. I once heard some old babushkas singing Russian folk songs for money in St. Petersburg, and seven years later I still remember the minor-key, three-quarter-time melody of the chorus—it was, after all, designed to get under your skin that way and be passed down through illiterate or semiliterate generations. But Beethoven's Seventh could not be passed down this way. The melodies are too extended, develop too idiosyncratically, and in too many variations, and the whole thing is simply too long to memorize, short of repeated listenings to people performing it—which they can only do from written scores. In addition, each of over a dozen instruments has its own part. There could be no classical music without pen and ink.

Classical music is, in this sense, unnatural, like elevated oratorical style, classical poetry, and densely constructed prose. Classical music takes painstaking, extended training and serious effort to produce, and requires close attention and practice to appreciate. Beyond the listener-friendly warhorses like Vivaldi's *The Four Seasons*, Mozart's *Eine Kleine Nachtmusik*, or the first movement of Beethoven's Fifth that one would have to be a corpse not to respond to on some level, classical is *hard*. Brahms's chamber pieces are gorgeous as texture, but they are rarely catchy, and only with training or repeated listens can one fully digest them as statements rather than a mere sound. And then when we move ahead to Schoenberg and his quest to bring classical music to a new level of development, his music can be downright irritating, and he worked at *not* being catchy. For many musically inclined people, even repeated listenings leave them deaf to his art. Classical pushes the envelope—hard.

The Boomer's Ear

Yet in an earlier America, despite its challenges, classical music had a place at the table. A larger segment of the public sincerely enjoyed it, and a general norm required the rest to sit through a lot of it—it was all but inescapable. There was a sense that to engage with music beyond the elementary level was part of being a respectable middle-class citizen. Here is a description of this America that I find especially apt; this world was

> northern, civilized, and white. (. . .) It was overwhelmingly middle class, a world created by self-satisfied shopkeepers and senior clerks, people with fine penmanship and clean collars and a knack with machines; a forward-looking world of skill and professionalism, of taste (according, as always, to prevailing standards) and restraint and deep sublimation. Its music had to be polite, asexual, and serious—but in no way intellectual, mind you.

In this America, the crucial difference between them and us is that the two main elements the listener pricked up their ears to were melody and harmony. Florid operettas like *Naughty Marietta* and *The Merry Widow* enchanted audiences despite ridiculous stories, overwrought lyrics, and cartoon acting because what they paid to enjoy were long-lined, ravishing melodies like "I'm Falling in Love with Someone" and "The Merry Widow Waltz."

Rhythm was garnish. Its prominence and infectiousness in ragtime and early jazz was received alternately as a strangely seductive oddity or as an incitement to debauchery for the very reason that the miraculous power of syncopated rhythm was new to its white audiences. There are few things quainter than ragtime song lyrics from before World War I marveling that listening to ragtime "you can barely keep your feet from tapping." It seems a rather odd thing to call attention to today—"I was listening to U2 and, like, I kept moving my leg to the beat!" But to people raised on marches, jigs, waltzes, and parlor ballads, the feeling of a rhythmic "groove" was as novel as the nasal rush from too much wasabi was for us twenty years ago when we started eating sushi. Abraham Lincoln and Emily Dickinson never knew jamming.

But even for the people hopped up on syncopation, melody and harmony still reigned. "The Maple Leaf Rag" was experienced not as a rhythm track but as a uniquely catchy *song*. Today, however, the American typically listens mainly for two things: 1) rhythm and 2) the vernacular authenticity of the singer's vocal tone.

Certainly we haven't tossed out melody and harmony altogether. But we can do without them if the beat is fine enough, whereas B.C. Americans could not have. Rap is exhibit A—and recall that 70 percent of rap's listeners today are white. The eternal pulsations of house music, in which lyrical fragments are sprinkled thin as mere decoration, take our rhythmic fetish to its logical extreme. The joy increasing numbers of people are taking in Third World popular music (World Beat) is also focused on rhythm; dance is central to most fans' relationship to such music. The rhythms in much Third World music may well be complex—but they are also endlessly repeated, or perhaps change at set intervals between which there is endless repetition. Rhythm is deeply, elementally seductive. But it remains a less elaborated form of expression than the long, musical line with subtle, shifting harmonies underneath that the classical musician sweats over. Mahler was complex not only within four-measure units, but also in these units' constant and unpredictable transformations throughout a movement. He didn't have the option of doing the same thing over and over again.

As to voices, there are refined ones we thrill to, but again we can do without them. We cheerily admit that Bob Dylan can't sing and still elevate him to bardlike status. Tom Waits's voice is downright grating, but then for his fans that's part of the point—in sounding like any old chain-smoking truck driver singing, he reads as "true." But in the old days, there was no such thing as a popular recording star who could not produce a refined vocal tone of some sort. Unless you were a comedian halfway talking your way through a song (Eddie Cantor, for example), you had to be able to carry a tune, and do so with a smooth tone soothing to the ear, of a sort that required training or a special gift to produce. In other words, you were not expected to sing like you talked. Today, the closer a singer can get to doing so the better—it's predictable that in our times rap, eliminating the singing entirely, became so staggeringly popular so quickly. And to most of us, the trained, legitimate voice sounds forced, irrelevant, best taken in small doses.

In our times, that cherish egalitarianism, multiculturalism, and skepticism of elite Western norms, there is an inevitable comfort in claims that music is music, and that Yo-Yo Ma and Bono are on different paths to the same mountaintop. But the simple fact is this: Whatever its power over us, music centered on repeated rhythm and a vocal tone that about one in five people could produce with the assistance of retakes and splicing is closer to a preliterate pole of musical expression than classical music. If one of the main things that grabs you about a cut of music is either the funky rhythm it starts with or the overall feel of the singer's voice, then nine times out of ten, that music is "oral." Like speech, it is based on short segments often repeated, easier to write and easier to process than classical music, making no serious demands on the listener. And when our sense of a voice's beauty is tied to how it speaks to our everyday, kitchen-sink essence, we again hearken to the oral—spoken language is more personal and subjective than written.

My intention is not, as so often in this book, simply to decry. I do like classical music, jazz, and theater music. But I am as bewitched by a good beat as anyone else. My CD collection includes a healthy amount of rock and soul and even a bit of rap, and I still have a stack of 45s that I collected in the eighties largely for how good the rhythms of the songs were. I myself happen not to be much of a voice fan as a rule; I listen for the instrumental aspect, and oddly for a linguist, I can hear a lyric twenty times and still not be able to sing it from memory. Yet if I had to choose between an operatic voice and Gladys Knight's, I'd take Gladys's—opera has its moments, but I can only take so much of it at a stretch (whether it's in English or not).

But that said, certain facts remain. To address and take to heart extended melodies and harmonic sequences that, without writing, could only fade into oblivion is to foster an artifice. To savor the cyclic beat and the personal relevance of a vocal ambience is to parallel the musical sensibility of an preliterate tribesman, his fundamental human sophistication acknowledged. And today, the latter description applies to most of the recordings featured on display at a Tower Records store. Many people sixty and under have never known an America where this wasn't true, and thus sense music centered on rhythm and vocal funk not as one kind of music, but as music itself, most of the other kinds processed as "for old people." One old girlfriend watched me closing my eyes and swelling a bit to the main theme of Tchaikovsky's Sixth and asked "What are you doing?" "Enjoying the music," I said. "Haven't you ever seen anyone savoring a melody?" "Yeah, old men," she replied—and within the only time frame she had ever known, her reaction was perfectly understandable.

Another old girlfriend recalled a male friend realizing that a new relationship wasn't going to work out when the woman turned out not to like the African World Beat dance music of Kanda Bongo Man. My girlfriend, the friend, and their crowd were entranced at the time with Kanda Bongo Man, as my girlfriend still was, jeeringly recounting the woman dismissing the music as "repetitious and monotonous." But while whether Kanda Bongo Man is monotonous is a matter of taste, repetitious it is—up, catchy rhythmic patterns cycled over and over and over, decorated with the singer's jolly, exotic chants in the Lingala language. But to my old girlfriend, to criticize this music as "repetitious" was like scorning a cat for being naked. For her, as for the millions who treasure house music, the repetition is the soul of music itself.

But before the sixties, America knew no commercially significant music in which brute repetition played such a key role. Just as we talk when we make speeches and write more and more like we talk, and just as our poetry imitates talking, we adore music that just talks.

Why Was Mickey Conducting an Orchestra?: Classical on the Wane

For example, the passage above about the musical sensibility of an earlier America comes from a discussion of the 1935 Mickey Mouse cartoon *The Band Concert*. Mickey conducts a raggedy brass band playing *The William Tell Overture*, repeatedly disrupted by Donald Duck playing "Turkey in the Straw" on the flute. Even this innocent scenario reveals a different

America: Why is Mickey conducting an orchestra? Today, what even *is* a band concert? In 1935, outdoor concerts by symphonic bands and local orchestras were still common in America. But today, the occasional band-shell Pops concert is a once-in-a-blue-moon occasion for most of us, hardly something one would write a cartoon about. Characters in new cartoons made for television are not given to conducting orchestras. There is no episode of *Johnny Bravo* where he takes up conducting a band to impress the chicks. Classical music has too marginal a place in our society for a plot like this to make sense today.

"Do You Like Music?"

Until the 1960s, for example, in middle-class America the default meaning of "music" *was* classical music. "Do you like music?" meant did you like Beethoven, not Rudy Vallee singing pop songs on the radio. A music lover was assumed to like the classics. In Harold Stearns's *Civilization in the United States* anthology, composer and music journalist Deems Taylor's contribution "Music" discusses classical music almost exclusively. This is not out of elitism, since he even defends musical-theater composer Victor Herbert's first-act finale of *Mlle. Modiste* against *Rigoletto*'s "La donna è mobile," which he calls "vulgar rubbish." It was just that in 1922, it was assumed that a discussion of music in America meant the classical music scene, however you felt about other music. Today, in such an anthology about the state of music in America, classical music would be treated as subsidiary at best. For us, music in the default sense is contemporary pop.

In an article from around when *The Band Concert* was made, theater orchestrator Robert Russell Bennett neatly signaled how different his era was in a revealing sidenote. Though classically trained, Bennett was writing about the art of expanding composers' piano scores into parts for a musical-theater orchestra, and thus felt the need to specify:

> For the purposes of this article, the word music will refer to what is known as "popular," "light," "commercial," etc., and is not to be confused with the great art of music for musicians and cultured listeners, who might pardonably wonder why we spend time on the details of the scherzo—so to speak—without taking up the profounder movements of life's symphony.

Bennett felt that caveat as natural, but after less than seventy years it is the quintessence of archaism. Today's cultured listeners would need no reminding that classical is not exactly at the top of most people's list when they think of music! Nor would most people cherishing their rock, R&B, hip-hop, country, and World Beat take kindly to a trained classical musician dismissing the music they love as mere "scherzos." In fact, no classical musician would venture such a gaffe, because now they are on the cultural defensive. Time was when pop composers looked up to classical, Gershwin being a prime example, and stride pianist James P. Johnson composing sadly obscure symphonic pieces being another. There was even an *Archaeopteryx* stage when some rock musicians were given to fashioning large-scale works seeking to equal the scale of the symphony. But the era of *The Wall* is long gone, and today the situation is reversed. The classical musician works to see as much value in modern pop as they can, and classical producers try to boost subscription rates with concerts uniting pop musicians with orchestral accompaniment.

Capitalism and niche marketing has had a lot to do with sending the classical world into increasing desperation. But again, mass culture itself is not incompatible with high culture. In Stephen Sondheim's musical *Follies*, set in 1971, when two middle-aged ex-lovers meet, the man recalls that the woman used to love listening to Toscanini broadcasts. This refers to the fact that from the thirties through the fifties, NBC had a top-class classical orchestra in residence giving regular concerts over the airwaves. Its conductor, Arturo Toscanini, was a megastar in his era, and not merely on the level of a Michael Tilson Thomas, but of a Madonna. People hung on his words. They wondered what he did in bed. He was considered larger than life.

Nor was the NBC Symphony mere window dressing. Classical music's presence went far beyond this on the pop-media scene of the time. *The Voice of Firestone*, focusing on classical music, began just as radio was becoming a mass medium in 1929, was transferred to television as soon as possible in the Uncle Miltie era of 1949, and ran until 1963. The similar *Bell Telephone Hour* began on radio in 1940 and ran on television until 1968, even bolstering rather than cutting back the classical section of the program as late as 1966. And of all things, on radio, the two shows formed part of a *block* of tony programming on NBC on Monday nights! Today's "Must-See-TV" blocks on NBC rise no higher than the level of sitcoms. Joan Sutherland made her "television debut" on the *Bell Telephone Hour* in 1961. When was Cecilia Bartoli's "television debut?" And who cares—because classical music has no place in network television today.

To an extent, PBS has taken over the classical wing of things. But how prominently do these broadcasts figure in the general consciousness more than occasionally? My sense is that the last orchestral PBS show with a national profile, whether you watched it or not, was *Evening at Pops* when Arthur Fiedler conducted it in the seventies. But even he proudly stuck to the classical music easier on the untrained ear, and the Boston Pops' music has gotten poppier by the decade since. And in any case, videos and the flood of channels now available have swept *Evening at Pops* out of sight as a national staple. Arthur Fiedler was a household name in the seventies, but today's conductor, Keith Lockhart, is the answer to a trivia question.

A Place in the Sun

Make no mistake: The fact that the networks let classical music go once PBS was available shows that its serious fans have always been a minority. The regular listeners to the *Bell/Firestone* block in 1950 numbered only seven million. On television, *The Voice of Firestone* was yanked as early as 1959 when Firestone got hungry for a larger viewer base to sell tires to. They restored it in 1962 after an indignant protest, but then buried it for good after one more season. Walt Disney came up with the idea for *Fantasia* while dozing at a classical music concert, and a few years earlier, Ethel Merman had gaily sung in a musical:

> I can't stand Sibelius or Delius,
> But I'd give my best pal away for Calloway!

Thus, Americans then weren't whistling Bruckner from house to house any more than they are now. And yet, right when Merman was singing that lyric in the 1930s, the place of classical music in mass culture was expanding rather than contracting. Radios and improved recording techniques made the music available in ordinary homes, and the music industry took advantage of this with aggressive marketing (including a focus on the more accessible works, mostly from the nineteenth century). Austrian pianist Artur Schnabel found American listeners untutored when he toured here in the early twenties, but ten years later noticed that audiences were more informed and enthusiastic. When movie theaters were wired for sound in the late twenties, the Warner Brothers actually chirped that they were hoping they could now bring classical music to every small town. The extent to which they followed up on this notwithstanding, that they would even claim it reveals the era as different from ours. No broadband proponent even pretends to be on the edge of their seat hoping to bless the American masses with classical music streamed through their laptops.

And in fact, a great many of Warner Brothers' early Vitaphone shorts, made just before sound on film became ordinary, were of classical musicians and opera singers;[21] they were seen as commercially valuable right alongside the vaudevillians. And before sound, orchestras accompanying films couched their repertoire in the classical sound: throbbing strings, flutes atwitter, French horns, not a nightclub dance band. Today, there is a growing trend to compose new scores for silents in jazzier idioms. Why not? But it wouldn't have occurred to anyone in 1922.

Classical music in this era, then, while hardly comfort food for most, was on the table, a player. This played out graphically in a pop cliché of the era, the battle between swing and legit. Judy Garland's first movie was a short (*Every Sunday*) pitting her pop against sweet little Deanna Durbin's light classical singing, and the result is a draw. The point of the short is not to diss Durbin, who went on to a sterling career of her own in a long series of films built around her warbling. The same year Disney made *The Band Concert*, he also made *Music Land*, where the prince of the Isle of Jazz falls in love with the princess of the Land of Symphony. And then there were the Looney Tunes that trashed classical music: *A Corny Concerto* ("Gweetings, music wovers!"), *Rhapsody Rabbit* (Bugs playing Lizst at the piano), *Long-Haired Hare* ("FI-I-GAA-ROOOH! FI-GARO! FIGARO–Figaro-figaro-figaro-figaro . . ."), *Rabbit of Seville* ("Can't

---

21. Vitaphone was a system in which the sound portion of a filming was recorded on big record discs that were then played in synchronization with the film in the theater. The Vitaphone shorts are precious documents: The first human beings in human history that we can see and hear at the same time. Predictably, as soon as sound-on-film took over, the Vitaphone materials were either destroyed or scattered every which way. Today, the Vitaphone Project is scouring the nation trying to reunite the film shorts with their discs. Some of the restored performances cannot communicate meaningfully across eight decades, but quite a few are mesmerizing. These only make it sting even more that a great many Vitaphone shorts are lost entirely, while in other cases, all that is left is a silent film we will never hear, or a weird disc of talking and singing that we'll never be able to look at.

you see that I'm much sweeter / I'm your little señori-ter . . .") and of course, *What's Opera, Doc?* ("Kill da wabbit!"). These shorts tear classical to pieces, but the fact that it was even considered ripe for parody shows that it had a presence that it now does not. In the 1950s, Robert Russell Bennett had a joshing conversation with a Broadway composer that is now another one of those untranslatable moments. He describes telling Harry Ruby ("I Wanna Be Loved by You" [boop-boop a-doop]):

> "You know, the trouble with all of you popular songwriters is that you get an eight-bar phrase and you have to plug it all afternoon. You write a strain like 'Some enchanted evening,' and then you say a few bars later, 'All right, now in case you didn't hear it, you dumb clucks out there, "Some enchanted evening," here it is again.' And then a little bit later you say, 'All right, I know you've forgotten it by now,' so you say 'Some enchanted evening' again. But," I said, "you take a thing like 'La donna è mobile' from *Rigoletto*—listen to Verdi, he never goes back, never returns to the original statement; keeps on going, always something new!"

For a classical composer to tell a pop songwriter something like this to-day, even in fun, would come off as unspeakably unhip. We expect John Corigliano to treat his music and Bonnie Raitt's as just "different kinds of music"—at least in public statements. The very idea that "written" music and its challenges could possibly have anything to teach a pop composer has fallen away, in favor of a sense that a kickin' beat and a raw, earthy voice are realer than long-lined melodies and complex har-monies floating all over the place, especially for forty minutes.

And in this world, classical music stations are going off the air nationwide, and even National Public Radio stations are playing less and less of it. Polls show that people are most likely to prefer classical music as background, and music you brunch to sits no closer to your soul than your tiling and carpets. In early 2002, the government of Santa Cruz, California, actually started playing classical music over a PA system down-town to drive away loiterers! Gone were the days when a besotted Harry Truman would write to his wife in 1911:

> Do you think you could stand some Grand Opera? What? I have a desire to hear Lucia di Lammermoor or to see it, whichever is proper. Would you go? I don't believe that just one yelling match would be

unenjoyable. I have never seen Lucia and I am curious to know how much torture one has to endure to get to hear the sextet.

Truman was no more an opera lover than most people, but classical music hung in the air enough in his era that he had heard of the sextet from *Lucia,* and was game to experience it. And I hope Harry got to see it done, because it *is* good—it grabbed me the first time I heard it. It is perhaps most familiar from the Looney Tune where Porky Pig battles a cat singing on the fence outside his window while he's trying to get to sleep; after Porky kills the poor cat at the end, the nine cat souls ascending to heaven yowl through an abridged version before the fade-out. When *Notes to You* was made in 1941, it was assumed that audiences would get the joke. It says something that thirty-five years later, I first heard it watching this cartoon on TV!

American Popular Song: From "And Then He Wrote . . ." to "The Way She Sings"

We also see the shift to the oral in the fate of the vintage American pop song. There was a time when the best-loved pop songs were, while hardly as elaborated as classical music, little gems of rigorous craft. As Alec Wilder's classic analysis of hundreds of these songs, *American Popular Song* (1972), demonstrated, a standard by Gershwin, Porter, Berlin, Rodgers, Jerome Kern, Harold Arlen ("Stormy Weather"), or Burton Lane ("Old Devil Moon") is worth extended musicological analysis—these men were minor geniuses.

When "Written" Was State-of-the-Art

Certainly when these classics were new, for every one of them there were five hack toss-offs now justifiably forgotten, even if some were passing hits then. Paging through dusty stacks of sheet music in antique shops and thrift stores, we face the reality of the era as the immortal tunes are vastly outnumbered by dopey flotsam that only those around at the time will recall, like "Open the Door, Richard" and "Mister Five by Five." If I got my wish and spent a night in a Manhattan nightclub in 1936, I would not get to hear a sweet swing band glide through an endless procession of songs like "Easy to Love," "Pick Yourself Up," and "I Can't Get Started." I'd get maybe one of those songs plus a passel of pap I've never heard of and would wish I hadn't.

But actually, even these also-rans often evidence more sheer sweat in the creation than most pop music today. I, as an erstwhile semi-professional cocktail pianist, have often found myself working hard to wrap my fingers around the chord changes of the better throwaway songs of the time according to my personal standard. Golden Age pop composer Harry Warren, for example, is now best known for deathless little masterpieces like "I Only Have Eyes For You" (a tune every bit the equal of anything Puccini ever wrote) and "The More I See You," still cherished by jazz artists. But even his toss-offs were often fantastic in their minor way. I used to sneak some of them into my repertoire and found that even casual listeners would often single out these tunes as catchy (for the two or three readers afflicted with my malady, songs like "Plenty of Money and You," "I Don't Have to Dream Again," and "A Nice Old-Fashioned Cocktail").

From "I love a Gershwin Tune" to "Did You Know That's a Cover?"

Late in life Warren dismissed rock with "My dog could write a better song." Crabby, but he was referring to a genuine qualitative distinction, and one that parallels the difference between speech and writing. Most pop today is driven less by what the composer writes down than the performer taking raw materials and fashioning it into an individually charismatic performance.

What's gripping about Whitney Houston's hit "Didn't We Almost Have It All?" is not the melody or harmonies, which are so elementary that we couldn't care less who wrote them. A squadron of musicians have sold out to write such songs and live in luxurious anonymity in New York and Hollywood. The sheet music alone of many old pop songs is well worth playing to the note—the basic skeleton of the song, its melody and harmonies, can stand alone as a compelling statement. But buy the sheet music to "Didn't We Almost Have It All?" and take it home to play on the piano and it just sits there, making you wish Houston were with you to sing it. What that song is is Houston's pyrotechnic, gospel-tinged singing of it. In the same way, speech is immediate and personal when uttered, but loses its power when transcribed word-for-word on paper, denuded of its situational context and the nuances that intonation conveys. Written language is designed to communicate with much less dependence on context or intonation; it stands on its own. New pop is spoken music; old pop was much more written.

Rap, then, takes this spoken trend to its logical extreme, leaving no possible sheet to take home at all. We could almost predict that after the sixties, a form of pop music would emerge that is all about the performer talking over a beat. And because rap is so very much a "spoken" form, to sing it to yourself means not mechanically reciting the text, but imitating the speaker in all of his visceral, personal immediacy. Watch teens and twenty-somethings rapping along to themselves as they walk down the street and note the theatrical facial expressions, gestures, and vocal tics they adopt. No one actually talks in the very particular confrontational cadence now established for rapping: To ape this when rapping to one's self is to do the performer, not "the song." You imitate someone's talking, not their writing.

And it follows that modern pop songs are considered the property of the singer. If another performer ventures to record the song, it is an irregular event termed a "cover," considered opportunistic and gauche any sooner than about ten years after the original rendition. But there was no such thing as a cover before the rock era in the sense we have today. When the Golden Age composers published a song, they fully expected that several singers would record versions of it over the next few months. "Night and Day," for example, was not associated with any one singer— if anything, it was a "Cole Porter" song. But today there exist no pop composers with household names (other than performers who also happen to write their material). When producers put together a Broadway revue like *Smokey Joe's Café* gathering the songs of Jerry Lieber and Mike Stoller, it's news to us that "Ruby Baby," "Jailhouse Rock," and "Stand By Me" were all written by the same guys. We associate most of the songs with a particular performer. But in the old days, even if a singer happened to make a song their own (e.g., Bing Crosby's version of Irving Berlin's "White Christmas"), this was hardly seen as blocking legions of others from recording it as well.

This was to a large extent because the written aspect of the songs was substantial enough to make any professional rendition worth buying. If the song itself stands alone as a full statement, then it is worth hearing even if some anonymous stiff sings their way through it. But when the written part is just a suggestion of a melody and a skeletal sequence of harmonies, the expectation is that what will make it worth listening to is a particular singer filling it out with their personal improvisations and idiosyncratic charisma. Naturally, then, what that singer does with it becomes the song itself, and thereafter, for anyone to sing the song is less to render what was written than to imitate that performer. "Respect" is not a written song—it's a performance by Aretha. What its composer— Otis Redding, as it happens—wrote on paper was, in itself, not even meant to be heard. American pop now tilts oral.

There are exceptions aplenty at any given time. Burt Bacharach has always written what musicians outside of the pop world call "real songs," as have Stevie Wonder, Billy Joel, and Sting. In 2003, Norah Jones swept the Grammys with an album of nicely "written" songs— pointedly, however, bemused at her success on the pop market. And it is a continuum issue: They Might Be Giants' work is closer to songs in Harry Warren's understanding than the ones that Britney Spears is given (who composes songs like "Oops, I Did It Again"? And note that we have no reason to care). But all of these people are exceptions to a trend. Overall, the tilt in pop music toward the oral since the late sixties has been stark indeed.

You Can't Stop the Beat

It's interesting watching America's middle-aged *Together with Music* pop scene of the fifties first exotifying, then trying to tame, and finally getting devoured by rock music. First Ed Sullivan only films Elvis from the top. Then in the late fifties and early sixties, the old pop establishment treated rock as a cute novelty. The Chipmunks put semirock into the mouths of small animals with speeded-up voices. Cole Porter wrote "The Ritz Roll and Rock" for Fred Astaire to sing and dance to in the 1957 film version of *Silk Stockings*, trying to wrap rock up as just one more "everybody's doing it" dance craze like the Turkey Trot or the Jitterbug.

But the same year Mario Savio hit the headlines in 1964, the Beatles came to America, cutting up at Idlewild Airport turning a press conference into a "press conference." Something was blowing in the wind on that tarmac. While the 1965 cartoon series about the Beatles turned them into tame, lovelorn little darlings, the animated film *Yellow Submarine* three years later was the sign of something new. In this film, the Beatles are not coping with an alien world—they *are* the world.

The Beatles, though, were transitional figures like Savio: They did write "real songs." But just as the student protesters after Savio sacrificed the Socratic impulse to the theatrics, most of the people who followed in the Beatles' wake carried on the rhythmic addiction, the black-inflected diction, and the cheeky informality, but didn't bother with the artistic constraint. And because a culture busy getting down no longer required real songs, America ate this music up such that today, a good two generations have grown up with a musical sensibility based on beat and shaggy vocal passion. That is: Whatever residual response one has to the melody and harmony, take away the beat and the cool voice and we lose interest, while music based entirely on melody and harmony appeals only to the few. Enter spoken music as default—the rock era.

Paint It Black

And "the black thing" fed into this just as it affected mainstream language. Much of rock's character was drawn from not only black inflection, but the rhythmic prominence and meat-and-potatoes structure of the blues, much of this filtered in turn through the old-time rhythm and blues/country fusion of the Louis Jourdan "Caldonia" variety ("What makes your big head so hard?") and its descendant strains pioneered by Bo Diddley and Chuck Berry.

It wasn't that black writers have been by any means strangers to "real" songs. From the late 1800s through the 1930s, composers like Will Marion Cook, Bob Cole and the Johnson brothers, Eubie Blake, and Fats Waller gave their white colleagues a run for their money. The black presence was in fact a crucial element in the mix that became the Golden Age American pop song, so much so that Irving Berlin was accused of having a "colored boy" under his piano writing for him (why under instead of just beside?). And beyond this level, it would be hard to say that bandleader/composers like James Reese Europe and Duke Ellington were not at home in written music styles. Even the hardest-driving black bands of the time, less artistically ambitious than Ellington, were not just "talking" their music despite the hot drumming and blaring brass. Danceable and athletic though Count Basie and Jimmie Lunceford's music was, they used intricate arrangements crafted by trained musicians that took serious practice for a band to master.

But the swing-band era was dead by the sixties, and the most prominent form of black pop by then was the more elemental forms of doo-wop, Motown, and soul. "Dancing in the Streets" is less a song than a performance by Martha and the Vandellas; we couldn't care less who wrote it, and regard anyone who ventures a version of it to be covering Martha and the Vandellas. Thus to fetishize and ape the black sound as lovingly as bands like the Rolling Stones did in the sixties was to drink in a largely spoken kind of music, reinforcing the triumph of that general mode.

Certainly the black musical sound had been making its way into the white American soul as far back as the ragtime of the 1890s, and by the Jazz Age in the 1920s, the black thing was the pièce de résistance on the pop music scene in the urban hotbeds of interracial ferment—Ann Douglas's *Terrible Honesty* beautifully chronicles this in New York, for example. Then American pop took another hit of Negritude in the fifties as Bill Haley and the Comets, Elvis, et al. channeled Jourdan, Diddley, and Berry. In the early sixties, in that clip of Patty Duke doing the twist and chewing gum during the famous opening credits of her sitcom, it's clear that the music she is dancing to is neither Bing Crosby nor anything like the bouncy white-bread theme song. But like the Beatniks and Beat poetry, in this era rock and roll was just one of many voices. This was a time when whatever Patty Duke was dancing to, the cast album for *The Music Man* could still be a major seller.

It's one thing to stir the black essence into a form that remains white, as the Golden Age composers did, or to admit it as one of many genres, as when rock and roll was crazy youth music. But it's another thing to inhale the black sound as one's very musical soul and hold it close throughout adulthood. Zora Neale Hurston nicely captured the difference between B.C. and now in her description of the contrast between her relationship to twenties jazz and that of a white "Negrophile" "slumming" in Harlem in the 1920s:

> "Good music they have here," he remarks, drumming the table with his fingertips. Music! The great blobs of purple and red emotion have not touched him. He has only heard what I felt. He is far away and I see him but dimly across the ocean and the continent that have fallen between us.

There are millions and millions of white Americans today who appear to not only hear but feel B.B. King, Aretha Franklin, and Prince every bit as much as black Americans, and Eminem would certainly appear to feel as well as hear the essence of hip-hop. Only after the change in the mid-sixties would this become possible, when the black sound became less a fetish than the cross-racial bedrock of the American musical sensibility.

For most Americans under sixty, one of the hardest things to adjust to in 1936's mainstream America would be that the music would be too sweet, the rhythms too tame, the singers too arch and soppy. Counselors would have to work with applicants for weeks preparing them for "funk cravings" in a mainstream America that didn't know such music yet. In the same way, for an American brought from 1936 to today, after they figured out that bath soap was not considered sufficient underarm protection, one of the hardest adjustments would be a pop-music norm they would find melodically and harmonically barren and rhythmically barbarous.

Gallivanting Around: The Piano Bars Go Oral

I have also seen an ongoing drift toward the oral on the urban piano bar scene since the 1980s.

In the old days, theater music was part of the pop-music literature. There was no such thing as show tunes in the 1930s because the songs one heard at the theater were also played on the radio. During the medley overtures that preceded musicals, audiences often broke out into applause as the orchestra segued into songs that had become current hits. Robert Russell Bennett recounted such an event during the revival of *Show Boat* in 1946 when the overture slid into "Why Do I Love You?" which had become a standard since the original production of the show in 1927.[22]

But after the rock revolution, only the occasional theater song became a commercial hit (e.g., Sondheim's "Send in the Clowns" from *A Little Night Music* when Judy Collins recorded it). Show tunes cleaved off into a separate category, a cult phenomenon cherished especially by gay

---

[22.] So alien has the concept of the instrumental medley become in this age of songs based on vocal charisma that a dear friend of mine in the Stanford performing arts crowd, one of the most musically gifted people I have ever known, once bemused me by recounting hearing a medley overture that some savvy conductor had written for the annual musical campus satire. "The songs just flowed from one into the other—it was neat . . ." she said. But she was describing the standard-issue overture once staple to a musical theater performance, some of them performed in isolation at pops concerts. I doubt that a Stanford undergrad watching an edition of the *Gaieties* before about the 1970s would have found the genre of the instrumental medley so novel.

men. In the larger American cities, singalong bars arose catering to this crowd, in which a pianist plays theater songs all night while patrons sing, interrupted occasionally by a customer or waiter taking a solo.

There exists no such bar (i.e., that holds show tunes front and center) that is not a gay hangout. As such, the straight man who truly loves theater music finds himself in the odd position of getting used to going to mostly gay bars to hear the music played and sung live. In any big city there exists a small coterie of straight male piano bar regulars, who usually hang together and quietly establish themselves as off-limits *re* the inevitable pick-up aspect of such places (and also learn that they are actually not bad places to meet women, since there is so little competition!). I became one of those when I lived in New York in the mid-eighties, when a circuit of about seven such bars was thriving. But I write on leave for a year in New York fifteen years later, and I am struck by how much the scene has changed.

For one, many of the bars I knew have closed, and the situation has been even worse in San Francisco, where the seven bars that existed fifteen years ago are now down to about one and a half. In New York, most of the handful of bars still open have gradually shifted to focusing more on ordinary pop music than show music (and thus drawing increasingly straight crowds). A generational shift has occurred. In the eighties, the bedrock clientele of these bars were men then in their forties and fifties, who had come of age in the Stonewall sixties and had known an America where rock had not taken over yet. Today, this generation has aged beyond the inclination to gallivanting around late at night, and the generation replacing them never knew B.C. They are scions of the era of rock, rap, and karaoke, and it makes for a less cultish—and less written—piano bar culture.

I didn't know or care a thing about theater music until I graduated from college, when a friend took me to the marvelous Marie's Crisis in Greenwich Village. I was thunderstruck by the music, and started frequenting it to drink in this world of music I had barely known to exist until then, obsessed enough to put up with the occasional social awkwardnesses (made easier by the fact that I quickly found that I wasn't alone). Especially on the off weeknights when the crowds were thinner and the pianists would do lesser-known songs, Marie's Crisis became nothing less than a classroom for me. I picked up the literature, the lore, the standards of appreciation, and the guidelines of performance style from countless evenings at the feet of the pianists and regulars there, usually performers between jobs. These guys knew everything, and had been around to see a lot of the old shows when they were new.

But just fifteen years later, a twenty-year-old curious about musical-theater lore could not get that education at Marie's Crisis, nor anywhere else in Manhattan. The new pianists are dazzling technicians and stalwart toastmasters just as their equivalents in the eighties were. But they do not have the almost intimidatingly comprehensive command of the vintage musical-theater literature that the old ones did (when even the ones from the eighties were too young to have experienced much of the old-school literature as new). There is no pianist working Marie's these days who I even bother asking for songs from cult-cast albums of the forties through the early sixties or forgotten chestnut songs from earlier that once reigned as common coin on the piano bar circuit. They're all too young (forty-something or less) to have picked them up when they were current—and as products of their times, usually only faintly connect with such pre-B.C. tokens as lore. I recall one of them asking "Did you know Harry Warren was writing music for the movies even into the 1950s?" The guys I learned from in the eighties would have considered that assumed knowledge, and would have looked upon my not knowing it as jejune.

Nor are the customers as savvy as they used to be. One of the pianists once broke out into "They Won't Send Roses" from *Mack and Mabel*, a show whose music was written by Jerry Herman. Herman is best known for his megahits *Hello, Dolly!*, *Mame*, and *La Cage aux Folles*. But *Mack and Mabel*, a saga of silent film pioneer Mack Sennett and his love affair with the teens' version of Meg Ryan, Mabel Normand, is a cult classic among the cognoscenti. Or more accurately, the older cognoscenti. Hearing the song, one thirty-something casually yelled "What's this from?" "*Mack and Mabel*," the pianist informed him. More than a few people around the bar mumbled "Oh." "Oh"??? In 1986, all but one or two people in the room would have known this as casually as sports fans know that the Buccaneers are from Tampa Bay.

These days, most of any crowd at Marie's on a busy night would rather hear shows from after the rock transition, written in an idiom informed by modern pop. A clump of diehards trill enthusiastically through the songs from *Oklahoma!* and *Gypsy*, but the room truly comes alive when the pianist launches into songs from *Little Shop of Horrors* and *Jesus Christ Superstar*.

This shift is not merely cosmetic. It's not just that time goes by, because time had certainly already gone by in 1985 and yet the old stuff was still cherished. These modern scores, couched in a modern pop idiom, tend to be less intricately crafted than older ones. As dear to the hearts of millions of Americans as many of them are, songs like "I Dreamed a Dream," "I Don't Know How to Love Him," and "Don't Cry for Me, Argentina" are, in terms of formal musical structure, dishwater. The best-loved songs from older shows often leave one wondering just how the composer came up with such a perfect sequence of notes and how the lyricist managed to match those notes so perfectly with words. Jerome Kern and Oscar Hammerstein's "All the Things You Are" is often mentioned as an example, but this was a pinnacle. One senses the same "Where did he *get* that?" even in many of the also-ran gems.

Imagine yourself assigned to write a love song for Fred Astaire to sing to Ginger Rogers for *Swing Time* in 1935. In 1935, you are not thinking of it as "a golden classic starring two eternal icons," but as just "the new Astaire picture that will play for a few months and make me enough dough to buy me another summer house." You think, "I love you," "you're so pretty," the moon, "Oh, God," etc., with last year's song for the couple in that vein, "Cheek to Cheek," floating around in your head. But Irving Berlin already wrote "Cheek to Cheek," and you can't just crank out some knock-off of that one like "With Your Little Head on My Chest." So—what would you write down?

Jerome Kern came up with "The Way You Look Tonight," an utterly true, warm, solid, beauteous clincher of a melody. It didn't exist until he put it down on paper in some apartment in Manhattan—but it sounds like it has existed from the dawn of time. Even if you are a trained classical composer who can write intricate twelve-tone opuses, or an accomplished jazz player who can negotiate chords so inverted they're perverted and in any key and at top speed, could you write a melody as ineffably perfect as "The Way You Look Tonight," where the melody does not just go where your whim or idiosyncrasy happens to take it, but where every note sounds like it just had to fall right where it did? It's a very special gift.

"I Dreamed a Dream," "I Don't Know How to Love Him," and "Don't Cry for Me, Argentina" do not produce this impression on a musician. Any composer of decent talent could bang out melodies at this level, and I imagine that a computer could be taught to crank out even better ones. I once performed in a special centennial edition of the Stanford *Gaieties* student-written revue, resuscitating Gaieties songs from the teens up into the eighties. A lot of them, one-shot deals never heard again after a weekend or two on Stanford's campus and written by moderately talented undergrads who went on to *About Schmidt*-style lives, were more carefully crafted than anything in *Les Miserables* or *Evita*. Jerome Kern and Irving Berlin were minor geniuses. Andrew Lloyd Webber is just lucky.

And that judgment stems neither from Anglophobia nor discomfort with the money Lloyd Webber has raked in. It's simply that his work is less written than the older composers'. He does have a way of coming up with one or two good melodies per show—although often it would be more accurate to call them ideas for melodies. One of his best is the one for "Unexpected Song" in *Song and Dance*, but instead of developing it into a statement of thirty-two bars or longer, he just repeats the same sixteen bars over and over again, changing the key each time. It's a highly effective and thoroughly cheap trick, disqualifying the song as serious work.

Lloyd Webber also has little concern with going to the trouble of making his melodies and lyrics complement one another in a fashion that requires effort in the composition. One of the clumsiest moments in *Sunset Boulevard* is when chorus members are having a jaded, sarcastic conversation, and Lloyd Webber scores it with a bland, bouncy tune in a major key that sounds like people saying hi at a Fourth of July picnic in Omaha. Even in an era when characters in musicals were more generically drawn and songs were less thematically specific, the better composers didn't allow things like this. In 1939, Kern and Hammerstein did a now-forgotten gem called "All in Fun," in which the singer wryly describes how what began as just "having fun" with someone has come to mean more than that to her. Kern's melody, chromatic and angular yet warm and contained, is, of all things, *a musical summation of wryness*, perfectly complementing the lyric. That was art, and Lloyd Webber couldn't pull such a thing off at gunpoint.

Lloyd Webber is English and *Les Miserables'* composer is French, but then American listeners adore these men's music. And besides, they are not alone—here in America, theater music is rarely written to meld music and words as carefully as in "All in Fun" today, and few need it to be—the rabid fans of Frank Wildhorn's thin, paint-by-numbers scores for *Jeykll and Hyde* and *The Scarlet Pimpernel* reveal themselves as A.D. products. Shows with more elaborately written music may attain passing hit status for a year or three and then fade into regional and college productions, such as *Nine, City of Angels,* or *Ragtime*. But they do not achieve megahit status and stand firm on the Great White Way for a generation or so like *Les Miserables, Miss Saigon,* and *Cats,* held dear by legions of fans who are not otherwise especially taken by theater music.

One even gleans the new musical sensibility in how audiences relate to those respectable also-rans. In *Ragtime,* the ballad "Wheels of a Dream" is one of the most musically elementary pieces, capped by the easy score of a man and a woman singing to each other loudly about a rather generic sentiment. This song elicited the biggest reaction of the evening from audiences while the show ran. But the score itself has not made its way into the canon—it is rarely done at the piano bars and its recording has scarcely approached the runaway sales of that of *Rent.*

The one song from *Ragtime* that has achieved an approximation of classic status among musical-theater fans is the plangent ballad "Your Daddy's Son," and it is indicative that it is in minor key. Modern American listeners thrill to the minor in a way that they once did not: The default mode for vintage pop was major, even when the lyric was less than sunny ("Bewitched, Bothered, and Bewildered," "But Not for Me"). Minor key was a special tool in the composer's kit, rather like marjoram in the spice rack. The song "Forty-Second Street," describing the fascinating lowlife of an urban stretch, would sound trivial in a major key. But Warren's couching it in the minor renders it a more layered celebration of those "sexy ladies from the eighties who are indiscreet." But today the minor has a special currency in pop music. When I used to play the piano in a dorm-basement lounge in college, I used to watch the people sitting around the room prick their ears up spontaneously when I launched into a minor-key vamp or ostinato, and observe that if I played the same passage in a major key a few days later it would have no such effect on their subconsciouses and they would just keep on chatting. We associate the minor key with sincerity—because the minor sounds sad, sadness is a form of alienation, and alienation is a form of cool. Hence "Your Daddy's Son" stands out in *Ragtime,* and in the same way, the closest thing to standards from *Nine* and *City of Angels* have been the minor-key ballads "An Unusual Way" and "With Every Breath I Take," respectively.

Meanwhile the youngest generation of theater composers, having known nothing but an America where music talks, often write vamps (repetition) and burbling ostinatos (more repetition) in the left hand and place a melody on top that is euphonious enough, but hardly so specifically turned and polished as to leave you wondering just how they came up with that particular sequence of notes mated to those particular harmonies. Some, like Jason Robert Brown and William Finn, appear incapable of creating self-standing melodies of the sort that appear dictated from on high as opposed to just inoffensive. Others, like Adam Guettel and Michael John LaChiusa, sense self-standing melodies as corny, and write theater music often so willfully quirky and determinedly unpretty that their work could be taken as the equivalent of postmodernist prose or serialist classical music. It is written for themselves, a tiny coterie willing to listen to the cast albums fifteen times to let the work get under their skins, and a slightly larger group who, their ears dulled by the rock aesthetic, cheer such scores for their "energy" or the people performing them. Neither these composers nor their fans are listening in the way their grandparents would. They are all products of their times.

We see the difference in sensibility between then and now in how singers approach even older show music in the cult realm of cabaret singing, when singers put together evenings of standards to perform in a small venue. In a cabaret workshop in New York in fall 2002, the teacher told a student not to stretch the word *somewhere* in "Somewhere Over the Rainbow" over two long-held notes. "You would never talk that way," the teacher said. Okay—but this would never have occurred to Judy Garland in 1939, despite the fact that much of her appeal lay in how one could always hear a real person talking in her voice. Our sense of natural lies much closer to ordinary speech than it did for our grandparents.

That song "All in Fun," for example, was written the same year Garland sang "Somewhere Over the Rainbow," for the musical *Very Warm for May*. The scene preceding it contrasted perfectly with the cabaret class episode. A director is coaching a singer at a rehearsal for a musical-within-the-musical, and after she has sung a few bars of the verse (prelude before the chorus) of "All in Fun," he stops her:

Johnny: Uh, wait a minute—what'd you do that for?

Liz: What?

Johnny: That business with your hand—what was it?

Liz: I don't know—it's just a gesture.

Johnny: Well, what's it *mean*?

Liz: Well, nothing in particular. I've seen lots of singers do that.

Johnny: Well, so has everybody else.

Johnny says "All I want you to do is figure out what the words mean, and then sing them as if they were your own." He wants her to sing naturally. Liz tries the song again. The singer playing Liz, Frances Mercer, sang with the diction typical of theater singers of the period: "Just a fellow ahnd a girl, we have hahd a lit-tle whirl . . ." And yet to Johnny, *this* is singing as if the words are her own. "That's *good!*" He smiles. There's natural and there's natural.

"Cool!"

In a society where classical music and jazz exist, the person who only truly cherishes music that 1) can be danced to and/or 2) is sung in a raw, unaffected style that makes the person sound like someone you could have a beer with, is like a person raised on hot dogs and Coke. Hot dogs are good, of course. As is Coke—I pity earlier Americans who did not have this exquisite-tasting beverage.[23] But in the end, hot dogs and Coke are simple stuff—almost anyone likes them on first tasting, worldwide. Asparagus is odd-looking and vaguely reminiscent of genitals; oysters on the half shell look like mucus sitting in a pool of saliva on a rock; bourbon really doesn't taste good at all and is more about smell and sensation—these take more acclimation, but are well worth the effort. Just as an earlier America had more room for bourbon ("cocktail hour" in those John Cheever homes), it had more room for music that takes an especially high degree of concentration to write, perform, and listen to.

Serendipity once set me in the middle of an almost uncannily perfect illustration of the contrast between before and after in musical America. In 1997, the Museum of Television and Radio in New York was showing a rare tape of a concert by the Rat Pack. In the row ahead of me were two women around seventy; in the row behind me was a twenty-something couple in T-shirts. At one point, Sammy Davis, Jr. did a Mario Savio/*Archaeopteryx* version of "I've Got You Under My Skin." He started by

---

23. I understand that I am referring to a drink that has become an emblem of American imperialism. But I also submit that a great many who reflexively scorn Coke because of its corporate associations, if they first encountered it in a distant village in New Guinea as a warm, local brew made in earthenware pots and called something like *aktiip'a*, would cherish it as a masterful coca-flavored "indigenous creation" and eagerly seek to reproduce it for dinner party guests when they got home!

singing the song straight, accompanied by the orchestra. But he followed this with an extended scat-esque sequence, using the lyric as a skeleton for rhythmic chanting in a slit-eyed, trancelike state, arms extended, fingers snapping, head tilted back, eyes half shut. In other words, Sammy was getting down, in a style reminiscent of Bobby McFerrin.

About halfway through this part, one of members of the couple behind me said "Cool!" And right after this—I swear—one of the old women in front of me said "Enough of this is enough." The dowagers had liked Frank Sinatra and Dean Martin singing songs the way they were written in clean diction—they were used to a tradition in which music was a written affair, when the singer was expected to "do the song." But the scenesters behind me were used to jamming, when the singer gives us the song filtered through their visceral, spontaneous, unscripted essence, with no Egyptians interjecting with "La, la, la!" They therefore felt more at home with Davis's fantasy on Porter than with anything else in the special. They were used to music that just talks.

Education did not create this contrast. If these women had taken the "clapping for credit" music appreciation classes once common in American schools, these had introduced them to Rachmaninoff, not Bing Crosby and Glenn Miller—obviously people of this vintage cottoned to Crosby and Miller whether they had been steeped in classical or not. Nor was it that the twenty-somethings' America is dumber than the older women's had been. These ladies had swooned to written pop music as bobby-soxers in an America that the scholars and critics in Harold Stearns's anthology had condemned as antiintellectual back in 1922. Moreover, that was an America that had long ago richly drunk in the Romantics' conception of the natural.

The difference between the row in front of me and the row in back of me was the result of a specific cultural transformation in how Americans relate to authority, and its implications for what kinds of expression we regard as compelling.

And the date of the special: the year everything changed—1965.

CHAPTER SEVEN

Conclusion

It would be so easy! "We must overhaul the teaching of language skills in the schools!" "The time has come for a revolution in the world of arts and letters!" And so antiempirical, useless, formulaic, and irresponsible. Brass tacks: All indications are that the trends I have described will increase rather than decrease, and that there is little that can be done about it. I write that not out of any disinclination toward evaluating. I sense that I have made it clear in this book that I know what I like and why. But both our technology and our culture are pointing ineluctably away from the print-centered one of an earlier America, and the standards of language use that were bound within it. The issue is not whether this will continue, but where it will take us.

Technology on the March, Gutenberg on the Ropes

From Cellular Phone to Cell: The Great Enabler

A condition stems from an initial cause, but is then nurtured by enablers. There could be few better enablers of our slide toward the oral than the triumph of the cell phone.

As recently as 1993 I was rehearsal pianist for a musical when at one point the characters, going through a pretentious phase, took out what we called cellular phones. These were intended as signaling the characters' obsession with business, and the propmaster had to buy the phones—most people did not have ones of their own in 1993. By 1998, as cell phones began to percolate into ordinary life, columnists and comedians had a hard time shaking this association between cell phones and showing off. But in the summer of 1999, as I sat in a train car full of people nattering into their cells about the mundanest of things and realized that this was now an ordinary condition, it was clear that the look-at-me analysis was obsolete.

The cell phone is now as default a possession as a toaster. The millions of people using them today are no more showing off than they are when using Discmans. The reason Americans spend so much time on the phone today is basic human craving for contact. The cell phone is a cure for loneliness.

In hunter-gatherer societies, our concept of personal space is virtually unknown. Humans are social animals, and in indigenous societies, life is a fundamentally communal endeavor, where a small group of people who have known each other lifelong talk to one another all day long every day. In many societies, the absence of talk occasions discomfort—for people not to acknowledge one another's presence with talk is processed as chilly and unnatural. Hence the elaborate greeting formulas in many societies, required at each passing encounter, leaving many immigrants to the United States baffled by our quick, unfelt "How are you?" or mere nod or raise of the eyebrow.

Civilization and technology create ample circumstances for solitude. One reads or writes alone. The scholar, who reads and writes for a living, works in isolation, thanking his family in acknowledgments for putting up with this. Easy travel leaves more people alone more often than natural human conditions ever occasioned. Before the late nineties, humans in Western societies had come to accept as normal an amount of solitude in their lives that most people in the world would find strange.

The popularity of the cell phone reveals how unnatural our lives in fact were. Cell phones allow people to return to our natural state—talking casually during as many of our waking hours as possible, recreating the conversational ambience of a preindustrial village. A passage on the Web site of the Social Issues Research Centre beautifully captures both this advantage and the true meaning of the cell phone:

> The space-age technology of mobile phones has allowed us to return
> to the more natural and humane communication patterns of pre-

industrial society, when we lived in small, stable communities, and enjoyed frequent "grooming talk" with a tightly integrated social network. In the fast-paced modern world, we had become severely restricted in both the quantity and quality of communication within our social network. Mobile gossip restores our sense of connection and community, and provides an antidote to the pressures and alienation of modern life.

The elemental urgency with which people seek that sense of "connection and community" at all times now that technology allows it is almost striking, compared with the illusion of spiritual independence the technology of just a few years ago gave us. In train stations and airports today, one often catches what was until recently an unusual sight: The person who sits down in a waiting area, takes off their coat, stretches their legs and sighs, obviously readying themselves for a good hour or so of downtime—but without a newspaper, magazine, or book in their hands. Ten years ago, they would have had either this or at least some knitting—even a Game Boy would be better than just looking at the wall for an hour. I have gradually learned that this oddly empty-handed person will regularly take out a cell phone and talk on it for the entire hour. They *did* bring something to do—what most people would rather do than anything else besides have sex.

Of course many people insist that they are doing important business at such times. But then, just a few years ago they would have had to wait till they got home or to the office and this wasn't considered a problem. "Hello, Sean? This is Justin. I'm just checking in—I was wondering whether that inquiry from yesterday . . ."—whatever that call is about could have waited. As recently as 1998, it would have had to. What Justin is really doing is, indeed, checking in—reassuring himself of his connection to other humans. The business about the inquiry and the like are just excuses, in their way. The caller, and the person on the other end who has come to expect such calls, are, at heart, just warding off loneliness in a way that they could not have before.

Not long ago I had occasion to notice a man talking casually on his cell phone while in a public bathroom stall. Technically, why not, after all? Waste elimination is one of the few occasions when even hunter-gatherers suspend the conversational impulse briefly, preferring to take care of the task off by themselves—it is another human universal to approach human waste and its processing with a certain privacy. But the cell phone eliminates, so to speak, the visual and olfactory concerns that condition that universal, and therefore, why not talk then? It was only a matter of time.

Why Read If You Can Talk?

Of course, time was when in a literate society one often read a paper or magazine in that situation. But once there's a way to talk instead, there's no contest. And this reveals that while the cell phone does make it easier to keep up with one's children and frees us from the danger of winding up stranded on distant roads miles from a pay phone, it is also a siren call ever tempting us away from engaging written text.

There are readaholics and introverts among us—but they are a minority. I would venture that for not just some but most people, given a choice between spending an hour reading—anything—and talking on the phone, they would choose the latter. My impression is also that among the educated, this may temper somewhat but remains relevant— I have known academics of this tendency. Many might claim otherwise, but then I wonder how easy they might find it to resist that cheery ring even if the caller ID was not from a family member or good friend? Just a few years ago it was common for people with cell phones to claim "I only use it for emergencies and making plans"—but one hears this less and less, and quite a few of the people who were saying this in 1999 now gladly spend an hour initially allotted to a good read to talking on the phone.

And this is, literally, natural. We are social animals. Reading is an artificial activity, entailing engagement with an artificial representation of human speech and removing us from social engagement. Talking is what we are hardwired to do. The people in old films of crowds walking down the street are in their own heads. They had to be: Their era's technology did not allow them to talk on the phone on the street and they couldn't have imagined any such thing. But if we could go back and give them cell phones, they would have taken to them immediately—deep down, they'd have rather become villagers just like us. Hence, the increasingly common sight of people on the street with headset cell phones, so that even having their hands full does not impede them from talking— checking in with Justin—all the time.

Thus with the cell phone always available, engaging text while waiting, riding, or flying is an option rather than a virtual necessity to ward off solitude and boredom. People have always chosen talking over reading in such situations when they could. I recall a scene in a foreign-language textbook I used twenty years ago where a group of passengers traveling together on a train trip bought magazines at the station to read on the way. Even back then, I wondered—in real life, how much will any of those people want to read magazines when they will be sitting there facing one another? Certainly they will want to talk; I could only imagine a train traveler buying a magazine if he was alone. But now we can even talk when we *are* traveling alone, and so we do.

When the day comes that people are allowed to use their cell phones on airplanes, I predict that airport bookstores and newsstands will start reporting sharp drops in sales, as people gradually realize that they aren't going to read anything they bring on the plane anyway (give it about two years after cell use is permitted). We can also expect newspaper sales to continue to plummet rather than leveling off, no matter how clever ad campaigns are. Freed from the artificiality of solitude and silence, increasing numbers of people will spend the time they once had no choice but to kill with a newspaper talking on the phone.

"Just a Second—That's My Other Line"

Many modern Americans can also spend a lot more time on their landlines than was once possible. Even at my age I can remember the days when you would walk into a room when someone was on the phone and start to ask them something only for them to carefully shush you with "This is long distance"—too expensive to waste even half a minute. If you started a relationship and one of you moved across the country, then if you wanted to hold on to each other, you resigned yourselves to the prospect of truly massive telephone bills, one's tolerance of which was taken as an indication of commitment. And forget transatlantic romance—even if you shelled out the money, you got a low-volume, echoing connection that barely seemed worth it.

But with deregulation and technological advances, long-distance plans now allow us to keep in touch with people very far away for a thoroughly manageable expense. International phone cards allow immigrants to talk with their relatives on the other side of the world more cheaply, comfortably, and frequently than someone in California used to be able to talk with someone in New York just twenty-five years ago. This means more room for talk, and less reason to have to content ourselves with the abstract, mediated kind of human contact that reading text lends. If the cell isn't ringing, the landline will—and pick up we must.

It's sobering to recall that just one presidential administration ago, the situation for most people was that as soon as you left your house, no one could call you and the only way you could call anyone was to use a public pay phone. Now we can talk whenever we want to and many of us feel as naked without our cell as without our pants (I resisted for a while, but must admit having fallen into that state over the past year or so). The cell phone heaps several spadefuls of earth upon the coffin of what once was a print culture in the United States.

Orality in the News

Because the insta-phone phenomenon distracts us from having to engage text, Americans will therefore rely increasingly on radio and television to get their news. But then this will only take us even further away from written language and the print culture. While newsspeak is hardly as scruffy and telegraphic as casual speech, it is written in bite-size sentences designed to be taken in at speed by ear, and news language becomes more casual each year.

But more to the point, there is also a great deal more of the oral-leaning news available on television around the clock than there was before CNN and its imitators—in 1975, you could not get a guaranteed news fix on TV at just any old time of day. And reinforcing that is that television is permeating public spaces more and more as time goes by. Not very long ago, one largely watched television at home and in sports bars. Today, there are TV sets in train stations and in airport waiting lounges; television shows and informational broadcasts are increasingly available *on* planes; bars and cafes increasingly have television sets running around the clock channel-surfed by the person mixing drinks; and personal, carry-around television access on electronic devices is on the horizon.

Before radio or television, the only way one could possibly learn about the world beyond one's immediate purview on a regular basis was to engage written text. Beyond this, one could only hope to catch the occasional lecture (notice that "attending a lecture" is now an increasingly marginal activity, and that to the extent that we do partake of it we tend to call it "a talk," signaling how much less formally composed such events now tend to be). Then for a long time after radio and especially television were invented, they were only engagable in certain spaces of our lives, and only offered but so much news and talk in any given day. Now we are inundated in talking—often just talking—heads almost everywhere we go, to an extent that would overwhelm someone brought to our time from as recently as 1980. We live in a global village indeed these days, and in a village, people talk—all the time.

Iceberg in Hell: The Print Culture in Twenty-First Century America

"A man may love his country, Monsieur, and forswear its rulers."

The educated class are the main stewards of a nation's language. As I have noted, norms of usage have drifted away from the rigorously elaborated to the extent that this class has developed a deep skepticism of the moral legitimacy of the nation and its missions. Despite the renewed sense of patriotism documented among undergraduates and in polls of ordinary folk across the nation, I see no signs that anti-Establishment skepticism will decrease in the realms of journalism or education, whose practitioners today often choose these very careers out of a sense of a mission that tilts left. As such, there is little reason to suppose that America will come to love its language any time soon.

For example, all indications are that over the next ten years at least, our country will be engaged in combat with various groups and nations, Arab ones especially prominent among them. That certain peoples are dedicated to our annihilation warms the heart of no American. But this enemy hates us in part because of our imperialist ventures past and present. Because this is a bedrock of the brief against our government that many thinking Americans have long held, there is an identifiable sense among more than a few that this enemy on some level has a certain point. Seeing Palestinians shot by Israeli soldiers, recalling that not very long ago the White House was supporting Saddam Hussein, and watching as the Bush administration quietly backburnered the rebuilding of Afghanistan once the immediate threat of the shelterers of Bin Laden had been eliminated, it is impossible for many to revile Bin Laden, Al Qaeda, and their supporters as unhestitantly as Americans did Hitler. A common feeling is that Bin Laden is a bad guy, but that America is an evil nation.

As such, our battle against this foe will continue to inspire a vigilant, prickly sort of ambivalence among the educated. That our enemy is located in regions rich with oil will give any of our operations there a taint of the mercenary. To a thinking class for whom opposition to discrimination has been a defining aspect of their identities as intellectuals and moral people since the 1960s, nasty incidents of anti-Arab bigotry in the wake of 9/11—which will certainly sadly occur here and there—will stand out as indictments of America's essence in a way that equivalent incidents did not for a less enlightened World War II America. The nature of modern weaponry is such that, increasingly, we will likely be obliged to engage in preemptive strikes rather than responses to immediate threats—which will leave the necessity of the attacks eternally debatable. A President many assume to be underqualified and illegitimately instated will likely be elected for a second term.

In such a context, Speaking Truth to Power will remain a powerful and dominant reflex among the people best situated to present and impart higher levels of language to future generations. Somehow Oscar Hammerstein keeps coming back on me in this book: In the spring of 2003, there was a brief revival in New York of his creaky old operetta *The New Moon*. The dopey plot mechanics and corny lyrics were too dated to register with the audience as anything but camp, and there was but one moment the whole night when the audience truly connected with what was happening on stage. One character had occasion to declare "A man may love his country, Monsieur, and forswear its rulers." The Bush administration had gone to war with Iraq two weeks earlier, and delighted by the parallel, the well-heeled, educated audience erupted into one of the longest bouts of noisy applause I heard during that whole theater season. The only similar moment in my experience had been when heroine Tracy Turnblad in *Hairspray* squealed in response to a certain narrative twist "Manipulation of the judicial system to win a contest is un-American!"—another Bush swipe, and another show-stopping storm of hoots and clapping. The love for their country these theatergoers have is filtered; long gone is the sense that we were in good hands under "Mister President." The oppositional consensus this audience represented will continue to elevate Doing Our Own Thing as the enlightened position in our times.

The Black Thing

At this writing, I have seen *Hairspray* no fewer than five times, I must admit—I adore every second to an extent that almost embarrasses me. And there are other moments in it that signal the new America we live in. As a coda to an extended number featuring both white and black cast members ("Welcome to the Sixties"), three black chorus girls dressed as the Supremes step out to the footlights and riff vocally for about thirty seconds. All five times I have seen the show, the overwhelmingly white middle-class audience has gone insane for this quick little sequence unrelated to the plot—the Motown sound is now imprinted as a whitebread American delight. Later in the show, the heroine's friend has gotten involved with a black boy and sings "But now I've tasted chocolate and I'm never going back!" accompanying the declaration with an angular from-the-torso gyration, with "testifyin'" hand in the air, palm facing front, usually associated with black female singers defiantly bringing down the house. Again, the white audience screams with approval— a long way from 1968, when Petula Clark touched Harry Belafonte's arm on a TV special only for sponsor Plymouth to threaten to pull the plug on the show.

We've come a long way on race in America, and not just in black people "becoming whiter." A certain few continue to insist against all evidence that America remains deeply opposed to black people and their progress. But despite the fact that we are not quite where we would like to be yet, the melodramatic nature of this brand of self-medicating alarmism becomes ever more clear, and meanwhile white America becomes a blacker place by the year. Black-white marriages continue to burgeon. Black-white romantic relationships arouse increasingly little comment. Increasing numbers of children of black and white parents are identifying themselves neither as white nor black but "biracial," incorporating elements of both in a new race entirely. A whole generation of white young people have grown up in an America in which rap is just music, along with a new generation of "wiggers" who deeply embrace black speech, body language, music, and dress styles. On *American Idol*, the typical white singer sings in a black cadence and musical style—with this now processed as just general pop style.

Even aspects of black body language are becoming mainstream. Watch many non-black women about thirty and under and notice that to underscore a point in a feisty, "don't mess with me" kind of way, they often do the swivel-neck gesture formerly associated with the black "sis-tah." I have seen this in the very whitest of young women, in reserved Asian ones—and do not get the feeling they are even aware of it as a black incor-poration. The gesture has just gotten around, like *man* and the high-five. Too often assessments of the state of race relations in America imply that the situation between Americans of about fifty, stamped by experiences at an earlier state in our racial story, is "the way it is." But in the literal sense, the future of race in America is with the kids, and they are living in a United States quite different from the one we remember when we were their age.

Ironically, though, this heartening news will also help preserve our linguistic status quo. As wonderful as this evidence that we are truly get-ting past race is, it also means that increasing numbers of Americans are taking as a badge of authenticity a speech style that, with all of its mar-vels, is very much a spoken one. "Ebonics" is increasingly a lingua franca among Latino and some Asian teens as well as black ones, for example. More and more, we associate genuineness, honesty, and warmth with a kind of English that falls further from the written pole than white-bread spoken English does.

In this, America is undergoing a process of contact between speech varieties that has happened often worldwide. In contact between groups, intimate cross-cultural bonds often thrive amidst a context marked by conflict, and the result is cultural hybridicity. This extends to language, in ways counterintuitive given the prevalence of subjugation and misery. When Dutch settlers colonized South Africa, they took on indigenous Khoi ("Hottentots") as slaves and servants. White children were often reared by Khoi nannies, and in general Khoi became as deeply entwined with whites socially as black slaves were in the United States, and they left their mark on the whites' language. Afrikaans is an offshoot of Dutch, but has a double negative construction that Dutch does not: *Sy eet nie pap nie* "She doesn't eat porridge," or, word-for-word, "she eats not por-ridge not." Afrikaans inherited this from the Khois' language, which has the same construction: Khois spoke Dutch this way, and children heard their rendition as much as if not more than the native Dutch one, and incorporated into the Dutch they grew up to speak. Today this is proper Afrikaans, enshrined in the most formal of grammar books. History would lead one to suppose that the Khoi were about the last people the settlers would have modeled their grammar upon, but language changes from below as much as from above.

In a situation more parallel to the one in the United States, German teens are increasingly using Turkish slang to signal coolness. Relations between Germans and resident Turks are extremely rocky, but then that's the point: To sprinkle one's German with Turkish signals rebellion against the Establishment, a trend well-established among young Germans in response to the grimmer aspects of the nation's history. Here, we can see an artistic summation of the equivalent in America in the film *Head of State*, when Chris Rock's presidential candidate character lights up America's audiences with speeches climaxing with "That ain't right! That ain't right!" The character's audiences are quite mixed, not just black. And yet with all allowances made, the notion of middle-class whites jumping into chanting that slogan rings true today, whereas it would not have to the same extent fifty years ago. Interestingly, when the character first hits on the watchcry as he improvises a speech, he self-consciously "corrects" himself and says "That *isn't* right," acknowledging the wary eyes of his handler. But times have changed—it is more rhetorically effective for him to slide back into *ain't*, and before long the slogan is being printed for banners and advertising.

An interesting contrast: There is a photograph from the late 1930s of black women picketing in front of the White House. The women were quite likely warmly comfortable in some level of Black English, as most black Americans always have been. But the signs are couched in doily language: One of them reads "Down with Dastardly Practices!" These women spontaneously sensed the spoken/written gulf of their era—black identity or not, you wrote and spoke publicly in a way different than you spoke on the phone. The Chris Rock character in *Head of State*, like many black public figures in real life, is comfortable speaking in public the way he talks. And America loves that character as they love Chris Rock; the character and Rock live in what Stephan Talty has called Mulatto America, and thank God. But the particulars of history have it that a Mulatto America will be a more spoken one. Crucially, the Rock character's disapproving handler is played by black actress Lynn Whitfield: The white audiences get it while Whitfield's starchy Establishment cog doesn't, black though she is. The vernacular flavor Rock dwells in is portrayed as less black than race-neutrally real.

The New Immigration

One more thing that will encourage our drift away from the written is another by-product of something wonderful. This country is in the midst of a massive influx of immigrants, which will surely continue for several decades to come. That we can offer them a harbor from the glum circumstances too common elsewhere is a blessing, especially since our country has too often been responsible for the circumstances in question. But it can also only further discourage a sense of personal allegiance to this language.

For a vast proportion of Americans now and surely for a good long time beyond, English will be a language they had to work to learn and never spoke perfectly, or a language that they grew up with in school but did not use in the home with their closest intimates during their formative years. Yes, earlier immigrants wholeheartedly embraced English when they came here. But they came to a B.C. America with a more apple-cheeked sense of itself and its legitimacy, where the word *multicultural* did not exist and *diversity* had yet to take on the wary, sociopolitical tenor we associate with it.

And then on top of this, to the extent that the progeny of our new immigrants become American, they are increasingly identifying with a youth culture that cherishes gestural rebellion against the Establishment, with hip-hop as its music and Ebonics-lite as its language. In other words, they become, well, *American*. However that rubs you, elevating the crafted rendition of standard American English is decidedly not one of the hallmarks of that cultural space.

Schools As Symptom

These currents, technological and cultural, have awesome power. As such, to call for a revolution in how English is taught in the schools would be a tinny, formulaic gesture. Our educational establishment marinates in a national context in which the elaborate forms of English once thought of as the bedrock of respectability are considered archaic and irrelevant. This will only be reinforced as our populations of schoolchildren become increasingly polyglot and multicultural, given that a major strain in our educational establishment is committed to respecting diversity over fashioning foreigners into "good Americans." Then add the strain in the ed world that overtly distrusts English and America as imperialist threats to a child's developing a healthy, moral sense of identity. There is no room here for the casual assumption of another era that school was about teaching students to express themselves in a laboriously elaborate form of English; that fashion has gone the way of the garter.

The improvement of public education overall in America is one of our most daunting and urgent problems. But a realistic prediction is that to the extent that improvements proceed in language arts curricula (as they appear to be doing slightly), they will never go as far as producing students who write with the elegant fluency of the French Revolutionary polemicists, the Civil War writers, or the workaday journalist who dictated a letter to Marian Anderson to his secretary in prose like "I hesitate to suggest the expenditure of any sum of money which might seem to you considerable, and yet if it aids in the securing of larger audiences, it might be considered justified." This standard is alien to the generations of people working in and running the educational and textbook bureaucracies, just as it is to most of us. We will no more see a return to this era than men will go back to kissing women's hands. The times have changed, permanently.

What About Him?

Importantly, my desire is not to hector, but to describe what I believe is now an integral part of being an American. And as such, I might note that I sense myself as suffused with the same lack of linguistic self-love I have chronicled around me. I certainly would not want to listen to Edward Everett talking for two hours. Many readers may well have wondered at times in this book "What about the way he writes?" and my writing indeed hearkens to casual language much more than it would if I were writing forty or more years ago. From an early age I thrilled to nonfiction writers who wrote rather like we talk, and in that, was an American of our moment. If I were writing in 1920, I would write the way people of letters wrote then—I would know nothing else and would feel a slangier style as gauche. But I missed 1920. Even with my private-school education, English has been presented to me on paper plates instead of china. The only way I can write with a sense of pleasure or purpose is to play the written and the spoken against each other. I toe the line in my academic work because I couldn't get published in academic journals otherwise. But when writing for the public, the strictly formal prose that many writers restrict themselves to would feel as alien to me as walking into a 7-Eleven in top hat and tails, and I often wonder how more formally oriented writers keep themselves awake at the keyboard. Stare at the past though I tend to, when it comes to language, I am imprinted by my zeitgeist's imperative to Do My Own Thing. I would venture to say that much of why I became a linguist is out of a sense that any language must be better than this one—or better, out of a desire to hitch on to languages whose speakers seem to cherish them so much, given that no one seems to care much about mine.

The Good News

The Word on the Street

But the news is not all bad. The narrowing of the spoken/written gap has its benefits. As with most artifices, more than a little blind tradition congeals around written norms.

As I have noted before, it can be frustrating for a linguist to see how deeply entrenched the notion is that sentences like "Billy and me went to the store" or "There's lots of apples in there" are illogical and erroneous. As such, to a linguist the development of writing can sometimes seem a mixed blessing. Yes, standards are here for good whether we like it or not, and all should be taught them, especially in writing when so many people are especially prickly on the issue. But the fact remains: These standards are as arbitrary as fashion trends or the custom in some cultures (hardly universal) to close your mouth when you chew. In a better world, people would see things like "there's apples" as alternates suitable for casual conversation, rather than lapses of sound mental functioning.

Spoken America nudges us closer to this ideal. There will always be grammar hounds out there. But the general antipathy toward the formal makes people ever more comfortable using alternate constructions even in public settings. This is not a threat to communication, because these constructions occasion no loss of clarity. Whether or not it sounds good to one, "There's lots of reasons for that" is in no sense less logically effective than "There are lots of reasons for that." Through the eyes of a linguist, the less people go around fearing that an error may fall out of their mouths at any second the better. There are enough logically baseless ways in this world for people to look down on one another.

Overall, our times allow a celebration of the art in spoken language that was discouraged before. The fluent vernacular speech of many of playwright David Mamet's characters is a fine example: Mamet studiously writes his characters using actual everyday speech patterns. And *studiously* indeed; pulling this off requires a great ear and a lot of polishing—if only a playwright had written this way in 1600 and allowed us to see how ordinary people really talked back then. In his scripts, Mamet even uses parentheses to indicate the way we set off pieces of what we're saying to make a broader comment on the subject. Here is Teach in *American Buffalo*, really *talking*:

> Then let her *be* her partner, then. (You see what I'm talking about?) Everyone, they're sitting at the table and then Grace is going to walk around . . . fetch an *ashtray* . . . go for *coffee* . . . *this* . . . and everybody's all they aren't going to hide their cards, and they're going to make a show how they don't hunch *over*, and like that. I don't give a shit. I say the broad's her fucking partner, and she walks in back of me I'm going to hide my hand.

"And everybody's all they aren't going to hide their cards"—that's perfect. Proper English would have "Everybody is making it look like they aren't going to hide their cards," but this does not convey the scene as vividly or precisely as Mamet's thoroughly *articulate* language. In a distant day, a character of Teach's station would either be written speaking in a textbook English that flouted social reality, or in a cartoon William Bendix "palooka" dialect that would discourage relating to the character as a whole human being. Mamet's art would gain nothing from either of these old conventions. That it is now considered legitimate, rather than pushing the envelope, to draw characters using the language people actually speak must be counted an as artistic advance.

Minding the Gap

As artful as it can be, the gap between spoken and written language can also become a burden upon learners. It's one thing when literacy is largely the property of an elite with the time and energy to devote to laboriously mastering a refracted version of natural speech. But the required effort becomes a burden if literacy and education spread in a nation's population to ordinary, busy people.

A Moroccan can be one of the most articulate young people in her village, but then go to school and find that it is considered high comedy to put a great many words she is familiar with on paper, and that written Arabic is basically a different language altogether (talk about bilingual education!). This situation is the result of historical happenstance. The written form was established at a certain time and associated deeply with a signature religious document. Over time, in people's mouths the language developed into various new ones from place to place. In Europe, Latin underwent the same process, but on a continent where new nations formed, each one developing the local variety into a written language and leaving Latin behind. But in the Arab world, nationalism exerted less sway, and with no separation of state and religion, the Koran, written in that one antique stage of Arabic, retained its cross-regional authority. Hence a situation where one writes in one language and speaks another, although both are called Arabic. Arabic is a marvelous castle of a language: There's a *lot* of it, as one Semiticist pal of mine puts it. But in a more ideal world, the humble Arabic-speaking learner would not have to learn a whole new language to communicate beyond the hearth and the street. From our perspective, our Moroccan schoolgirl grows up speaking English and then goes to school in Anglo-Saxon. Of course, written English has never been that far from spoken, but it was once farther. The person who wanted to express and disseminate their views in writing in a socially acceptable way had more to learn—recall W.E.B. Du Bois taking the composition class despite already writing rings around most of today's college graduates. But as pretty as that writing looks to us from a distance, there was still considerable arbitrariness in how far it had drifted from how people spoke.

For example, nuances of vocabulary is one thing, but alternates like *rest* and *repose*, in which the sole difference is social tone are cute, but not necessary. The more such pairs there are, the closer we get to spoken versus written Arabic. Many such pairs are the accidental result of the fact that when French speakers ruled England, they left behind a lot of synonyms for English words from their own language. Sometimes, the two words diverged into different meanings—English *pig* for the animal, French-derived *pork* for the meat. But even then, strictly speaking, is there a *benefit* in that distinction? Thousands of languages do not make it. And in the meantime, just as often the result was a doublet in which the only distinction is barefoot versus shod: *rest* and *repose*. Okay, this means we have lots o' words. But really, cases like this are mere accident—

they did not occur as the result of any preordained goal. And if today no one expects us to ever say or write the word *repose* except in a word game or in irony, I'm not sure I sense a grievous loss. We've got plenty more words!

Sentences weaving subordinate clauses with main ones can get a point across more economically and precisely than strings of short utterances. But when sentences take this ball and run with it, the result is sentences running line after line, requiring artful intonation to convey in speech and tortured, snail-pace reading for all but an elite to read. This is again an accidental drift, like the baggy-pants fashion among teenagers—it starts with baggy jeans, but then why not even baggier, and then, well, why *not* jeans literally hanging off of your butt? They don't fall off, after all. But when your back pockets are hanging somewhere behind your knees, we are simply defining deviance downward for the hell of it—whatever the joy in it, function is no longer the issue. Yes, tapeworm sentences are possible: but are they advisable? What, precisely, do we gain from them, after all?

People spreading their views today do not have to master as stringent a set of standards and constructions in order to be considered worthy of reading or hearing. In all of its cacophony, this is a more democratic situation than the earlier situation. This is all the more urgent given the massive numbers of immigrants America has received since the Immigration Act of 1965. Most immigrants do not have access to the quality of schooling that inculcates the highest levels of English easily, and are not in a position to provide the print-rich homes that steep a child in written language throughout their formative years. A narrower spoken-written gap makes it easier for the immigrant and their child to achieve a degree of accepted articulateness in society, widening employment opportunities and easing participation in artistic realms.

A wide spoken-written gap can even be seen as evidence of conservatism and stasis, in the barrier it places between the masses and knowledge. In his "A Reader's Manifesto," B. R. Myers usefully recalls a character in Aldous Huxley's *Those Barren Leaves*[24] associating a large spoken-written gap with, of all things, the unlearned and indigenous:

[24.] Boy, there's a title that makes you want to dig that one up! This reminds me of a Broadway musical of 1970 titled *Cry for Us All*. Did the creators really think something with that title could possibly run longer than ten minutes? "What are you all doing tonight, Justin?" "Oh, we're going to *Cry for Us All*."

Really simple, primitive people like their poetry to be as . . . artificial and remote from the language of everyday affairs as possible. We reproach the eighteenth century with its artificiality. But the fact is that *Beowulf* is couched in a diction fifty times more complicated and unnatural than that of [Pope's poem] *Essay on Man*.

Myers draws an analogy to European peasants' frequent discomfort when goodly priests decided to preach to them in the spoken language rather than a high one they barely understood (i.e., French rather than Latin, at a time when they were still close enough to be processed, albeit somewhat athletically, as the same language). It is worth considering that education and information permeate a population more to the extent that the spoken-written gap narrows. The huge spoken-written gap in Arabic is not unrelated to the hierarchical and repressive nature of many Arab nations. An America where the newspaper was written in archly florid prose was an overtly classist one in which education was spread much thinner than any of us could approve of today.

The Lesser News

Yet as most of us spontaneously sense, there are repercussions from our new linguistic culture that are harder to process as progressive. I close by observing a few more trends in modern America that result when a culture loses its love for its language.

E-mail—Writing for an Oral Era

So it is, for instance, that even when technology has provided us with a new way to write, we approach it through a carefree, spoken filter that our ancestors likely would not have.

There are few questions a linguist learns to expect more often from media interviewers and the general public than what e-mail's impact on language will be. What strikes the layman is the notoriously riotous spelling and neglect of capitalization and punctuation, but these are technically issues of decor. A recording of someone reading aloud a message replete with spelling errors and devoid of capital letters would be indistinguishable from a recording of the same passage spelled and capitalized properly. But along with these cosmetic issues go the choppy sentence structure and elementary vocabulary that we see as appropriate in an e-mail, which Theodore Roosevelt and Susan B. Anthony would have considered unthinkable. Even in e-mails written somewhat more carefully, we tend strongly to write in a way that would sound natural if read out loud. We write e-mails like we talk.

There is a tendency to assume that e-mail *causes* us to neglect the written level of the language. But this presumes that for some reason, composing letters on a computer rather than by hand or on a typewriter, and then sending them over phone lines instead of through the mail, is incompatible with the norms of written English. But if you think about it, we would expect that computers would *encourage* observing those norms, since correction and revision are so much easier (no more erasing and whiting out).

The fact that we are so comfortable writing e-mails this way is a symptom of how our relationship to English has changed. If Americans in 1901 had developed e-mail, they would likely have composed the same kind of elegant missives that they had been writing as letters (telegraphese was a cost-cutting measure, not mere neglect). In that world, written English was a crucial social grace—recall the way the professor wrote to Du Bois in a mere comment scratched onto a composition draft. To these people it would have been gauche to send someone an e-mail in fragmentary, everyday language. One imagines ad copy in a 1901 Sears catalogue for an Underwood Tele-typographical Machine, complete with the weird italicizing typical of the period: "For a mere few cents' worth of electrical current, so effortlessly can the writer correct *stylistic infelicities* and polish the *expression of his sentiments* that this *novel device* will draw *elegant prose* from the fingertips of *every American*." Today the situation is the opposite: To insist on couching one's personal e-mails in textbook English would alienate friends.

And with e-mail, the letter becomes obsolete. E-mail style is a symptom, but the demise of the letter actively contributes to the death of the print culture, as letters were once a prime opportunity for practicing written language and were one of the prime showplaces for it. Between the cell phone and e-mail, the letter has become as historical a concept as elocution or the recitation. There is no more reason to pen an epistle to someone when you can now either shoot them an e-mail or better, ring them up at any time for minor expense. Giving someone your home address after meeting them is becoming a more formulaic gesture by the year, and I haven't written a personal letter since 1997.

Finally, we drift even further from old written norms with the rapidly jelling traditions of instant messaging. Here, technology does encourage the change, as the small keyboards and screens make abbreviations like *U* for *you* and *C* for *see* expedient, and make composing elaborate written syntax feel rather like packing too many clothes into a suitcase. Add the air of up-to-the-minute playfulness that the abbreviations carry—another signal of independence from higher authority—and we have another nail in the aforementioned coffin.

A New "Discourse"

Another symptom of our new linguistic America is that so much of the prose our academics write is inaccessible beyond the ivory tower and aesthetically barren even within it.

Of course, this development would actually seem to contradict the written-goes-oral analysis. It could hardly be said that the way postmodernist academics have come to write has the slightest resemblance to the way anyone talks. UC Berkeley gender theorist Judith Butler won the journal *Philosophy and Literature*'s annual Bad Writing award in 1999 for this sentence:

> The move from a structuralist account in which capital is understood to structure social relations in relatively homologous ways to a view of hegemony in which power relations are subject to repetition, convergence, and rearticulation brought the question of temporality into the thinking of structure, and marked a shift from a form of Althusserian theory that takes structural totalities as theoretical objects to one in which the insights into the contingent possibility of structure inaugurate a renewed conception of hegemony as bound up with the contingent sites and strategies of the rearticulation of power.

And there is nothing extreme about that passage as postmodernist writing goes. What always strikes me whenever I come across the usual criticisms of this kind of prose is how utterly *ordinary* it is today among many academics. Literature professor Paul Fry casually writes in a book "It is the moment of non-construction, disclosing the absentation of actuality from the concept in part through its invitation to emphasize, in reading, the helplessness—rather than the will to power—of its fall into conceptuality." Decidedly little orality here.

Crucially, this kind of writing took hold of academia in—you guessed it—the late 1960s, amidst the rise of the deconstructionist school and its quest to turn literary analysis toward Speaking Truth to Power. Under this school of thought, language is incapable of conveying pure meaning. Instead, the text is most interesting as a source for evidence of the unconscious biases, agendas, and ideologies of the author, those concerning power relations and their abuses most of interest. For the person working under this model, not only are the aesthetic aspects of language of little inherent interest, but English is the language of an oppressive, imperialist nation. Inevitably, the stewardship of that language that earlier generations of academics took for granted will have no meaning for them.

So far, we have seen how this sentiment has usually driven formal language toward the informal pole. But technically, this is not the only direction the change could go. Languages in general, for example, both simplify and complexify over time. English was once a language with as many conjugational endings on verbs and gender marking on articles as its relative German, but simplification over time has eliminated these; the same things happens in other languages all the time. But then, on the other hand, our use of *do* in questions (*Do you have a Scottie who is a surgical problem?*) and negated sentences (*You do not have a Scottie who is a surgical problem*)—is a complication that has emerged in English over time. Note that no language besides English that you have learned or grown up with uses *do* in this way.

In this light, once a culture loses a sense of its public language as something to cherish, then a shift toward the less elaborated, the spoken, is one possible result. But another is that the formal, written variety is allowed to drift into a hyperelaborated mode. It's perfectly natural, after all. That is: first, it's *possible*, there is no logical sense in which the elaborate phraseology of nineteenth-century English prose is the absolute limit of how dense prose can get. Second, for the few whose education and gifts allow them to use such language, it's *handy*: Packing complex ideas into single sentences is economical. These writers value this language like we all value that person who has a knack for getting the entire contents of our dressers into one carry-on bag. Finally, and crucially here, for these writers it is *permissible*, since in our America, its ungainliness does not offend its writers' sensibilities the way it would have for their pipe-smoking, blazered predecessors.

Butler has demonstrated this in her way, responding to detractors that revolutionizing ordinary modes of thought, the goal of the leftist, requires "difficult and demanding" language. But does it actually require language *this* difficult and demanding? Most postmodernist prose could rather easily be recast in learned but accessible language, and before the late 1960s, leftist thinkers as eager to change paradigms of thought as today's postmodernists wrote in language that did not require doctoral training to comprehend. But there would be no reason for today's postmodernists to bother. After all, *they* have mastered this artifice-on-overdrive, and meanwhile, their very politics marginalizes any concern with the potential beauties of this imperialist monster of a language.

That is: the *permissibility* factor is key here, in distinguishing what can happen today from what could have happened before the 1960s. As long as their colleagues understand them, it wouldn't occur to the postmodernist scholar that there could be anything inappropriate in academic prose so demanding that no one can learn from it beyond their coterie, and so utterly unconcerned with euphony, rhythm, or style. An English professor before the 1960s would never cast their ideas in prose of this kind, no matter how complex or nuanced their ideas might be, because the public norms of American society placed a high value on graceful prose composition. To put a point on it, the scholar under the old regime would have been embarrassed to write the way modern postmodernist thinkers do. But the public norms of linguistic expression that drove that embarrassment are now a thing of the past. And after that, the deluge.

It has become fashionable to accuse scholars of this ilk of willfully writing opaquely either to reaffirm their status or camouflage muddled thinking. But this is a cheap shot. These people have adopted terms to their own ends and assign them highly specific meanings that the scholar trained in the jargon understands. As such, postmodernists' language makes perfect sense to them and their colleagues (although there are times when even academics in on the lingo admit being a tad winded by the more extreme examples). I have had occasion to observe scholars engaging in dialogues with one another in a spoken approximation of this kind of language, and have seen them discuss one another's papers and books written in it. And in them I detect not the slightest sense of smugness in the use of these terms and the endless sentences. On the contrary, in my experience, such scholars use this language with the utmost urgency and sincerity. I once watched a professor discussing Rodgers and Hammerstein's also-ran bonbon musical *Flower Drum Song* in high Bad Writing style. Occasionally interjecting warm, colloquial comments about how much she had always adored the film version as a child, she gave off not a hint of imperiousness. She was simply communicating in a language she had taken in by osmosis in today's academic culture.

While attributing this prose to ego runs up against the wide range of personalities who use it in real life, attributing it to drift is supported by historical parallels. At its height, the Roman Empire was very much a culture of rhetoric. A core intelligentsia, along with a goodly chunk of the public, actively appreciated artful use of Latin in speech and writing. But as the empire declined, Latin's sphere of influence retreated into the scholarly and liturgical, no longer used on-line as a living language. By the sixth century, there were two developments. First, as we might expect, there were preachers like Caesarius of Arles and Gregory of Tours who wrote Latin in a more oral style than ever before and insisted on the legitimacy of doing so. But then on the other hand, from writers like Cassiodorus and Venantius Fortunatus came an opposite strain of Latin: soulless, hyperformalized writing that was dense without being beautiful or clever. This had always been possible, but by this time it was also permissible because a community of people who cared about good Latin writing no longer existed.

While it is not cynical, then, postmodernist prose is self-indulgent—but based on the same impulse that leads so many of us to indulge ourselves just as much in our shift toward the oral in our prose as well as in public speaking. Not that we do so deliberately, anymore than a modern woman indulges herself by not wearing the corsets she never knew. But the postmodernists don't know any better anymore either, as most of them today never knew an academia in which this kind of writing didn't exist.

The postmodernists are like a pair of twins who create a baroque little private language—but coming of age in an alternate universe in which social norms allow even adult twins to walk around talking in a weird way full of fussy tics fashioned by and for themselves. The postmodernist academics are innocents just like the rest of us. We all operate under an imperative to do our own thing, permeating our souls so deeply that we are no more aware of it than fish are aware that they are wet. That is as clear in "The move from a structuralist account in which capital is understood to structure social relations in relatively homologous ways to a view of hegemony in which power relations are subject to repetition, convergence, and rearticulation brought the question of temporality into the thinking of structure" as in *Eau de fcuk*.

But the fact remains that this kind of language renders these people's work all but inaccessible to any but the tiny elite who happen to want to become university professors like them. Before the 1970s, the writing in articles and books by academics was much less often so forbiddingly opaque to the layman. The sad fact is that today, the equivalent of books like Richard Hofstadter's *Anti-Intellectualism in American Life* (1964), Carter G. Woodson's *The Miseducation of the Negro* (1933), William Whyte's *The Organization Man* (1956), or Betty Friedan's *The Feminine Mystique* (1963) would likely be written in prose so dense and so keyed to academic culture that few beyond the ivory tower could learn from them. Their authors would be required to couch their ideas in bristling academese on the peril of having their books dismissed as not scholarly, under a new assumption that substance is antithetical to comprehension by even the intelligent layman.

Pick up Michael Hardt and Antonio Negri's *Empire* (2000), for instance, and see how hard it is to glean meaningful ideas from the knots of jargon and graceless sentences. Even many people game for a chapter or so will get winded beyond that. The brie-and-subtitles set may be celebrating the book as a landmark, but its ideas will never penetrate beyond that little world—for the simple reason that the book was written with blithe disregard for readability. Hardt and Negri may have ideas worth our nation's taking to heart, but no one will ever know beyond campuses and coffeehouses. The authors came of age in a time when our pride in language was at such a low ebb that even our intellectual elite no longer see it as necessary to impart their thoughts with grace and clarity. That is, because they lack the old sense of linguistic skill as a social grace, they have no reason to be concerned with how their language plays to the world at large, and this leaves them open to the temptation of composing their prose in a fashion opaque beyond their guild.

This is an especially uncomfortable fact given how much of this work purports to celebrate disenfranchised peoples and provide them with strategies for overcoming oppression. But then, that very political commitment in turn illuminates how this "Bad Writing" fits into our broken love affair with the English language.

"I Love the Way He Uses English!" (?)

It is also predictable in B.C. America how little we value articulateness. We're not entirely deaf to it, but we weight it less in evaluating a person than people in many countries do.

It can be easy to live with a failing relationship day by day. One way of realizing it's time to move on is spending a weekend with a happy couple. In the same way, a useful way of understanding the nature of our relationship to English is comparing it with how many foreigners feel about and use their languages. They often express an open admiration for the use of their language in crafted form that is all but nonexistent in the United States. Their observations in this vein would be as hard to translate into English as it would be to effectively render a *Seinfeld* script in another language. Imagine conveying Elaine describing seducing someone who just got dumped as "First you just let them know you're there for them. Then next thing you know, you're *there!*" I've seen *Seinfeld* dubbed into French, and it just kind of falls flat.

Similarly untranslatable into English would be a Russian friend of mine telling me, unprompted and long before I ever thought of writing this book, about a former boyfriend that "But the main thing that made me fall in love with him was his Russian. Oh, the way he could speak the language." Picturesque in Russian, but actually rather ordinary among them. Russians are given to extolling the glory of their language—and even in Russia, not just when pining over it after moving here. Until recently, the recitational tradition even still ruled in Russian schools, complete with rigorous training in the language's rules of grammar and the mastery of the formal level of what they cherish as their "great, mighty" language. (However, a long-simmering skepticism about rote learning that traces back a century is now eating into the rhetoric training.)

Related to this sense of language is that in Russia, the spoken/written gulf has long remained reminiscent of the one in America of a century ago, with the creeping of slangier language into print since the fall of Communism received as a titillating shock. In one of my favorite Russian grammar books, the author realizes that the gap is large enough to be as much of a challenge for the foreign learner as mastering the spoken basics, and outlines various levels of Russian that seem almost different languages. Written Russian is a bristling confection of endless sentences packing together information in ways whose mastery is nothing short of a mind game. Or, to convey this without dragging us through yet another passage of Russian and translating it, the previous sentence could quite plausibly come out as: *But written Russian constitutes itself as an elaborate confection of endless, in ways the mastery of which is nothing short of a mind game information packing-together sentences.* Wrap your head around that—any educated Russian is used to it. A Russian I once mentioned this kind of thing to immediately said that the difference between casual and formal speech is bigger in Russian. And her sense of the reason was that in America "the desire to maintain the lowest common denominator is quite strong"—precisely what I think has made the difference.

Another example is Turkish. For this language I must admit having prompted a pertinent answer, discussing my plans for this book with a Turkish linguist and political dissident. I can do no better than to quote her directly:

> We love our language and I remember many instances when I and others have said "Wow, I love the way s/he uses Turkish." My mother was telling me only yesterday that she loves the way some far cousins of her speak the language. To prove her point she called them and asked me to chat with them! They (two sisters and a brother who have not gone to college) have this very sophisticated, artistic style.

That phone call is utterly inconceivable in any American home. Really, translate it: "Wow, I love the way she uses English!" Impossible even among Americans who had lived in a foreign country for years. You might miss speaking the language you were born with, but never would you be moved to say that. But then it wasn't always thus: Recall Booker T. Washington praising Charles Eliot's English—not abroad, but in America! Or how about a young woman cooing "But the main thing that made me fall in love with him was his English. Oh, the way he could speak the language." Not even the finest American actress could even begin to render that statement in a plausible way.

The same is true of French. Speaking French well is tightly bound into the French's conception of their culture. Legions of Americans are familiar with functionaries in France switching imperiously to English the second you get a noun's gender wrong. As an African from the Central African Republic poignantly put it, "When you don't know the French language, you aren't a human being."

He was on to something. The French waiter who processes the smallest mistakes as an injury to a precious artifact has a conception of his language fascinatingly distinct from ours. Picture being fluent in French and waiting tables and getting a French customer. You and he fall into speaking French, to his delight, but then he decides to try to practice his English with you. Now imagine that the second he said *I shouldn't drink any more because tomorrow I will go on a river cruise* instead of *I shouldn't drink anymore because tomorrow I'm going on a river cruise*—subtle, isn't it? But the *will* immediately marks the foreigner—you switched back to French to put the poor fool out of his misery. In reality, you would indulge the guy longer that that—*much* longer—no matter how good your French was.

Africans who speak both English and French often say that they prefer English because English speakers put up with accents and mistakes more readily. The soul of being French is to elevate "proper" expression in the language—and always has been, right down to the quixotic mission of the Academie Française to root out encroachments from English. Granted, this aspect of the culture is not always socially pleasant, and the French operate under the same misconceptions about the nature of bad grammar that English speakers do. But the fact that they are so very sensitive to how their language is handled reveals a cultural value attached to the elaborated form of their language that we do not have.

Russia, Turkey, and France show us that the way we feel—or do not feel—about English in America is not default. Throughout the world humans embrace, cherish, and monitor their languages like children. It's us who are different.

Here would seem to be the place where I am supposed to launch into a fulmination about how inarticulate George W. Bush is. Many have rued that Bush's almost bizarre clumsiness with the English language ("I know what it's like to put food on my family," etc.) comes off as folksy and accessible to voters, which would underscore my point about our devaluation of articulateness. But Bush's malaprops go far beyond the rustic or relaxed, and from what I see, Americans of all political stripes see high comedy in Bushspeak. It is more to the point that the way he talks has not *prevented* him from becoming president. Candidates bite the dust for being untelegenic, dour, visible present-day philanderers, too strident, or looking silly posing in a tank—but both Bushes show that having trouble rubbing a noun and a verb together is not considered a mark against one in applying for the leadership of the land.

It is in fact impossible to say with certainty whether or not a president could have gotten away with being so swivel-tongued before the late 1960s. Before that time, presidents were not recorded when speaking off-the-cuff nearly as much as they are today. And to the extent that a candidate may have fallen into Bush-style gaffes, the custom used to be to clean up public figures' speech for print, and the press were much less prone to highlighting such figures' humbler idiosyncrasies in general. However, all indications from the B.C. linguistic culture strongly suggest that if, say, Warren G. Harding had stood on daises upending the language day after day, and there existed the communications technology and practice to bring this regularly before voters, James Cox would have become president. As it happened, Harding was a fine speaker, and in his era, this was part of what brought such a mediocre figure to such prominence.

So It Is and So It Will Be

Thus we will continue to thrill most to English yoked to orally based charisma. The visceral and spiritual thrill of the black sermon will come to mind most readily when we think of the orator, while the pointedly persuasive "written" speech will remain as rare as a comet sighting. The livest presence poetry will ever again have in this nation will be the *Spoken* Word scene, while most written poetry will leave a great many people wondering just what the big deal is. Reviewers will eat up Dave Eggers's "spoken" writing style as vivid in contrast to reviewers in 1920, who would have found his prose so slapdash that they'd have had him deported under trumped-up charges in the Palmer Raids. Meanwhile, the cut-glass elegance of prose like this by Jacques Barzun:

> This is to say that cultural absolutes do not exist, pro or con. Nobody in the Renaissance circles so far looked at was shocked by the rise to eminence of the women whose mention here is far from closing the roster. The names of others are known and their lives recorded in detail; their deaths memorialized in poems, letters, and other expressions of praise and grief. The debate in *The Courtier* suggests that the reality was ahead of the stereotype and this fact was the spur to the arguments in defense of equality for the sexes. (88)

will remain the hallmark of a very old man who spent his first thirteen years in France.

It isn't that we will be deaf to verbal energy of any kind. Surely many admire the hot sermon for the preacher's use of language; Spoken Word fans relish spending an evening at a festival of language; people snap up Eggers's work, admiring his language. But when we admire these uses of language, we do not vibrate to these uses of *the English language* specifically. And because we will thrill most to language used to Speak Truth to Power, we will continue to be moved more by how charismatically someone flouts the rules of the standard language than how deftly they work within them. It is now an established cultural hallmark: *The American typically relates warmly to the use of English to the extent that it summons the oral, while passing from indifference to discomfort to the extent that its use leans toward the stringent artifice of written language.*

When a round-the-clock chatting device and high levels of immigration meet a country uniquely skeptical to authority and in thrall to a dialect emblematic of the oppositional, American English becomes a new kind of language in human history—a naturally born Esperanto. Esperanto was created on paper in the late 1880s as a universal language intended to promote world peace, designed to be easy to learn while still a full, living tongue. It lives today among about two million dedicated speakers. Although there are now a small number of children being brought up in Esperanto along with another language, usually the Esperantist grows up with a native language and then acquires Esperanto later in life as a tool to communicate with foreigners who have also chosen to learn it.

There is a small Esperanto literature, and it is a lovely and fascinating language that I have thoroughly enjoyed since I was a teenager. Nevertheless, few speakers would claim that the language occupies the space at their emotional core that their native language does. They did not learn their first words in it, usually do not pass it on to their children, and no matter how fluent they become in it, they will always express themselves most fully in their native tongue. Esperanto is a tool.

In the same way, American English is a tool. Countless millions utilize it, but whereas Esperanto speakers treasure the language, most of us do not cherish English emotionally anymore than we do a screwdriver. We are not proud of English. Hearing it after a year living abroad in another language, we may feel a certain relief and pleasant rush of familiarity, but we do not sigh in rapture at hearing its lovely particularities. We do not value English as a communal possession to decorate, to push to be the most that it could possibly be, as one does with what one loves.

For all but an increasingly lonely few of us, regardless of class, race, or educational level, American English is merely a quotidian conduit through which we Do Our Own Thing.

Interestingly, this is not the first time English has undergone a diminishment of resources. English is the only language in all of Europe that has no gender marking of the *le crayon/la plume* type, and it's not an accident that it is the only language in its subfamily, Germanic, whose spoken variety has no distinction between words like *here* and *hither* ("to here") or *where, whither,* and *whence,* as well as many other noisome, hair-splitting constructions that bedevil us when learning German, Dutch, Swedish, and the gang. The reason for this is most likely that when Scandinavians began invading and occupying Britain in the eighth century, there was a period when so many people were speaking English as a second language that children grew up hearing foreigners' incomplete versions of it as much as the natively spoken variety. They ended up adopting foreigner's English as their native language, and in a society in which literacy and education were marginal, elite activities, the language was then passed down the generations this way forever. English remained complex in many ways (as any foreigner learning it will attest!), but it had gotten a close shave, many of its complications worn away by people speaking it the way Americans speak French or Spanish when they learn it in school. This has happened to many languages around the world when history has it that for a time, more people speak it as a foreign language than as a native one. Modern Hebrew was similarly streamlined as it was revived by immigrants to Israel, and Swahili, long spoken by most as a second language rather than first one, is a strikingly user-friendly member of a litter of sibling languages like Zulu that are more elaborated.

Thus conditions can intervene to block a language from being passed down the generations fully intact. Today, there is nothing blocking the preservation of *spoken* English over time: Immigrants' children almost always learn perfect, native-sounding English from their American peers. But the artificial written variety is passing through a bottleneck. The late twentieth century has been the locus of a new lurch on English's time line in America, where oratorical, poetic, and compositional craft of a rigorously exacting nature has been cast to the margins of the culture. And just as foreigners tend to leave out the quirkier aspects of a language because they are so challenging to master deliberately, our wariness of crafted language stems from a rejection of the challenge that it poses, out of a sense that we will benefit more from following our visceral inner muses. As such, we increasingly become foreigners in the outer reaches of our own language. English becomes Esperanto indeed, as Esperanto's creator deliberately made it as free of difficult rules as possible in order to make it easy to learn.

The other day, newsstands in New York were bedecked with the *New York Daily News'* pithy eruption of a headline announcing the United States armed forces' penetration of Baghdad, WE'RE IN. With that headline ringing in my head as I walked down the street, I caught an old cinema lobby card in a shop window announcing a beauty contest presided over by Rudolph Valentino of beauty queens "Selected from the Principal Cities of the United States." That language alone, contrasting so sharply with the bleat of the *Daily News* headline, immediately marked the card as ancient, and in fact that contest was exactly eighty years ago as I write, 1923. Some months earlier President Harding had made one of his last speeches, on saving Alaska from oil drilling (*plus ça change!*), intoning the likes of "Words seem inadequate to portray the grandeur, to measure the magnificence, to express the mightiness, or acclaim the glory of monumental mountains and their jeweled valleys." The month after that, W. C. Fields became the toast of Broadway as a small-time hustler in *Poppy*, entering a new fairgrounds with the line "This is evidently the scene of our future labors." This show set the mock grandiloquence that would define the Fields persona we are familiar with, and though the verbosity was intended as a joke, the fact is that the joke registered in 1923.

But in 2003, *Letterman* tapes up the street from where I saw the *Daily News* headline, and neither Letterman nor his guests trade on hyperelegant language to milk laughs. Eighty years later, up is out in favor of in. We've tuned in; we're in ourselves and seeking to make our way in to the people around us. The barriers are down. "We're in," indeed—in oral America, to be precise.

Small-town, poker-playing Harding was no highbrow. His election was exhibit A in what motivated H. L. Mencken to indict the American populace of just that time as a thoughtless "booboisie." But "boobois" or not, in those days, in public one spoke and wrote "up" if one wanted to be taken seriously. As to *Poppy*, in terms of artistic substance it occupied roughly the level of *My Best Friend's Wedding*. But Fields's dictionaryspeak tickled audiences of 1923 because humor springs from truth. For his audiences, fancy language was at the table. It had a place in their hearts.

We, on the other hand, can't even laugh at it, because for us there is no truth in it at all.

References

x. **Everett's oration:** Garry Wills, *Lincoln at Gettysburg* (New York: Touchstone, 1992), 213–47.

xi. **1917 silent film:** *Tillie Wakes Up*, with the marvelous Marie Dressler.

xv. **Jonathan Swift and *rebuked*:** Jonathan Swift, *Proposal for Correcting, Improving and Ascertaining the English Tongue* (1712), (R. C. Alston, ed., English Linguistics 1500–1800, Menston, England: The Scolar Press, Ltd., 1969), 21–2.

xvi. **Roebling's letters:** David McCullough, *The Great Bridge* (New York: Touchstone, 1972) 155–7.

xxii. **Hendrik Hertzberg comment:** "The Silence of the Historic Present," *New York Times*, August 11, 2002.

xxiv. **Bob Dylan:** Well, think about it.

1–2. **Gullah and Black English:** for an up-to-date defense of the case, see John R. Rickford, "Prior Creolization of African American Vernacular English? Sociohistorical and Textual Evidence from the Seventeenth and Eighteenth Centuries," *African-American Vernacular English*, ed. by John R. Rickford (Malden, MA: Blackwell, 1999), 233–51; for reservations, see John McWhorter, 2001, "Strange Bedfellows: Recovering the Origin of Black English," *Diachronica* 17: 389–432.

6. **Vocabulary size:** a useful summary is David Crystal, *The Cambridge Encyclopedia of the English Language* (Cambridge: Cambridge University Press, 1995), 123.

7. **Lokele drum talk:** John F. Carrington, *La voix des tambours: comment*

comprendre le langage tambouriné d'Afrique (Kinshasa: Centre Protestant d'Éditions et de Diffusion, 1974), 41–2.

9. J. K. Rowling, *Harry Potter and the Goblet of Fire* (New York: Arthur A. Levine, 2000), 12.

10. **Hedge passage:** Wallace Chafe and Jane Danielewicz, "Properties of Spoken and Written Language," *Comprehending Oral and Written Language,* ed. by Rosalind Horowitz and S. Jay Samuels (New York: Academic Press, 1987), 89.

11–12. **Black-and-tan puppy passage:** M.A.K. Halliday, "Spoken and Written Modes of Meaning," *Comprehending Oral and Written Language,* ed. by Rosalind Horowitz and S. Jay Samuels (New York: Academic Press, 1987), 59.

12. **Post-conference transcript:** I'm not telling!

13. **Junior college students:** Edward C. Carterette and Margaret Hubbard Jones, *Informal Speech* (Berkeley: University of California Press, 1974), 390.

14–15. **Leo Tolstoy,** *Anna Karenin* translated by Rosemary Edmonds, (London: Penguin Books, 1954), 343.

16. *A house is building* as **"proper English":** a crisp summary of the issue, including the knee-slapping joke, is in Richard Bailey, *Nineteenth-Century English* (Ann Arbor: University of Michigan Press, 1996), 221–5.

17. **Tomatoes:** are indeed fruits.

19. **Hebrew Bible versus translations:** presentation inspired by an observation in Walter Ong, *Orality and Literacy: The Technologizing of the Word* (London: Routledge, 1982), 37.

21. **Silent reading and spaceless classical texts:** Naomi Baron, *Alphabet to Email* (London: Routledge, 2000), 33–4.

23. **Swift on simplicity:** Jonathan Swift, *Proposal for Correcting, Improving and Ascertaining the English Tongue* (1712), (R. C. Alston, ed., English Linguistics 1500–1800, Menston, England: The Scolar Press, Ltd., 1969), 32–3.

24. **Labov quote:** William Labov, "The Logic of Nonstandard English," *Language in the Inner City: Studies in the Black English Vernacular,* ed. by William Labov (Philadelphia: University of Pennsylvania Press, 1972), 201–40 (quote is on page 213).

24. **Repetitious passage:** Basil Bernstein, *Class, Codes and Control: Theoretical Studies Towards a Sociology of Language* (New York: Schocken, 1971), 135.

25–27. **Itchy Bernstein passages:** Bernstein, 32 and 151.

26. **Du Bois's terminology:** Try *The Philadelphia Negro: A Social Study* as a prime example, in which we marvel at an academic sociologist casually designating certain people as "lazy," etc.—hardly unusual at the time.

26. **Bernstein's clarifications:** Examples at Bernstein, 136, 178–83.

26. **Bernstein on restricted versus elaborated code:** Bernstein, 146–8.

27. **"What did the justice of the peace do?":** Tolstoy (Edmonds translation), 354.

29. **Lewis and Clark:** David Simpson, *The Politics of American English* (New York: Oxford, 1986), 119.

30. ***Main Street* teens:** Sinclair Lewis, *Main Street* (New York: Bantam Books, 1996 edition [1920]), 118.

31. ***Candid Microphone:*** episode of July 14, 1947.

31. **1947's bestsellers:** Michael Korda, *Making the List* (New York: Barnes & Noble, 2000), 95.

CHAPTER TWO

33. **Joke:** This was sent to me in an e-mail message by someone who wrote me about *The Power of Babel*; I immediately copied the joke into the file of my notes for this book, but deeply regret finding that I no longer have the message itself and thus cannot thank this gentleman by name. But he knows who he was, and Go Bears.

35–37. **Zuni ceremonial language:** Stanley Newman, "Vocabulary Levels: Zuñi Sacred and Slang Usage," *Language in Culture and Society*, ed. by Dell Hymes, (New York: Harper & Row, 1964), 397–406.

37. **Ceremonial language often taught:** Wick R. Miller, "The Ethnography of Speaking," *Handbook of North American Indians (vol. 17)*, ed. by Ives Goddard, 222–43 (Washington, DC: Smithsonian Institution, 1996), 229.

37. **Aristotle:** *The Art of Rhetoric*, trans. H. C. Lawson-Tancred (London: Penguin Books, 1991).

39. **Pomo reminiscence:** Edwin M. Loeb, 1926. "Pomo Folkways." *University of California Publications in American Archaeology and Ethnology* 19 (2). Berkeley: UC Berkeley Department of Anthropology.

40. **Bryan quote:** Ronald F. Reid, *Three Centuries of American Rhetorical Discourse* (Prospect Heights, Ill.: Waveland Press, 1988), 601–606.

41. **Comment on Bryan's intelligence:** Stephen Jay Gould, "William Jennings Bryan's Last Campaign," *Bully for Brontosaurus: Reflections in Natural History* (New York: W.W. Norton and Co.), 416–31.

41–42. **Du Bois speech:** Herbert Aptheker, ed., *Against Racism: Unpublished Essays, Papers, Addresses, 1887–1961 by W.E.B. Du Bois* (Amherst: University of Massachusetts Press, 1985), 14–6.

42. **Booker T. Washington on Eliot's English:** Booker T. Washington, *Up from Slavery* (New York: Dover Publications, 1901 [1995 edition]), 145.

42–43. **Eliot at Harvard:** Naomi S. Baron, *Alphabet to E-mail* (London: Routledge, 2000), 146–8.

43. **McGuffey excerpts:** William Holmes McGuffey, *McGuffey's Fifth Eclectic Reader* (1879 edition) (New York: The New American Library, 1962), 26–7.

44. **Maya Angelou's oratory contests:** Maya Angelou, *Gather Together in My Name* (New York: Bantam, 1974), 113.

44. **Congressional speeches:** *United States of America Congressional Record, Proceedings and Debates of the 77th Congress, First Session, Vol. 87, pt. 9* (Washington, DC: United States Government Printing Office, 1941), 9520-7.

45. **Tapes of session:** Hearty thanks to John McDonough for copies of the Mutual and CBS radio feeds.

45. **Sam Brownback quotation:** "Excerpts of Speeches Made on Senate Floor Regarding Resolution on Iraq," *New York Times,* October 4, 2002.

46. **Franklin D. Roosevelt address:** history.acusd.edu/gen/WW2Text/ fdr_speech_420106.html.

46. **George Bush's State of the Union address:** "Hypertext on American History" Web site.

47. **Mark Gerson quote:** *Esquire,* December 2002, 156.

51. **Norma Millay learns how to cuss:** Nancy Mitford, *Savage Beauty* (New York: Random House, 2001), 163.

52-53. **Joseph McCarthy speech:** "History at Illinois" (University of Illinois at Urbana-Champaign) website.

53. **Newton Minow speech:** "American Rhetoric" website.

55. **Ed Koch speech:** "History Channel.com" website.

55. **Michael Eisner speech:** American Society of Newspaper Editors' website.

56-57. **Savio speech:** transcribed from video on the Media Center page of the "Free Speech Movement Digital Archive" Web site.

57. **Savio and the "forum":** Reginald E. Zelnik, Mario Savio: Avatar of Free Speech, *New York Times Magazine,* December 29, 1996.

57. **Savio as "Socratic teacher":** Henry Mayer, "A View from the South" The Idea of a State University," *The Free Speech Movement: Reflections on Berkeley in the 1960s,* ed. by Robert Cohen and Reginald E. Zelnik, 157-69 (Berkeley: University of California Press, 2000), 164.

57. **Savio's stutter and later conversational style:** Doug Rossinow, "Mario Savio and the Politics of Authenticity," in Cohen & Zelnik 533-51.

58. **Savio as language lover:** Lynne Hollander Savio, "Remembering Mario," in Cohen & Zelnik, 552-6.

58. **Du Bois and notes:** David Levering Lewis, personal communication, November 2002.

58. **Savio and notes:** Editors' preface to Mario Savio, "Thirty Years Later: Reflections on the FSM," in Cohen & Zelnik, 57-72.

61-62. **Emma Goldman's speech:** "Gifts of Speech: Women's Speeches from Around the World."

62. **Emma Goldman newsreel clip:** "The Emma Goldman Papers" website.

64. **Sermon excerpt:** Bruce A. Rosenberg, *Can These Bones Live?: The Art of the American Folk Preacher* (Urbana: University of Illinois Press, 1988), 301.

65–66. **Sermon on paper versus "translation":** ibid., 145.

66. **Folk preachers' intuitive approach:** ibid., 36–7, 157–8.

67. **Mohave oratory:** Leslie Spier, *Yuman Tribes of the Gila River* (Chicago: University of Chicago Press, 1933), 168.

67. **The decline of the sermon:** Dean Smith, "An Era When the Art of the Sermon Has Declined," *New York Times*, March 30, 2002.

68. **Raymond toast:** David McCullough, *The Great Bridge* (New York: Touchstone, 1972), 475.

69. **Anthony quotes:** Ida Husted Harper, *Life and Work of Susan B. Anthony* (Vol. 2) (Salem, NH: Ayer Co., 1983; orig. 1898), 996–1003.

CHAPTER THREE

74–75. **Gioia book (including 1991 article):** Dana Gioia, *Can Poetry Matter?* (St. Paul, MI: Graywolf Press, 2002).

75. **Millay career highlights:** Nancy Milford, *Savage Beauty* (New York: Random House, 2001), 298–9, 367, 470.

75. **Dorothy McGuire's spare time:** Richard Severo, "Dorothy McGuire, Steadfast Heroine of Film, Dies at 83," *New York Times*, September 15, 2001.

76. **Howard Dietz's doggerel:** Terry Teachout, *The Skeptic* (New York: HarperCollins, 2002), 151.

76–77. **Adolph Green:** Jesse McKinley, "A Broadway Farewell? That's Entertainment," *New York Times*, December 4, 2002.

77. **Marie Dressler's recitation:** Matthew Kennedy, *Marie Dressler* (Jefferson, NC: McFarland & Co., 1999), 74.

77. **Millay's mother's bedside manner:** Savage, 25.

79. *Fatal Interview* **on bestseller list:** Michael Korda, *Making the List* (New York: Barnes & Noble, 2001), 65.

79. **Dorothy Thompson:** Savage, 434.

79. **Ruth Draper monologue:** "On the Porch in a Maine Coast Village," on the CD *Ruth Draper and Her Company of Characters: Selected Monologues.* (This woman was truly a genius: Buy this!)

80. **Brodsky in the classroom:** Carol Muske-Dukes, "A Lost Eloquence," *New York Times*, December 29, 2002.

81. **Yugoslavian bards:** Milman Parry, "Whole Formulaic Verses in Greek and Southslavic Heroic Song." *The Making of Homeric Verse: the Collected Papers of Milman Parry*, ed. by Adam Parry (Oxford: Clarendon Press, 1971), 376–90. (Originally published in Transactions of the American Philological Asssociation 64:179–97, 1933.)

81. **Human universals:** Donald E. Brown. *Human universals* (New York: McGraw-Hill, 1991).

83. **Berryman excerpt:** David Perkins, *A History of Modern Poetry: Modernism and After* (Cambridge, MA: Harvard University Press, 1987), 90–1.

83–84. **Baldwin poem:** James Campbell, *Talking at the Gates* (London: Faber & Faber, 1991), 16.

84. **Salter on Collins:** Mary Jo Salter, "You Are Not the Pine-Scented Air, O.K.?" *New York Times Book Review,* October 20, 2002.

85. **Collins excerpt:** "Osso Buco" in Billy Collins, *Sailing Alone Around the Room* (New York: Random House, 2001), 49.

85. **Nehring comment:** Christina Nehring, "Last the Night: The Abiding Genius of Edna St.-Vincent Millay," *Harper's,* July 2002, 74–81.

86. **Shulevitz:** Judith Shulevitz, "No Callers, Please—We're Poets," *New York Times Book Review,* September 22, 2002.

87. **Somalian poetry:** John William Johnson, "Somali Prosodic Systems," *Horn of Africa* 2: 46–54 (1979).

88–89. **Barth comment:** John Barth, "The Literature of Exhaustion," *The Friday Book: Essays and Other Nonfiction* (New York: G. P. Putnam's Sons, 1984), 62–76. (Essay orig. published 1967).

89. **Perkins:** Perkins, 345–6.

89. **White House poetry event:** Elisabeth Bumiller, "With Antiwar Poetry Set, Mrs. Bush Postpones Event," *New York Times,* January 31, 2003.

90. **Class poet in Millay's youth:** Savage, 42.

90. **Bishop excerpt:** Elizabeth Bishop, *Geography III* (New York: Farrar, Straus & Giroux, 1976), 3.

91. **Jefferson quote:** Margo Jefferson, "The News from Poetry," *New York Times Book Review,* May 11, 2003.

91–92. **Millay and sisters washing dishes:** Savage, 4.

93. **Hart lyric:** "To Keep My Love Alive," music by Richard Rodgers, from *A Connecticut Yankee* (1943 revival).

94. **"Put On a Happy Face":** music by Charles Strouse, lyric by Lee Adams, from *Bye Bye Birdie* (1960).

94. **"The Girlfriend of a Boyfriend of Mine":** music by Walter Donaldson, lyric by Gus Kahn, from *Whoopee* (1928).

94. **Audra McDonald's comment:** Jesse Green, "Diva of the Difficult Song," *New York Times,* November 11, 1999.

95. **Cobain's scrapbooks:** Kurt Cobain, *Journals* (New York: Riverhead), 136–41. (The poor boy must be rolling in his grave that anyone published these.)

96. *My Favorite Husband* **episode:** "Liz Writes a Song," January 27, 1950.

98. *War and Peace* **supertitles:** Matthew Gurewitsch, "Supertitles Are Starting to Become Part of the Act," *New York Times,* February 10, 2002.

100. **Luhrmann on** *Bohème* **and English:** William Wright, "Giving More Puccini to the People," *New York Times,* December 8, 2002.

103. *Così* **translation:** Ruth and Thomas Martin translation (Schirmer edition, 1951), 11.

106. **Hammerstein's recollection:** Oscar Hammerstein II, *Carmen Jones* (published libretto) (New York: Alfred Knopf, 1945), xiii–xiv.

109–110. **Baraka and Williams:** Werner Sollors, *Amiri Baraka/LeRoi Jones: the Quest for a "Populist Modernism"* (New York: Columbia University Press, 1978), 38.

110. **Moore excerpt:** Zoe Anglesey, ed., *Listen Up!: Spoken Word Poetry* (New York: One World, 1999), 62.

110. **Morris poem:** ibid., 81.

111. **"Chamomile Tea":** J. H. McWhorter, © 2003.

113. **Komunyakaa:** ibid., xi.

113. **Baraka and the Beats:** Amiri Baraka, *The Autobiography of LeRoi Jones* (Chicago: Lawrence Hill, 1984), 219.

116. **B. R. Myers, *A Reader's Manifesto*** (Hoboken, NJ: Melville House, 2002), 10–23.

117. **Baraka excerpt:** Widely quoted in media sources after Fall 2002.

119. **Barth comment:** John Barth (same citation as above).

CHAPTER FOUR

121. **Gershwin letter:** Joan Peyser, *The Memory of All That* (New York: Simon & Schuster, 1993), 103.

123–124. **New York newspaper letters on Jewett murder:** Patricia Cline Cohen, *The Murder of Helen Jewett* (New York: Alfred A. Knopf, 1998), 44, 330.

123–124. **Richard Robinson letters:** Cohen, 225–6, 280.

123. **Civil War letter:** " 'My precious Loulie . . . ': Love Letters of the Civil War" Web site (on Virginia Tech's American Civil War Resources site)

124. **Stanton letter:** Ellen Carol DuBois, ed., *Elizabeth Cady Stanton, Susan B. Anthony: Correspondence, Writings, Speeches* (New York: Schocken Books, 1981), 69.

125. **Teddy Roosevelt letters:** H. W. Brands, ed. *The Selected Letters of Theodore Roosevelt.* (New York: Cooper Square Press, 2001), 74–5, 474.

125. **Marian Anderson letter:** Allan Keiler, *Marian Anderson: A Singer's Journey* (New York: Scribner, 2000), 253.

128. **Railroad trip passage:** David McCullough, *The Great Bridge* (New York: Touchstone, 1972), 66.

128. **John Roebling passage:** ibid., 91.

128. **"Principal orations":** ibid., 520.

129. **Williams and Walker review:** Thomas L. Riis, *Just Before Jazz* (Washington, DC: Smithsonian Institution Press, 1989), 121–2.

129. **Assistant's reminiscence of Toscanini:** Joseph Horowitz, *Understanding Toscanini* (Berkeley: University of California Press, 1987), 293–4.

130. **Professor's comment on Du Bois's paper:** Herbert Aptheker, ed., *Against Racism: Unpublished Essays, Papers, Addresses, 1887–1961 by W.E.B. Du Bois* (Amherst: University of Massachusetts Press, 1985), 20.

130. **Mencken passage and reviewer comment:** Terry Teachout, *The Skeptic* (New York: HarperCollins, 2002), 71–2.

130. **Associated Negro Press director to Marian Anderson:** Keiler, 107.

130. **Toaster booklet excerpt:** James Lileks, *The Gallery of Regrettable Food* (New York: Crown Publishers, 2001), 171.

131. **"Sisters" letter:** Letter to the editor, *Village Voice*, 9/12/68 (published

in Randall Kennedy, "Interracial Intimacy," *The Atlantic Monthly*, 12/2002, 106; thank you to Randall Kennedy for giving me the date of the letter's appearance).

134. **Savio and "Fuck" sign:** Greil Marcus, personal communication, December 2002.

134. **Mencken on Harding:** Baltimore's *The Evening Sun*, March 7, 1921, quoted in Jonathan Yardley, "The Sage of Baltimore," *The Atlantic Monthly*, December 2002, 139.

134. **Edna St. Vincent Millay on her mother's "English":** Nancy Mitford, *Savage Beauty* (New York: Random House, 2001), 143.

135. **Comment on Angelou's "English" and Angelou memorizing *Hiawatha*:** Maya Angelou, *Gather Together in My Name* (New York: Bantam, 1974), 42, 40.

135. **Menand quote:** Louis Menand, "Life in the Stone Age," *American Studies* (New York: Farrar, Straus & Giroux, 2002), 164.

135. **McElhone article:** Brantley Bardin, "A Heavenly Creature," *Premiere*, December 2002, 107.

136. ***The Onion* quote:** December 4, 2002 issue.

136. **Judge Reinhold interview:** Claude Brodesser, "Q&A" column, ibid., 34.

136–137. **Bette Davis interview:** Kirtley Baskette, "The Girl They Tried to Forget," *Photoplay*, May 1935, reproduced in Richard Griffith, ed., *The Talkies: Articles and Illustrations from a Great Fan Magazine* (New York: Dover, 1971), 121, 278.

137. **Robert Taylor plug:** uncredited writer of "Ask the Answer Man" section, May 1935, reproduced in ibid., 171.

138. **Marie Dressler interview excerpt:** Matthew Kennedy, *Marie Dressler* (Jefferson, NC: McFarland & Co., 1999), 70.

138. **Dressler letter:** ibid., 140.

138–139. **Dressler memoir excerpt:** ibid., 119.

139. **Kirk Douglas interview:** Brantley Bardin, "Idol Chatter," *Premiere*, December 2002, 132.

140. **Julianna Margulies quote:** James Barron, "Boldface Names" column, *New York Times*, November 8, 2002.

141. **Lifebuoy ad:** *Photoplay*, July 1929, reproduced in Griffith, 349.

142–143. **Myers article and McCarthy and Guterson passages:** B. R. Myers, "A Reader's Manifesto," *The Atlantic Monthly*, July/August 2001.

143. **Myers "andelope" reference:** B. R. Myers, *A Reader's Manifesto* (Hoboken, NJ: Melville House, 2002), 45.

143. **Study on increasingly short sentences:** Brock Hausssamen, "The Future of the English Sentence," *Visible Language* 28: 1994, 4–25.

145. **Du Bois composition:** Aptheker, 16-7.

146. **Kansas eighth grade examination:** So many newspaper articles, Web sites, and widely distributed e-mail messages that it would be arbitrary to cite any single one of them; the test fairly swarms all over the Internet.

147. **Truman letter:** Robert H. Ferrell, ed. *Dear Bess: The Letters from Harry to Bess Truman, 1910–1959* (New York: W. W. Norton & Co., 1983), 73.

148. **Reading primer excerpts:** Sandra Stotsky, *Losing Our Language* (San Francisco: Encounter Books, 1999), 19, 1–3.

150. **Commager on McGuffey readers:** Introduction to William Holmes McGuffey, *McGuffey's Fifth Eclectic Reader,* 1879 edition (New York: The New American Library, 1962), x.

151. **Dartmouth conference:** ibid., 37–8.

151. **Social-dialogic model:** Naomi S. Baron, *Alphabet to E-mail* (London: Routledge, 2000), 150.

151. **"Big, smart English" proposal:** Stotsky, 212–3.

152. **NCTE's name-change proposal:** ibid., 223.

152. **Edward Lee Thorndike:** Stotsky, 16–7.

152–153. **Quail passage:** William Post Hawes, "About Quail," reprinted in McGuffey (1962 reprint), 192.

154. **Richard Atkinson speech excerpt:** The 2001 Robert H. Atwell Distinguished Lecture, delivered at the 83rd Annual Meeting of the American Council on Education, Washington, DC, February 18, 2001. (Accessible at University of California Office of the President Web site, at www.ucop.edu/pres/prespeeches.html.)

154–155. **Dowling quote:** William C. Dowling, "Enemies of Promise: Why America Needs the SAT," *Academic Questions,* Winter 1999/2000, 8.

155. **SAT questions:** Dowling, 14, 16.

155–156. **Charles Eliot comment:** Stephen N. Judy, *The ABCs of Literacy* (New York: Oxford, 1980), 33–4.

157. **Krehbiel passage:** Horowitz, 61.

157–158. **Charles O'Connell passage:** ibid., 293.

158. *Time* **passage on FDR:** *Time,* January 7, 1935, 11.

158. *Time* **passage on Churchill:** *Time,* January 2, 1950, 29.

159. *Time* **passage on Eisenhower:** *Time,* January 4, 1960, 11.

160. *Time* **story on Middle Americans:** *Time,* January 5, 1970, 10–17.

160. *Time* **passage on King Faisal:** *Time,* January 6, 1975, 2.

160–161. *Time* **passage on Ayatollah Khomeini:** *Time,* January 7, 1980, 3.

161. **FDR and response to the Fireside Chats:** Lawrence Levine, ed., *The People and the President: America's Extraordinary Conversation with FDR* (Boston: Beacon Press, 2002).

163–164. **French Revolution writers:** David Bell, "Words and Tumbrels," *The New Republic,* November 26, 2001, 41.

165. **Lewis comment:** Bernard Lewis, " 'I'm Right, You're Wrong, Go to Hell,' " *The Atlantic Monthly,* May 2003, 38.

CHAPTER FIVE

167. *Great Gildersleeve* **episode:** "Wooing Amelia Hooker," June 28, 1942.

168–169. *Let 'Em Eat Cake* **sequence:** Recording of Brooklyn Academy of Music production conducted by Michael Tilson Thomas, 1987, CBS Records, M2K 42522.

169. **Onion parody:** Scott Dikkers, ed., *Our Dumb Century* (New York: Three Rivers Press, 1999), 11. The "comedian" is "Dapper Dan Dugan doing his "Dapper Dan's Old-Time Musical Minstrel Revue"; the name, nickname, and show title all sound dead-on authentic for the period—is somebody at the *Onion* a Victor Herbert buff?

170. **English sentences since 1600:** Douglas Biber and Edward Finegan, "Drift and the Evolution of English Style: A History of Three Genres," *Language* 65: 487–517 (1989).

171. **Hernani episode:** Jacques Barzun, *From Dawn to Decadence* (New York: HarperCollins, 2000) 493.

171–172. **Barzun statement:** ibid., 496.

172. **Hazlitt:** William Hazlitt, "On Familiar Style," *Table Talk* (London: Dent & Sons Ltd., 1959), 242.

172. **Transcendentalists and the folk:** Barzun, 506.

173. **Elocution book:** Margaret P. McLean, *Good American Speech* (New York: Dutton, 1928).

176. *Dr. Christian* **episode:** "Prelude to Thanksgiving," November 22, 1939.

177. **Barzun on mass culture:** Jacques Barzun, "The Tenth Muse," *Harper's*, September 2001.

178–179. **Comments on education over time:** Stephen N. Judy, *The ABCs of Literacy* (New York: Oxford, 1980), 33–4.

180. **Education in Finland:** Jouni Välijärvi, Pirjo Linnakylä, Pekka Kupari, Pasi Reinikainen, Inga Arffman, *The Finnish Success in PISA—and Some Reasons Behind It* (University of Jyväskylä: Institute for Educational Research, 2002).

183. **Menand on counterculture:** Louis Menand, "Laurie Anderson's United States," *American Studies* (New York: Farrar, Straus & Giroux, 2002), 243.

184. **Stearns quote:** Author's preface in Harold E. Stearns, *Civilization in the United States: An Inquiry by Thirty Americans* (New York: Harcourt, Brace & Co., 1922), vii.

184. **Mob at McKinley's assassination:** Eric Rauchway, *Murdering McKinley* (New York: Farrar, Straus & Giroux, 2004).

186. **Todd:** He was also sometimes named Chad; today he is often named Justin.

188–189. **Enoch Powell on the BBC:** Thank you to my friend and partner-in-creolist-crime Anthony Grant for this observation.

195. **Podhoretz comment:** Norman Podhoretz, *Doings and Undoings* (London: Rupert Hart-Davis, 1965), 147.

CHAPTER SIX

197. **Drummer in Egypt:** William Nothdurft, *The Lost Dinosaurs of Egypt* (New York: Random House, 2002), 132.

199. **Description of early musical America:** David Wondrich. "I Love to Hear a Minstrel Band: Walt Disney's *The Band Concert*," *The Cartoon Music Book*, ed. by Daniel Goldmark and Yuval Taylor, 67–72. (Chicago: A Cappella Books, 2002), 68–9.

203. **Deems Taylor article and comment on Herbert vs. Verdi:** Deems Taylor, "Music," in Harold E. Stearns, *Civilization in the United States: An Inquiry by Thirty Americans* (New York: Harcourt, Brace & Co., 1922), 209.

203. *Robert Russell Bennett:* "Orchestration of Theatre and Dance Music," *"The Broadway Sound": The Autobiography and Selected Essays of Robert Russell Bennett*, ed. by George J. Ferencz (Rochester, NY: University of Rochester Press, 1999), 285. (The date of the essay is uncertain, but Ferencz dates it to the late 1930s, a judgment with which I, for whatever it's worth, concur.)

204. *The Voice of Firestone* **and** *The Bell Telephone Hour:* John Dunning, *Tune in Yesterday* (Englewood Cliffs, NJ: Prentice-Hall, 1976), 633–4, 58–9; Tim Brooks and Earle Marsh, *The Complete Directory to Prime Time Network and Cable TV Shows, 1946–Present* (New York: Ballantine, 1995), 89–90, 1098–9.

205. **Merman musical:** *Red, Hot, and Blue!*, music and lyrics by Cole Porter, 1936.

205. **Classical explosion in 1930s:** Joseph Horowitz, *Understanding Toscanini* (Berkeley: University of California Press, 1987), 260–1.

205. **Artur Schnabel:** ibid., 262.

207. **Bennett to Ruby:** Robert Russell Bennett, "The Autobiography of Robert Russell Bennett," *"The Broadway Sound": The Autobiography and Selected Essays of Robert Russell Bennett*, ed. by Gerorge J. Ferencz (Rochester, NY: University of Rochester Press, 1999), 93.

207. **Santa Cruz and classical music:** National Briefing, *New York Times*, January 26, 2002.

207–208. **Truman and** *Lucia di Lammermoor:* Robert H. Ferrell, ed., *Dear Bess: The Letters from Harry to Bess Truman, 1910–1959* (New York: W. W. Norton & Co., 1983), 62.

213. **Hurston passage:** Zora Neale Hurston, "How It Feels to Be Colored Me," *Zora Neale Hurston: Folklore, Memoirs, and Other Writings*, ed. by Cheryl Wall (New York: The Library of America, 1995), 828–9.

220. **Cabaret vignette:** Joseph Berger, "In Their Secret Heart, Life is a Cabaret," *New York Times*, November 29, 2002.

220. *Very Warm for May* **excerpt:** from script by Oscar Hammerstein, transcribed from the radio performance of the show distributed as a recording by American Entertainment Industries (AEI), 1985, AEI-CD 008.

CHAPTER SEVEN

224–225. **Cell phone comment:** Social Issues Research Centre website.

233. **Photo of black protesters:** Richard Wright, *12 Million Black Voices* (New York: Thunder's Mouth Press, 2002 [orig. pub. 1941]), 142.

237. **Mamet excerpt:** David Mamet. *American Buffalo* (New York: Grove Press, 1976), 15.

239–240. **Huxley quote:** B. R. Myers, "A Reader's Manifesto," *The Atlantic Monthly*, July/August 2001.

242. **Judith Butler passage:** Denis Dutton, "Language Crimes," *Wall Street Journal*, February 5, 1999.

242. **Paul Fry passage:** Paul Fry, *A Defense of Poetry: Reflections on the Occasion of Writing* (Palo Alto: Stanford University Press, 1995).

244. **Judith Butler on "difficult and demanding" language:** Judith Butler, "A 'Bad Writer' Bites Back," *New York Times*, March 20, 1999.

245. **Change in Latin writing style:** Erich Auerbach, *Literary Language and Its Public* (Princeton: Princeton University Press, 1965) (trans. Ralph Manheim from 1958 German version).

247. **Russian grammar book:** bravo to Derek Offord, *Using Russian* (Cambridge: Cambridge University Press, 1996), Chapter One.

248. **Russian friend:** Maria Polinsky, personal communication, October 2002.

248. **Turkish friend:** Gulsat Aygen, personal communication, July 2002.

248. **African's comment on French:** William Samarin, 1986, "French and Sango in the Central African Republic," *Anthropological Linguistics* 28: 379–87.

250. **Barzun quote:** Jacques Barzun, *From Dawn to Decadence* (New York: HarperCollins, 2000), 88.

251–253. **English language history:** I should note that this claim is not the general consensus among specialists in the history of the English language, but I have recently argued this point in detail in John McWhorter, 2003, "What Happened to English?" *Diachronica* 19.2., and with all humility, especially given its positive reception so far by assorted scholars, believe my case to be valid. The analogous analyses of Hebrew and Swahili are of longer standing.

253. **Valentino contest:** Emily W. Leider, *Dark Lover: The Life and Death of Rudolph Valentino* (New York: Farrar, Straus Giroux, 2003), 290–1.

253–254. **W. C. Fields in *Poppy*:** James Curtis, *W. C. Fields: A Biography* (New York: Alfred A. Knopf, 2003), 151.

Index

Acknowledgments

Writing this book required tracking down more than a few oddly specific facts. I am endlessly grateful to the following people for taking the time to pin down the answers to seemingly niggling questions I have had, or pointing me to obscure source materials no sane person has any right being interested in, all of which were in fact very helpful to me in crafting my argument: Bill Beeman, Diana Biris, Robert Cohen, Irina Galichenko, Randall Kennedy, Neil Kozodoy, David Levering Lewis, Jim McDonough, Johanna Nichols, Maria Polinsky, Sarah Sarasohn, Sandra Stotsky, and Bettina Tragl.

Special thanks to my friend Eric Rauchway for reading chapters and providing me with innumerable insights and pieces of data.

Finally, hats off to my agent, Katinka Matson, for going to bat for me for such an odd proposal, to William Shinker for believing in it, in anticipation to my publicist, Jean Anne Rose, for putting up with me on the book tour, and to my editor, Brendan Cahill, for burnishing my argument and presentation with eager mind and eagle eye.

Permissions